MOVING YOUR INVISIBLE BOUNDARIES

the KEY *to* LIMITLESS LIVING

MOVING YOUR INVISIBLE BOUNDARIES

the KEY *to* LIMITLESS LIVING

DR. JAMES B. RICHARDS

True Potential Publishing
REACH THE WORLD

Moving Your Invisible Boundaries: the Key to Limitless Living

ISBN: 978-1-935769-44-6

Library of Congress Control Number: 2013938149

Printed in the United States of America.

© 2013 by Dr. James B. Richards

True Potential, Inc.
PO Box 904
Travelers Rest, SC 29690
www.truepotentialmedia.com

DEDICATION

This book is dedicated to the three people who were key to helping me become the person I am: my mother, Josephine Johnson, who showed me I could overcome any obstacle. My sister, Patricia McLellan, who showed me I could learn anything, and my wife, Brenda Richards, who showed me how to love.

I am constantly asked how I came to discover these insights. The spiritual answer to that question is rooted in the fact that I came to Jesus knowing I needed to be saved from me. I was the problem. I had no desire for the life I lived or anything it had to offer. But that really did not come to fruition to a great degree until I found myself in a marriage with someone who loved me when I had little or nothing to offer. For the first time I believed I was loved, with no agendas.

Brenda's love for me made me want to be a better man. In fact, it brought me back to my roots. Any of my residual problems would only be resolved to the degree that I died to self and came alive to the love of God. Her love made me willing to face my chauvinism, my ability to overpower, my need to be right, and my deep rooted hidden fears.

Mom, right now you are in Heaven seeing the fruit of your life's investment in me. Because of what you showed me I don't know how to quit, no matter how hard it gets. Sis, every time I face a new challenge it is what you taught me when I was too young to even remember much of it that makes me say, "I may not know how to do this but I can learn!"

Brenda, for most of my life my broken heart forced me to push everyone away! Somehow, you loved me through it all. Because of what you showed me, millions of lives will never be the same. I may have been the one to put this into words but you were the one that showed me what it looked like in real life.

I am a deeply appreciative son, brother, and husband!

CONTENTS

Read This First ix

1. Making the Heart Journey 17

2. Defining the Heart 23

3. Why You Do What You Do 31

4. The Pursuit of Life 39

5. The Way of the Disciple 47

6. The Quantum Leap: Death to Self 57

7. Renewing the Mind: The Information Exchange 67

8. Spirit, Soul, and Body: A New Look 79

9. Believing on Jesus in Your Heart 91

10. Healing the Broken Heart 101

11. Where the War Rages 113

12. Why I Really Hate Being Wrong 125

13. Knowing God in Your Heart 135

14. Laws of the Heart 145

15. Growing the Word in Your Heart 155

16. Living in Harmony 163

17. Hardness of Heart 171

18. Entering the War Zone... 181

19. Entering the HeartZone 191

20. The Way of Peace 203

21. Biblical Meditation.. 213

22. Gathering Evidence... 221

23. Controlling the Process 231

24. Christ in You: The Starting Place.............................. 241

25. Participating in the Exchange 249

26. Put Off – Put On 255

27. Life Without Limits 265

28. Making Your Own Journey 273

READ THIS FIRST

Understanding the heart may lead to the most significant spiritual revelation of our day! In fact, many ministers and researchers, both Christian and non-Christian, who actively study and teach personal development agree that a more biblical understanding of the heart could be the single important aspect of human development, while ministers feel it is the key factor to usher us into the *'move of God'*[1] believers have sought for so long! For you, connecting with God in your heart as opposed to your mind will be your key to moving the invisible boundaries that have defined the extend or your personal growth,   health, happiness and success!

After all, God is a *heart* God; we are instructed to believe on Jesus in our *heart*; the Word must be sown in our *heart* to bear fruit; God speaks to us in our *heart* - the list of biblical references to the heart's effect on every aspect of life seems endless. It can be said there is nothing God does in the life of a believer that occurs outside of the realm of the heart! Yet very few Christians have ever been taught anything about the heart! Is it possible that the one missing ingredient required to actually experience all spiritual reality has been ignored through two thousand years of religious legalism, tradition and carnal thinking?

Heart belief is the prerequisite and the condition that allows us to participate in any good thing God has given including the new birth, operating faith in the promises of God and living the resurrection life! Since the Kingdom of God is a spiritual phenomenon only accessible internally, it stands to reason the door to the Kingdom is a *heart* that believes, not a mind that is informed. The heart is not another *doctrine* we must believe to receive from God; it is *how* and *where* we believe thereby allowing us to receive from God. The heart is where the invisible transforms into the visible, the impossible is made possible and spiritual reality explodes onto the physical plane!

The heart is like an automobile ignition. It doesn't matter how big and well-tuned the engine, the tank may be filled with high octane fuel, the tires are top of the line and the paint job is impeccable; without an ignition to light its fire, all you've got is a well built paperweight. The car looks good, but doesn't really do anything. In our Christian life we've got truth, we've got doctrine, we have volumes of knowledge but let's face the dismal reality … too often, it's not working as it should. Even when we manage to get aspects of the Word of God to work, it's kind of hit and miss. We're not really sure why it does or doesn't work! We are lacking the consistency that should be present in a God that is never contradictory or chaotic.

In today's religious quagmire spirituality gives way to intellectualism! Control has replaced power! Mysticism is the new miraculous. Positive thinking is the fad substitute for faith in the heart! We are told to close our eyes, confess the truth a million times, be full of remorse for all our sins and if God is in a good mood the last anointed prayer prayed over us might kick in! This 21st century gospel doesn't even resemble the message of Jesus or the early church. What we call spiritual is so bizarre we're embarrassed for our friends to see what we do in church. Unlike Jesus, who performed miracles out in the open among the lost, we hide behind church walls because what we do only works with those initiated into the club, who speak the language and have bought into the culture! What's worse is the absence of a personal moral lifestyle that should be the organic expression of our belief in Jesus Christ. We know we have the truth; it just doesn't show in our lives!

We aren't seeing believers exhibit the fruit of a godly life. Christians continue to struggle with sin, doubt, distress, and confusion. The body of Christ is tossed to and fro with every wind of doctrine. Regardless of the latest spiritual fad that promised to be the answer, we are left feeling there is always something lacking, one more step, or one more formula we must learn. Sadly, the issue of the heart, or more specifically, the beliefs of the heart have been consistently omitted from the application of spiritual truth! It seems the one central truth is missing, "If we don't believe God's word in our heart, our hopes of living in His promises are in vain.

Coming to understand and apply the truth of the heart opens the door to all we have learned about God. It doesn't cause us to discard the truth we have known; it brings it into perspective. It puts the application of God's Word within our reach - no longer something that seems far off and unattainable. And it certainly doesn't require some spiritual guru to supply it to us.

Over the last several decades, so many wonderful biblical truths have been restored to the body of Christ. The problem is, however, the restoration of information has not actually translated into *transformation*. More information hasn't necessarily translated into better quality of life (spiritual fruit) in the believer! In fact, this flood of information has given rise to a negative backlash. After hoping in so many failed doctrines, believers succumb to the many dangerous paths that simply lead to more frustration, desperation, and vulnerability.

The acute awareness of God's promises that we can't seem to put into action leads to deep unresolvable insecurity. The subsequent frustration often leads to rejecting the promises of God, which are our only means of *'escaping the corruption that's in the world.*[2] Even worse, some are giving up on God completely. When believers fail to receive the clearly stated promises written in God's Word, they can fall prey to a mentality of doubt that declares, *"If this didn't work, none of it works."* Even more frightening is how believers frustrated over failed promises become vulnerable to destructive heresies.

The issue of the heart has been eluded the majority of believers in every generation from Moses until this very day. Whether consciously or subconsciously the masses seem to be determined to hold to their self-life and only surrender to God externally. This is why the children of Israel struggled in the wilderness.[3] The legalist point to disobedience as the issue, but God's word is clear that the disobedience is the result of a heart of unbelief. Likewise, the early church soon departed from faith in the risen Lord and gave itself to every imaginable heresy. As the early church distanced itself from Old Testament Scripture they had no Biblical basis for interpreting the New Covenant. Like those who came before them, they became ignorant and arrogant. They rejected God's Word, God's purpose, and God's promises. In the absence of resurrection power the scriptures were subjectively interpreted based on *'personal revelations'* or cult philosophies which resulted in extrapolating truth into destructive heresies, destroying the listener.

The great majority of the 21st century church has rejected the finished work of Jesus as the absolute basis for knowing and experiencing God. Instead of believing on the cross, i.e. the death, burial and resurrection of Jesus, in our hearts we are asked to intellectually agree with the information. Then we wonder why there is no power. We would do well to consider Paul's insight

> *For I determined not to know anything among you except Jesus Christ and Him crucified. I was with you in weakness, in fear, and in much trembling. And my speech and my preaching were not with persuasive words of human wisdom, but in demonstration of the Spirit and of power, that your faith should not be in the wisdom of men but in the power of God* (1 Cor 2:2-5, NKJV)>

We refuse to examine our faith in light of the outcome for fear we will not pass the test. We want God, but we don't know how to experience Him. We are overrun with error that sounds good philosophically (the wisdom of men) but contradict the character of God, His clearly expressed Word and bear no fruit.

Then there are those who are so discouraged they cannot deal with another personal failure. Consequently, they justify their failed experience by inventing a legalistic doctrine of prerequisites pushing God's promises beyond reach! There is, however, a much deeper destruction at work. When we can't get the truth we believe to produce the promised result, our hearts are injured.[4] Repeated failures make it increasingly difficult, if not impossible to trust God.

But what if the promises of God we've learned but can't get to work in our lives really are true? What if they're already ours because we are in Jesus? What if every wonderful thing God has ever done is for us *today* and can be experienced in the *'here and now'*? What if all we need is one key factor to make every good promise from God come alive in our lives? What if we already have sufficient faith to live in God's truth? I've got good news – as born again children of God, we do!

Man's religion has tried to make this all harder than it really is. You have sufficient faith! God has given to *every man a measure of faith*! You just haven't been shown how faith actually works from the heart.[5] Our externally focused, carnally minded culture has confused the functions of the heart and the mind. We operate in intellectualism and call it faith. Our problem isn't a lack of faith. Our problem is pretty simple: first, we are not clear about the conditions and provisions of The New Covenant. Second, we attempt to use our faith to get what Jesus has already given us, thereby denying the finished work of Jesus. Our faith must be in the finished work of Jesus, not our works. Last and by no means least, we must learn that true, effective faith comes from our heart, not our head.

This book is not about doctrine; it is about getting your doctrine to *work*, provided your doctrine is rooted in the finished work of Jesus. I will walk you step by step through the biblical concepts of the heart. At the end of each chapter will be a short application segment with tips for putting what you just learned into practice. You must understand, in this book I will be using Jesus' teaching style. When Jesus taught, especially about the heart, He used conceptual, metaphoric language. If we attempt to turn each detail of Jesus' parables into a doctrinal point, we miss the concept. Likewise, many of my concepts are not meant to be a literal explanation. In portions of this book I may attempt to convey concepts for which there are no accurate English words. Try to simply understand the concept without worrying too much about the details. It is more important that you learn to live from the heart than to explain the heart!

As you make this journey, you will discover, as thousands of others have, that connecting with God in your heart is the answer you have been seeking. It is the missing piece to the puzzle! You are about to begin an incredible journey. Walking with God from the heart makes every day an adventure. Because there is no end to His greatness or goodness, this is your key to limitless living.

We all seem to put subconscious limits on how good we believe life can be, how much we can prosper, how much energy we have, the extent of our happiness and even our capacity to enjoy loving relationships. We call these self-inflicted limits 'invisible boundaries'. One of the most exciting aspects of this new journey you are about to begin is the ability to move your invisible boundaries. *Moving Your Invisible Boundaries* more than a book title; it is your new approach to limitless living.

Because I am reintroducing some biblical concepts that may be foreign to many 21st century believers, I have included scripture references at the end of each chapter along with other footnotes. Some readers may just want to read through the material, others may want to study the scripture references and other notes. Including the scripture references and footnotes at the end of each chapter allows the reader to study the relevant scriptures without having to leave the book.

This book references several Heart Physics® tools. Please don't think you must purchase these tools to benefit from this book. You can do just as I have done; look up scriptures and experiment through trial and error to discover your own way of connecting to your heart. You have enough material in this book without any of the support material to make a major life transformation. The Heart Physics® resources, however, were developed for two primary reasons. After teaching these methods to individuals and groups over more than thirty years I realized how many more people this teaching could reach and help by committing it to a developed program. But most importantly, I realized that by including certain facets of this teaching into the programs I can help students reach a level of effectiveness in just a few weeks that took me years to attain. There's no sense in it taking ten years to learn and experience what you could in a month!

There are exercises at the end of each chapter designed to move you experientially through the material as it is learned. The Bible teaches that information, independent of heart-developed faith and application, is pretty much useless. As Paul said, *"knowledge puffs up but love builds up"* (1 Cor. 8:1)! No truth, doctrine or theology has the power to change your life just because you know the information. It must be believed in the heart. This happens by immediately finding ways to take ownership of what you hear. Commit to it. Envision your life with these concepts working. Express your desire and intention to God to live the truth you learn!

Please don't mistake developing your heart with *'behavior modification'.* Behavior modification is usually done through a form of conditioning. Conditioning is not altogether wrong; it is only wrong when it is a substitute for a true change of heart. Grace - God's power, capacity, and ability, which comes through unmerited favor and works from the heart, is what makes us able to be, do and have what God promises. Grace only comes through faith in the heart. We do not want you to totally reject the value of conditioning. Like almost anything else, conditioning can bring value when used properly. It is a great basic development tool when coupled with heart development. More on the subject of conditioning is addressed in my book, *Leadership That Builds People.*

References are made to *'developing the heart'* or to *'heart exercises'*; some of these exercises directly influence the heart, some indirectly. Don't try to figure out which is which. That will become more obvious as you learn to make a clear distinction between the *voice of your mind* and the *voice of your heart.*

Now! Get ready for the most incredible experience of positive, painless, permanent transformation you ever imagined. You are moving to a realm with the potential to know and experience God like never before. You are about to enter the HeartZone! In the HeartZone you will not just move past your invisible boundaries, you will move the boundaries and enlarge every aspect of your life… this is limitless living!

Endnotes

i. The idea of a move of God is not actually scriptural within the New Covenant framework. The idea that God is not moving and we could somehow do enough to get Him to move is a legalistic concept fraught with self-destructive deception and doctrinal error. God has done all that needs to be done through the finished work of the Lord Jesus. We, not God, are the ones who need to "move." We need to move ourselves to immovable heart beliefs concerning the Lord Jesus and His resurrection.

ii. 2 Peter 1:3-4, His divine power has given to us all things that *pertain* to life and godliness, through the knowledge of Him who called us by glory and virtue, by which have been given to us exceedingly great and precious promises, that through these you may be partakers of the divine nature, having escaped the corruption *that is* in the world through lust. NKJV

iii. Ps 78:18-19, And they tested God in their heart By asking for the food of their fancy. Yes, they spoke against God: They said, "Can God prepare a table in the wilderness?
Ps 78:37, For their heart was not steadfast with Him, Nor were they faithful in His covenant. NKJV

iv. Prov 13:12, Hope deferred makes the heart sick, But *when* the desire comes, *it is* a tree of life. NKJV

v. Rom 12:3-4, God has dealt to each one a measure of faith. NKJV

Free Online Support!

Want to put what you're reading into practice right now? Please visit this link (http://www.heartphysics.com/MYIBsupport/) for free online cognitive support, exercises and chapter questions.

1

MAKING
THE HEART JOURNEY

Every person goes through life with the deep awareness that there is more! We know internally that we could be experiencing more of what the Bible promises. We know that we live on the edge of something far greater than we have ever seen. We even experience brief glimpses into that realm, but like dreams in the middle of the night, they escape our memory when we awaken, leaving us with only a vague sense of having touched something holy! From time to time we even experience something in our life that is miraculous. When the rejoicing stops, we are left with the feeling that this should be a way of life, not an occasional mountaintop experience.

The fact that you are reading this book says one thing… you still have hope! We all know that those who seek, and keep on seeking, find.[1] But what we often forget is that those who keep seeking have a secret motivation… hope! Those who stop seeking do so because they no longer maintain the confident expectation of finding the good outcome they once expected! Hope is the confident expectation of good things.[2] It is intertwined with an attitude that says, "There is a solution to my problem. I will not give up until I find it!" This expectation causes us to keep looking when society, science, and religion have all said that there is no way! Hope believes it will find a way, even when there seems to be none!

Those who have hope will try all kinds of things. They are not daunted by failure. When hope stays alive, we tend to view those things that didn't work as an elimination process. It is a fine-tuning of the remaining options. Because people of hope don't quit, they tend to eventually find more solutions than the average person, but they also have more disappointments. They can even be gullible at times. They live by the adage: if I don't swing the bat, I'll never hit the ball. So they keep swinging at the ball. Sometimes they get home runs; sometimes they strike out! They often face criticism from the cynics who have stopped looking, whose only relief is found by smothering the hope and optimism of others, those who need company in their misery. But outside sources are not the greatest enemy of hope.

The supreme enemy of hope is an internal paradigm shift. This only happens if there are enough disappointments. Disappointment has the potential to negatively influence our heart! Hope deferred makes the heart sick![3] When the heart becomes sick, it loses its capacity to hope, to confidently expect good things. Hope is the springboard to faith. Faith, which is the secret weapon of the heart, emerges from things hoped for. Without hope, it is impossible to move on to faith. However, the ultimate tragedy is found in the fact that a sick heart loses its ability to hear, sense, and follow God into an experience of His power, provision, and promises!

> THE SUPREME ENEMY OF HOPE IS AN INTERNAL PARADIGM SHIFT.

The Bible says the heart becomes sick when hope is deferred. This heart sickness, according to one source, is a condition resulting from being worn or wounded in battle. It can also be the result of grieving.[4] Grieving is what happens when we experience loss, whether real or imagined. In other words, the day-to-day struggle with the same issues can wear us down, affecting our heart like a wound that occurs in the battle of life. The result is an overwhelming sense of loss, lack, or failure. This feeling of loss is what we feel when hope is gone. We don't just lose hope; we lose our hope of the outcome that is so desperately needed or desired! It is as if something has been forcibly taken from us and the loss wounded us so deeply we are unwilling to hope again!

This book is not full of empty promises. I'm sure, like all of us making this journey in pursuit of solutions, you've had your share of disappointments, of hopes deferred. But you picked up another book which means you are still seeking! You are still fully capable of continuing the journey in the continuum of hope, faith, and fullness of life! This journey is only possible when one learns to live in constant contact with their heart. Hearing and knowing the voice of your heart is the first step of learning to hear and know the voice of God. The one promise I will make is that I will give you tools you can use to begin this journey of living from your heart!

I can also promise this: if you use the tools, principles, and processes I provide, and effectively influence your heart, your world will change. You will walk into a new, never-ending dimension of discovery that is beyond anything you've ever seen, heard, or imagined.[5] The heart is the inner path to the Kingdom of God[6] and all its resources. Apart from learning to live from the heart, our knowledge of God is little more than information with the occasional, inconsistent breakthrough of the true Life of God!

Learning to live from your heart does not mean you will reject or disavow all that you have previously learned. It does mean you will make a paradigm shift whereby you are now able to use all that you have ever learned or experienced in a way that actually works. This new awareness becomes the matrix around which all of your life is now organized, empowered, and expressed. Everything can now work for you instead of against you!

However, I must give you this warning: the journey of the heart is not an intellectual endeavor. While the information you gain in this book is crucial. It is of no real life-changing value until you put it into practice. In fact, nothing you currently know is of any real value until you put it into practice from a heart perspective. That is the shortcoming of nearly all self-development programs. They may tell you what to do, but unless the change in behavior is

> THE JOURNEY OF THE HEART IS NOT AN INTELLECTUAL ENDEAVOR.

accompanied by a change in a heart belief, it will be little more than behavior modification. Behavior that is modified by effort lasts only as long as we are "motivated" to put forth the effort! But, one day we get tired, frustrated, or discouraged. On that day we are no longer motivated to put forth the effort. Or we encounter some opposition that is greater than our willpower, and our newfound behavior is crushed under the weight of circumstance!

The Bible promises a paradoxical place of rest. The place of rest is where we cease our own efforts. The paradox is, however, that we must labor to enter into this place of rest![7] In other words, once we do the work of entering the place of rest, the labor is over, and we begin to function under the power of positive, painless, permanent, effortless transformation! The Scripture clearly identifies the failure to deal with our beliefs as the cause of not entering rest. In the New Testament it is understood that beliefs are nearly always a reference to the beliefs of the heart as opposed to the thoughts of the mind. So I must understand that altering the beliefs of my heart has the potential to bring me to the place of rest where I experience what God has for me, completely independent of my willpower! So, this journey will be a combination of knowledge, application, and experience. Knowledge provides you with the truth you need to know. Pondering, contemplating, and meditating on that information from the perspective of application will bring you understanding. Seeing yourself able to live in this truth allows the heart to experience God's grace. The *Theological Wordbook of the Old Testament* says this about the verb, "knowing:"

> *The verb refers to knowledge which is superior to the mere gathering of data. It is necessary to know how to use knowledge one possesses (Pirke Abot 3:12). The verb y¹da± can also mean "understanding" in the sense of ability. It can also mean "to be perceptive," (Ps [8]73:22). However, yada' generally describes the process whereby one gains knowledge through experience with objects and circumstances. Bîn is a power of judgment and perceptive insight and is demonstrated in the use of knowledge.*

Information that is not gathered from the perspective of application is very deceptive and egocentric. It feeds all that opposes life from the heart! Jesus explained the way we know His doctrine is of God is the willingness (intention) to put it into practice.[9] Understanding moves us to godly application.

As the meditative application of understanding continues, wisdom emerges. Wisdom is the practical application of information. This comes directly from the mouth of God to your heart! God's wisdom moves us to navigate the pathway of application in a way that only God can provide. He knows all the factors, all the people, all the opposition, and all the resources. Walking with God and following His voice in your heart is wisdom. As we walk with Him, we experience the capacity and strength to make the journey, i.e. we remain in the place of rest through the entire journey!

The meditative process is the one constant in the entire progression of moving from information to application. It is the meditative process that keeps us in touch with our heart, in connection with God, and empowered by the Holy Spirit! Jesus taught that it was only the meditative process that determined the amount of life you would get from the truth you hear. [10] When we leave the meditative process, we return to

> ## WISDOM IS THE PRACTICAL APPLICATION OF INFORMATION.

the control of the mind. The mind doesn't hear the voice of God. It doesn't matter how much knowledge we have stored in our mind; while absolutely essential to our overall life, it is no substitute for hearing the voice of God in your heart!

So, I am not making you any offer that the Bible does not make. Nor am I suggesting any process that is not based on Bible wisdom and application. But I am offering to show you what I have learned thus far in my journey of the heart. Those who make the journey are never disappointed. The only frustration you may experience is when you try to take control of the process rather than following your Shepherd as He leads you down the path of life!

Endnotes

i.   Matt. 7:7, Keep on asking for something to be given and it shall be given you. Keep on seeking, and you shall find. Keep on reverently knocking, and it shall be opened to you. For everyone who keeps on asking for something to be given, keeps on receiving. And he who keeps on seeking, keeps on finding. And to him who keeps on reverently knocking, it shall be opened. (From The New Testament: An Expanded Translation by Kenneth S. Wuest, Copyright © 1961 by Wm. B. Eerdmans Publishing Co. All rights reserved.)

ii.   in a good sense: *expectation of good, hope*; and in the Christian sense, *joyful and confident expectation of eternal salvation*: (From Thayer's Greek Lexicon, Electronic Database. Copyright © 2000, 2003, 2006 by Biblesoft, Inc. All rights reserved.)

iii.   Prov. 13:12, Hope deferred makes the heart sick, But *when* the desire comes, *it is* a tree of life. NKJV

iv.   Theological Wordbook of the Old Testament. Copyright © 1980 by The Moody Bible Institute of Chicago.

v.   1 Cor. 2:9, "*Eye has not seen, nor ear heard, nor have entered into the heart of man the things which God has prepared for those who love Him.*"* NKJV

vi.   Luke 17:21, the kingdom of God is within you. NKJV

vii.   Heb. 4:11, Let us labour therefore to enter into that rest, lest any man fall after the same example of unbelief. KJV

viii.   OT:8394, Theological Wordbook of the Old Testament. Copyright © 1980 by The Moody Bible Institute of Chicago. All rights reserved.

ix.   John 7:16-17, Jesus answered them and said, "My doctrine is not Mine, but His who sent Me. If anyone wills to do His will, he shall know concerning the doctrine, whether it is from God. NKJV

x.   Mark 4:23, The measure [of thought and study] you give [to the truth you hear] will be the measure [of virtue and knowledge] that comes back to you — and more [besides] will be given to you *who hear*. AMP

2

DEFINING THE HEART

Defining that which can only be experienced but not seen is a challenge for the 21st century Western mind. We are such a left brain culture; we want everything to make sense based on the parameters of our cultural logic, ideas, and opinions. We are like the US Patent Office which will not grant a patent for something that does not fit into the currently accepted scientific norms. This means it is nearly impossible to get a new, revolutionary product to the marketplace. In the same way, we can't see what God is trying to show us because we have already decided how things should be!

When we want everything to fit into the way we already see things, it blinds us to that which is beyond our current opinion. When the Jews argued with Jesus about their sinfulness, Jesus explained that they were trapped in their current state for one reason: they insisted, "How we saw it was how it is!"[1] They closed their eyes; otherwise, they would have to see, understand, and repent (change their mind). The false security of being right was more comfortable than the sure security of following God! Like people today, they wanted a revelation from God without having to change their opinion.

Revelation is not what God finally shows us when we fast or make a compelling sacrifice. Revelation is when the veil is removed from our eyes because we surrender our opinion. Paul said the Jews had a veil over their eyes when they read God's word.[2] That veil was the way they held to and interpreted the law. God was trying to show them the very truth they had sought for centuries, but they refused to remove the veil of their opinion. God desires for us to see all He has for us today! But it is our attempt to find security in our opinions that keeps us from the revelation we need to launch forward into new dimensions.

It is my goal to talk about function. The Bible was written with a mindset that said, "If I do this and a certain thing always happens, then I have no need to explain how it happens." Much of the very destructive doctrine that exists today

> **THE GOAL IS FOR US TO DISCOVER HOW TO CONNECT WITH, INFLUENCE, ESTABLISH, GUARD, AND FOLLOW OUR HEART.**

is the product of people seeing the outward fruit and assuming to know the inner workings! It is possible to understand the inner workings of some things; in other instances we just know "this produces this." When I use examples, they are only examples. They are not necessarily fixed ideas. The goal is for us to discover how to connect with, influence, establish, guard, and follow our heart. That will happen because we grasp the concepts, not because we get all the details "right." All of my examples and illustrations are more for conceptual gain than literal information.

In order to attempt to define the heart, I must share a small portion of my personal journey. In the fall of 1972 as I sat reading and meditating on the Word, I read this Scripture: *For the LORD does not see as man sees; for man looks at the outward appearance, but the LORD looks at the heart"* (1 Sam. 16:7). In those early days I made no assumption that I could understand God's word as it applied to me apart from His help. As was (and still is) my practice, I meditated on the meaning of this verse, seeking to understand how it applied to my heart. I read, prayed, and pondered deep into the night and I emerged with one all-consuming reality: God is a heart God!

That night I came to realize that outward behavior was meaningless apart from what was happening in the heart. God wanted my connection with Him to be internal, not external. Reality with God was determined by what was real in my heart. I determined that I wanted to know God in my heart! The problem was… I had no real clue what the heart was from a biblical perspective.

My first pastor was a very godly man, but he was also very "old school." He didn't look at original language as an important factor. He preached a good message. He was loving, kind, and he was a good shepherd! The first time I met with him and shared my calling he said, "Let me see your Bible." I very embarrassingly handed him my stolen Gideon's motel Bible. He said, "If you're going to study the Bible, you need to purchase a good study Bible, a *Cruden's Complete Concordance* and a *Nave's Topical Bible*. With these three tools you can look up anything in the Bible and understand what it's talking about." I immediately went to the Christian bookstore, bought the reference Bible he recommended, and put the other two books on layaway. Because of this great introduction to Bible study, I developed effective Bible study skills very early.

After months of looking up all the verses that used the word "heart," I went to him for more insight. When I asked him what the heart was, his reply was something like this: "The heart is the inner man; it is the same thing as the spirit." His answer didn't set right with me. I really didn't know enough to know what question I should ask next, but I knew I had not found my answer. The months of reading and pondering the verses about the heart, along with the prompting of the inner voice of God, kept telling me there was more.

Since he was an interim pastor, it wasn't long until a younger man came as our permanent pastor. He was another wonderful man that helped me so very much in my next steps of following God. The first time we met he told me, "The Bible was not written in English. Never look up a word in the Bible in a *Webster's Dictionary*." He reached behind him and pulled a Greek-Hebrew lexicon from his shelf and said, "If you're serious about studying the Bible, get yourself one of these and use it in all your Bible study." That was my next purchase!

Based on my previous pastor's advice, I had already looked up all the verses for heart, soul, mind, and spirit. But I still didn't have the answers I needed. So, I asked my current pastor the same question. To my surprise his answer was the same: "The heart, soul, or spirit are all words that pretty much mean the same thing." I asked, "Then why are soul and spirit used in the same scriptures if they mean the same thing?" He had no answer, but he had armed me with a new tool…original language!

I was equipped with good research tools; but even more importantly, I was fully engaged with God through an intimate life of prayer, worship, and following Him as a disciple. My eyes opened by degrees. The thing that was most influential was not the word I read, or the definitions I discovered, nor what I felt the Holy Spirit was teaching me, but what I experienced as I applied all these truths. You never know if anything is true until you put it into practice and see the results. Through the study of this book and the journey of life, we must remember it is only information until we experience it through faith-based application. As we dive deeper into the biblical meanings of the concepts of the heart, this foundational truth will become the guiding rule of learning to live from your heart!

> YOU NEVER KNOW IF ANYTHING IS TRUE UNTIL YOU PUT IT INTO PRACTICE AND SEE THE RESULTS.

You will always take yourself through the process of information, understanding, wisdom, and application. Every phase of this is bathed in prayer, meditation, and faith!

So skipping ahead about four decades, how do I understand the heart? The heart, first and foremost, is the "real" me. All other factors of the heart are more about function. Functionally, it is the seat of all feelings, good or bad; the core of my understanding, the lens through which I see and interpret the world around me. It is the true guidance system of life. It is the place where I meet, commune with, and hear the voice of God!

If you had asked me 30 years ago, I would have said, "The heart may be what we know as the subconscious mind." My reason for that assumption was based on the similarities between the heart and the subconscious. While I was never fully convinced that they were one and the same, my thought that they might be was completely wrong. In fact, until I had a firm grasp on the difference between the heart and the subconscious, I was not willing to write this book; hence, the 40 year delay!

Like the subconscious mind, the heart is our automatic pilot. One primary difference between the heart and the subconscious is that the subconscious engages when we encounter situations that touch on past associations. In other words, when I meet someone that reminds me of a person who hurt me in the past, I have a wave of negative feelings. Those feelings are because of the similarities which, in turn, trigger subconscious feelings and thoughts. Basically, "subconscious thought" simply means, "below conscious thought or awareness."

The heart, on the other hand, is the master controller of our entire being. Regardless of our attempts at self-control, if there is deceit, adultery, hatred, or any other vile thing in our heart, it will "leak out" in our words and behavior.[3] As such, all habitual problems can only be permanently resolved when dealt with from the heart. Likewise, when righteousness is in our heart, our behavior tends to be more in harmony with the character and nature of God. Self-control can temporarily mask the good or evil that is in our heart, but eventually that which is in the heart manifests.

The heart, as I said, is the "real" me. As such, it is the seat of my identity. Who I experience/believe/feel myself to be is the key to the quality of my life. The heart communicates with the brain and with all the cells of the body. It is the master controller in every sense of the word. We know the cells of the body constantly receive signals that program the function of the cells. The scientists that discovered this do not, however, know where this signal originates. Based on what the Bible teaches and other emerging research, it is very probable that every time our heart beats it sends a signal to every cell in our body, programming that cell to fulfill the beliefs of the heart! The heart programs the cells!

Proverbs give us this wisdom: *Keep your heart with all diligence, For out of it spring the issues of life* (Prov. 4:23). The word "issues" could just as well have been translated as "boundaries."[4] The *Theological Wordbook of the Old Testament* says it could speak of a slave being set free. The idea being conveyed is this: the boundaries or limitations in your life are not a product of anything outside of you; they are the product of your heart. The only way you can cease being a slave to your present boundaries is to expand the beliefs of your heart. The only way to keep from making your life boundaries smaller and smaller is to guard your heart!

> YOU ARE ONLY COMFORTABLE LIVING A LIFE WITHIN THE BOUNDS OF WHO YOU BELIEVE YOURSELF TO BE.

Why would every boundary in your life come from your heart? Simple! If the heart is the real you, you are only comfortable living a life within the bounds of who you believe yourself to be. The skills I learn, the information I ingest, and the training I complete will do little to move me beyond my current circumstances unless I change the beliefs of my heart … change my sense of identity. This is why many people can help others, but not themselves. They pass along the information to those who will believe and apply it, yet they do nothing with it themselves.

Because we have focused on the external, we have spent our faith trying to move the external mountains. We think the boundary is out there. We think the circumstance is the mountain. But Proverbs says the mountain or boundary is my own heart. The unseen world functions differently than the seen world. To move a mountain in the seen world, we need a massive amount of power. It looks as difficult as the mountain is big. But in the unseen world, we don't really need enough power to move the mountain. We need enough faith to change the way we perceive ourselves in relation to the mountain.

With the advent of quantum science, the world discovered that the greatest release of power doesn't occur by making bigger bombs. It occurs by making changes at the smallest level… the atom! The most powerful bomb in the world was created by splitting the atom, not by bundling together more explosives. Such is the realm of the heart! If I see myself as a mountain mover, I move mountains. It's easy; it's who I am! But if I don't see myself as a mountain mover, it is unlikely I will muster enough faith to move much of a mountain!

The heart always moves you to live within the boundaries, harmonious with your sense of identity. We can venture beyond the boundaries of our identity. But when our life exceeds our sense of self, in a good or bad way, it causes stress and discomfort. That is when we expand our sense of self to fit the new circumstances, or we self-destruct. People who try and fail repeatedly do so because they are trying to bring about life changes from the outside instead of the inside. They are a slave to the boundaries of their heart. There is no cure other than changing the beliefs of the heart by changing our sense of identity!

There are many ways your heart can bring you back within the comfortable boundaries of your sense of self. You can find yourself having negative emotions, destructive behavior, or even physical illness. One source I read years ago stated that people often have their greatest physical struggles at their time of greatest opportunity. If you have unresolved guilt, shame, or any negative emotion that makes you feel unworthy, these feelings will overthrow your life's greatest opportunities. When your life becomes better than you believe you deserve, you will feel what the Bible calls "condemnation." Condemnation is the expectation of judgment. That's the feeling you have when things are going too well and you're just "waiting for the other shoe to drop." That dread and the sickness or destructive circumstance that follow is not God; it is your own heart.

You are not the only one affected by your heart. Scientists have attempted to determine how far from the physical body the signal of the heart can be detected. At this moment the answer is unclear. But I can assure you there are no limits. That signal which influences our brain and every cell in our body influences the world around us as well. It influences others to trust or not trust us, to say yes or to say no to our request.

Without speaking a word my heart, the "real" me, is influencing my mind to think within the boundaries of my sense of self. These beliefs are programming every cell in my body to function a certain way. And to some degree, they are telling the world around me to treat me in a way that is consistent with how I see myself. No wonder the writer of Proverbs chose a word that described the function of the heart to be like the boundaries that hold a slave captive or the doors that open to set him free.

Other than our personal relationship with Jesus, which is a heart issue, there is nothing we should understand more than our own heart. Jesus taught that whatever we are currently experiencing in our life is going to be what we get in the future, but He added one important addendum: you are going to get *more* of what you have. This seems to imply both quantity and quality. If you don't like what you have, it's time to change your heart. The only solution He offered to break the cycle of destructive patterns in our life was to learn how to influence our heart (not our mind) with the word of God.

> IF YOU DON'T LIKE WHAT YOU HAVE, IT'S TIME TO CHANGE YOUR HEART.

We are not abandoning the value of the left brain to gather information. But we are abandoning the left brain, intellectual approach to knowing God. And by all means, we must determine to resist allowing our intellect to lead us. We must connect to God in the only way that is real, which is the only way to move the boundaries, open the gates, and experience a better life than we have known. That is the purpose of this book. In this book we will learn what the Bible teaches about the heart and how we can change our heart's beliefs. You will acquire the information, principles, and tools that, when applied, will forever change your life! Using what you learn will expand the boundaries of your heart. This really does take you to the place where there are no limitations!

Endnotes

i.   John 9:41, Jesus said to them, "If you were blind, you would have no sin; but now you say, 'We see.' Therefore your sin remains. NKJV

ii.   2 Cor. 3:15-16, But even to this day, when Moses is read, a veil lies on their heart. NKJV

iii. Matt. 12:34, For out of the abundance of the heart the mouth speaks. Matt. 15:19, For out of the heart proceed evil thoughts, murders, adulteries, fornications, thefts, false witness, blasphemies.

iv.   (Biblesoft's New Exhaustive Strong's Numbers and Concordance with Expanded Greek-Hebrew Dictionary. Copyright © 1994, 2003, 2006 Biblesoft, Inc. and International Bible Translators, Inc.)

3

Why You Do What You Do

Living from the heart is living on automatic pilot. Based on your sense of self, your heart will always attempt to lead you in a direction that fulfills and expresses your identity. When I use the term "identity," I am referring to your believed identity. Your believed identity is the identity, or sense of self that you have developed over time. It is the result of the beliefs you have created because of your life experiences. It is your believed identity that your heart is always seeking to express and maintain. In Christ there is a monumental gap between your true identity and your believed identity! This contradiction is the source of every struggle in the life of a believer.

Proverbs 23:7 is probably the most quoted Bible verse concerning the heart. *For as he thinks in his heart, so is he.* The first and most telling part of this verse is the fact that no matter what a person is doing or saying, who they really are is who they are in their heart.

There is, however, another incredibly important concept revealed in this verse. The word "think" comes from a word that means "to split," as in a gate, door, or opening. It can also refer to a porter, janitor, or keeper. This is what we understand from this word: thoughts are the gatekeeper of the heart![1] There are two types of thoughts this verse is referring to: the thoughts of the mind or the deep thoughts of the heart. In the Greek New Testament, we see a distinction between these two sources of thoughts.

Regardless of the exact source of thoughts, there is something to be gained from either perspective. If this is a reference to the thoughts of the mind, this is saying that what we think about opens or closes the door to the heart. At one time, this is how I understood this verse, and based on many biblical teachings about our thought life, the principle is valid. However, the verse does specifically say *thoughts of the heart,* not thoughts of the mind!

The deep thoughts of the heart are the gatekeeper that determines what gets in and out of my heart. In the context of this verse, this means that no matter what I am doing on the outside, the gatekeeper will ultimately open the door and the true intentions of my heart will be expressed. This is why Jesus said it was, in fact, the things that flowed out of our heart that defile us. This also tells us that external behavior may not always reveal what is in our heart!

There is a struggle everyone faces: the gap between what I intend to do and what I actually do! There are two factors that not only guide us beyond conscious control, but even guide us in opposition to conscious intentions: the beliefs of the heart and the thoughts of the subconscious mind. Remember, the thoughts of the heart are more about your life paradigm, which is the direct expression of who you think you are. The subconscious thoughts are more about particular situations. In other words, there can be things I intend to do, yet no matter how much I pray and plan I end up doing something else. It's like resolving to talk to your spouse without getting angry. Then, for some unknown reason you find yourself out of control. We usually blame the actions of the other party for our behavior, but the truth is our unplanned behavior is always the product of the deep thoughts that drive our behavior.

> THE THOUGHTS OF THE HEART ARE MORE ABOUT YOUR LIFE PARADIGM, WHICH IS THE DIRECT EXPRESSION OF WHO YOU THINK YOU ARE.

The Book of Proverbs is a Book of Wisdom. It gives us insight into the practical application of truth. Among the many insights of this incredible book, there are precious gems that help us understand the way our heart affects our overall life experience. For example, Proverbs 12:25 says, *Anxiety in the heart of man causes depression…* Depression is not a one-time event. Depression is a general mood or feeling that negatively affects every aspect of our life. Like all life-dominating issues, depression has to do with the heart. This word for anxiety is a more correct translation than the word *heaviness* as used in the KJV. This word more precisely means an anxiety that tends toward fear. [2] If fear is in the heart, it can cause anxiety. Anxiety is a form of dread, i.e. condemnation: the expectation of punishment. When one has a foreboding feeling of things going bad, it can lead to depression and/or anxiety.

Some people live in a state of constant negativity or pessimism. They may take courses to help them think more positively and make positive affirmations, yet life still looks gloomy. And to add to the problem, life usually fulfills their gloomy expectations. Proverbs 17:20 explains, *He who has a deceitful heart finds no good, And he who has a perverse tongue falls into evil.* The ability to look at the world and find good is rooted in the condition of our heart. When we change our heart, we change our view of the world.

The eyes do not actually see. They absorb light, which is sent to the brain and the brain creates the images; however, the heart is the vessel of perception. The word for understanding is so closely related to the heart that the two words are sometimes interchangeable. We understand with our heart, and our heart creates the perception. While the brain creates the images we see, the heart interprets them. Thus, you have the "half empty or half full" life paradigm based on your interpretation of what you see. Your interpretation of what you see creates your emotional (felt) experience of the world. Your experience becomes your sense of reality.

YOUR EXPERIENCE BECOMES YOUR SENSE OF REALITY.

The word "deceitful," as used in the Proverbs passage, may best be translated *crooked.* Therefore implying, a person with a crooked heart does not see the world the way others may see it. There are many ways to describe and explain a crooked heart. For me, the best illustration is that of a prism. When light passes through a prism it is bent. According the degree of the bend, the light emerges a different color than it entered. Such is the light of the eyes; what we see and how we see it may be worlds apart. Proverbs 15:30 says, *The light of the eyes rejoices the heart.* In other words, how we see it can make the difference between pessimism and optimism, hope or dread!

Sadly, very good people with the best of intentions spend billions of dollars every year on self-help tools that, at best, only modify behavior as long as willpower is present. Until issues are resolved at their root source, i.e. the heart, they are not solved, they are simply managed. And managing problems is exhausting. Managing bad impulses is frustrating and discouraging. Managing temptation is never ending. Managing is coping. Coping is surrendering to the problem. It is like living with an abusive person because you don't believe there is any way to escape.

Interestingly, the words *upright* and *righteous,* as used in Proverbs, are often translated from the word *straight* in the original language. Just as surely as a crooked heart causes us to never find good, a straight heart leads us into the pathway of abundance, happiness, and peace. We can be on automatic pilot for good as well as bad. But modifying our behavior is not the key. The only key to abiding results in any area is to make the *crooked places straight! All the days of the afflicted are evil, But he who is of a merry heart has a continual feast* (Prov. 15:15). The options are affliction or feast, but the key is a merry heart!

I cannot emphasize strongly enough the limited benefits of behavior modification. When your behavior is destructive, by all means, use all your willpower and determination to modify your actions. At least you can have peace in your surroundings, which can give you the emotional freedom to work on your heart beliefs. But you must remember that even when your behavior is proper, only a change of heart can change the way you see the world; only a change of heart can change what you attract to yourself; only a change of heart changes the unspoken messages that your heart sends to your body and the people around you; only a change of heart puts an end to the internal struggle.

> I CANNOT EMPHASIZE STRONGLY ENOUGH THE LIMITED BENEFITS OF BEHAVIOR MODIFICATION.

The condition of your heart determines the ultimate outcome, regardless of your efforts or intentions. *The backslider in heart will be filled with his own ways, and a good man shall be satisfied from himself* (Prov. 14:14). A change in behavior does not alter how you see yourself to any significant degree. And whatever positive shift you initially gain is only lost when your behavior slips. On a larger scale, because of all the ways our heart beliefs affect us physically, emotionally, and environmentally, dynamics of a continuum are more all-inclusive than the cause and effect of behavior. When heart beliefs are accompanied by behavioral changes, the heart is at peace in the presence of God, and confident in the presence of man!

Dealing with each problem in our life is like picking fruit from an unwanted tree. No matter how many times we pick the fruit, it grows back. Dealing with the beliefs of the heart is like planting a new tree and filling your life with the desired fruit. The fruit falls off of a tree that has died at the root. Likewise, unwanted behavior falls away as the heart changes.

The only way to make all the pieces of your life begin to congruently and succinctly come together for your own good is to deal with the beliefs of your heart. *Make the crooked way straight!* Listen to just some of the benefits of taking the truth into your heart, listening to God in your heart, and hiding the word in your heart:

A sound heart is life to the body (Prov. 14:30). This is the key to altering the way our body does everything from digesting food, to circulating blood, to creating physical energy.

This verse shows the superiority of accessing God's wisdom in our heart. None of us are capable of protecting ourselves against all that is in the world. But when we believe, listen, and follow God in our heart, the benefits are incredible. This is the secret of limitless living! *When wisdom enters your heart, And knowledge is pleasant to your soul, Discretion will **preserve you**; Understanding will keep you, To **deliver you** from the way of evil, From the man who speaks perverse things, From those who leave the paths of uprightness* (Prov. 2:10-13). The person who connects to God in his or her heart seeking protection, simply follows their Shepherd as He

> WHEN WE BELIEVE, LISTEN, AND FOLLOW GOD IN OUR HEART, THE BENEFITS ARE INCREDIBLE.

navigates the valley of the shadow of death and leads them unharmed every step of the way.

Let your heart keep my commands; For length of days and long life And peace they will add to you (Prov. 3:1-2). When we relate to God out of our heart, instead of our mind or our behavior, we find everything we need and desire for an incredible life. The health, energy, and longevity that emerge from an emotional environment of peace emerge effortlessly for the person who holds God's truth in their heart. Proverbs 3:3-4 even says that when these things are in our heart we can find favor and high esteem. *Write them on the tablet of your heart, And so find favor and high esteem.*

Some people are paralyzed by their inability to be "led by the Lord." They turn it into a carnal comedy of errors. God is not far away. He is not hard to find. There are no magic formulas. There is no need for a mediator or specially anointed person. We simply have to meet Him in the one place He promised to speak, our heart! *Bind them continually upon your heart; Tie them around your neck. When you roam, they will lead you; When you sleep, they will keep you; And when you awake, they will speak with you* (Prov. 6:21-22).

When we ponder, consider, and meditate on God's Word from the perspective of how we would look, behave, and feel embracing a particular truth, we bind them to our heart. But we must remember, until we ponder God's Word from the perspective of how it affects our identity, it will not bind to our heart. Merely thinking about the right and wrong interpretation of Scripture has no positive influence on the heart. In fact, trying to sort our right and wrong interpretations usually leads to stress, anxiety, fear, and legalism.

So now you know, regardless of what you intend to do, you find yourself doing what is in your heart. Sometimes you act much better than you had intended to and you're amazed that you have such strength. Other times you seem to sink so far beneath your standard behavior and do things that surprise and appall you. Now you know that, by and large, your life is being guided by preprogramming... the beliefs of your heart. But also know that as sure as you have developed heart beliefs that are destroying you, you can develop new beliefs that put you on an autopilot course toward life at its fullest.

At this point I am asking you to do what you may not know how to do, and we'll get to the "how to." Right now you need to "decide to!" You cannot get understanding, wisdom, or grace for anything you have not yet decided to do.

But if you are ready to put yourself on a new course where life works as it should, it's time to say a prayer of commitment. In whatever way you want to say it, let God know you are finished with living from your mind. Acknowledge that you intend to know, follow, and commune with Him in your heart. Let Him know that He'll have to lead the way; He'll have to be your teacher and your strength. Then let Him know that every step of the way you are willing to surrender how you think it ought to be, so you can have it as He has made it to be! With this firm decision you are ready to move forward!

Endnotes

i. OT:8176 ru^v* **sha`ar** (shaw-ar'); a primitive root; to split or open, i.e. (literally, but only as denominative from OT:8179) to act as gate-keeper (see OT:7778): (figuratively) to estimate:
   (Biblesoft's New Exhaustive Strong's Numbers and Concordance with Expanded Greek-Hebrew Dictionary. Copyright © 1994, 2003, 2006 Biblesoft, Inc. and International Bible Translators, Inc.)

ii. OT:1674, The root d¹°ag signifies anxiety, with a shading toward the meaning of fear in some cases. (from Theological Wordbook of the Old Testament. Copyright © 1980 by The Moody Bible Institute of Chicago. All rights reserved. Used by permission.)

4

THE PURSUIT OF LIFE

The journey you are now beginning is nothing more than an extension of what you have held deep in your being all your life. You have always wanted more, known there was more, and the fact that you are reading this book says that you haven't given up; you are still making the journey. Everything you have read, prayed, seen, and heard has brought you to this very moment. Make no mistake; what you are experiencing is THE JOURNEY. It is the epic adventure of your life. This is the road every human was destined to travel. The journey of the heart is the beginning of a lifetime of transforming into who you are

> EVERYTHING YOU HAVE READ, PRAYED, SEEN, AND HEARD HAS BROUGHT YOU TO THIS VERY MOMENT.

destined to be: the real you, in Him! It is the process that fulfills in us the ultimate purpose of Jesus coming to Earth… that we could know God and experience every aspect of His Divine Life.[1] There is no end to this in scope, duration, or quality. You are created to walk the pathway of life!

Jesus said He had come that we might enjoy *life to its fullest.*[2] In another place He said, *And this is eternal life, that they may know You, the only true God, and Jesus Christ whom You have sent* (John 17:3-4). Man has always thought he was experiencing life, just as we think today. Just because we are walking, talking, and breathing, we think we know what life is. But life is not existence; it is not just the space between birth and death. Since the time man brought sin into the world, the entire human race has experienced a diminished quality of life. In the simplest experiential terms, sin is a diminished quality of life. It is the beliefs, feelings, or behavior that causes us to experience life to a lesser degree than it could be.

> IN THE SIMPLEST EXPERIENTIAL TERMS, SIN IS A DIMINISHED QUALITY OF LIFE.

Because you are starting to understand the heart, you now realize that destructive behavior is the product of a heart seeking to create a quality of life that perfectly reflects its sense of self. Thus, Jesus explained, all sin, i.e. destructive behavior, emerges from the heart. Therefore, the cure can only be found by the changes that occur in our heart!

No one has ever understood death like Adam. At one time he lived in the world as it was supposed to be. He knew God personally and he lost all of it. That was his death. His physical death, which took place hundreds of years after this event, was the result of what he lost in his life experience with God! Those who are outwardly focused say, "God told Adam he would die and he didn't!" From this flawed idea, which denies the word of God, they extrapolated, twisting their carnal logic into every manner of corrupt doctrine.

Make no mistake, Adam died. Sin didn't cause him to die; death, sin, fear, disbelief, and disobedience are synonymous; they are mere manifestations along the continuum of darkness and death. When we give belief to the lie of having or being less than we are, our actions are behavioral expressions of that belief, a behavior unbefitting of our true identity. Adam's existence after he left the garden was not life as it should be; it was merely existence. Since the fall of man, the human race has lived under the delusional idea that because we have figured out how to exist and bring a degree of happiness to ourselves, we actually have the capacity to make our life as good as it can get; or even worse, we think we can make it what God intended.

Adam didn't know life as good as it could be. God has always determined that our quality of life would be found in Jesus. Even if man had not fallen, we would have only experienced what God had in mind for us, and fulfilled our destiny through the Lord Jesus. Before there was a world, before there was a man, and before there was sin, it was predestined that Jesus would be the way to God's ultimate life![3] Make no mistake... Jesus has always been the focal point of all creation. His coming to bring mankind the abundant life was not an afterthought! It has always been the plan.

The life God is offering through His resurrection power is the only source great enough to fulfill God's purpose of expressing His great, limitless love. The life that God offers is not some inanimate object, nor is it a mere legal standing. This life is some of His very essence. Just as His breath, breathed into Adam, infused him with a life so powerful it has empowered the physical birth of every human being that has ever lived, this life in Jesus is God manifesting in the person of the Holy Spirit in us, with us, and through us. It is as if we are injected with a virus that invades our cells, bringing about a metamorphosis until every blood cell in our body has changed us as a species! The Scripture does say *the life is in the blood.* And our life is in the blood of Jesus!

The life God offers does not change things on the outside so that as our circumstances change we become happier. God's life changes us on the inside so that as we become happier, more content, and internally experience every other expression of healthy life, the outside world then conforms to harmonize with who we are! This is not merely our state of being; it is a divine influence, life, and power that permeates both our inner world and our outer world.

Jesus said He came to bring us eternal life. The traditional religious concept of eternal life has been reduced to simply living forever. But if living forever was all that was offered, to be honest I don't think we would find that very appealing after a few hundred years. To understand what God is offering and why this heart journey is so important, we must start with a proper understanding of what is being offered: eternal life! The word *eternal* is something that is without beginning or end, that which always has been and always will be.[4] *Strong's Concordance* says it is also used *of past time, or past and future as well.*[5] It is, however, when we look at the root of this word that the picture suddenly explodes into something beyond our capacity to grasp with our finite mind. The root of this word, which is usually translated as *world* can also mean: *vital force, lifetime, age, generation, time, and eternity.*[6]

MOVING YOUR INVISIBLE BOUNDARIES

This root word, *eternal*, is also used in reference to this world and to God's Kingdom. Without going into pages of language research and explanation, we need to understand the basic idea that the word *eternal* has some vague reference to our concept of time, but is much more than time. It can actually stand in opposition to time. To understand what God is offering, we must grasp the concept presented in these words: eternal life. Since this can describe the period before the creation of the world, the period since the creation of the world, the end of this period, and used in reference to the Kingdom, we understand that it is not just the period of time, but it is the force or power that makes that period of time what it is. It is the time period, but much more; it is the realm, the system, and the power that works in that realm!

God's Kingdom is not something that will come in the future. It is something that exists now. There will be an appointed time in history where the Kingdom will completely consume and overcome the world-system. At this moment, however, it is only found in our inner man. It is only seen in the world to the degree that we express it in the way we treat people, make decisions, and interact with the outer world! Because the Pharisees of Jesus' day had our same faulty paradigm of time, they looked for an event, a starting place marked in time when God's Kingdom would finally come. They were looking for a salvation that was external, which fit into our finite paradigm of existence. What God was and still is offering, however, is a salvation and deliverance that is, first and foremost, internal.

> GOD'S KINGDOM IS NOT SOMETHING THAT WILL COME IN THE FUTURE. IT IS SOMETHING THAT EXISTS NOW.

Notice in this interchange the same misconception that existed then and now. *Now when He was asked by the Pharisees when the kingdom of God would come, He answered them and said, "The kingdom of God does not come with observation; nor will they say, 'See here!' or 'See there! For indeed, the kingdom of God is within you"* (Luke 17:20-21). Those who look to the future for an external appearing of the Kingdom of God are missing the quality of life they could be enjoying in this life. They have already missed the appearing of the Kingdom. The Kingdom doesn't exist in time. It has no beginning or end. It exists in a realm. In that realm the power and resources of God are fully available. In that realm all the promises are realized. In that realm Jesus rules as Lord and King!

Those who do not make the heart-connection with God know very little of this realm and its subsequent experiences. They have the information but not the experience. It's like they have viewed a photograph but never made the actual journey. They can talk about it as if they have been there, but they do not experience the power of Kingdom living![7] They look ever outwardly, deeply longing for a time in the future when God's Kingdom will come and break off the oppression of the world's system. Yet, the very fact that they look outwardly or to the future shows that they are, in fact, operating under the laws that control the world's system. Those who look inwardly to find Christ experience the Kingdom now. They live in a paradox that *passes all understanding*; it doesn't make sense in light of the way we currently perceive and experience life. They find inwardly what cannot be seen outwardly.

The second word, *life*, only has its fullest meaning now that we have grasped the idea of eternal. The word for life in the New Testament comes from the rich Greek word "zoe" pronounced "Dzo-a." This word is more about quality of life than being alive. Zoe is true and actual life. It is the life possessed by God, actuated by the Spirit. It is a life worthy of the name – active, blessed, endless

ZOE IS TRUE AND ACTUAL LIFE.

in the Kingdom, and it denotes to living most happily in enjoyment of the theocratic blessings.[8] It is the quality of life God possesses. It is the quality of the Life given to Jesus which He, in turn, has given to us because of His presence in us.[9]

Vine's goes on to point out, "this life is not a mere principle or power, it has moral associations which are inseparable from it." To the outward-focused this would be twisted to mean we earn the life of God by the life we live, i.e. our behavior. This reversal of reality leads us to a faulty paradigm of cause and effect, which is actually part of the religious thinking that the New Testament labels as being of this world ('s system), and thereby opposed to God and His Kingdom. This life of God seems to allow for no distinction of who God is in character and what He experiences in quality of life. Likewise, our capacity to yield to (not earn) the quality of life that exists in the Kingdom is inseparable from yielding to

His character. Jesus is the light and the life. It is, therefore, impossible to embrace Him as one and not the other. (This gets into the mystery of righteousness, which will be discussed in future chapters.)

Cremer points out, "There is concentrated in the life of God every good which man can desire or enjoy." He also says, "This denotes the absence of anything that is a hindrance to the individual in the preservation and realization of His life, and thus it denotes a spiritual life which does not come under the power of any destructive influence such as death, and a life free from the effects of sin."[10] Even Cremer points out that this life is self-governing. It is not a possession we manipulate to do our will; it is something to which we yield ourselves and allow to unfold along the continuum of embracing the light and experiencing the life. In other words, I can't embrace the life for ultimate happiness *and* yield to the thoughts or behaviors that would neutralize that quality of life. On the outside, with casual observation, it seems like legalistic cause and effect. But those who make the heart journey realize it is a continuum that is experienced and embraced inwardly that manifests itself through all the outward dimensions of our being: spirit, soul, body, and eventually reaching our environment.

> THE HEART JOURNEY... MANIFESTS ITSELF THROUGH ALL THE OUTWARD DIMENSIONS OF OUR BEING ... EVENTUALLY REACHING OUR ENVIRONMENT.

All human beings want this quality of life. We all pursue it in every decision we make. There are those who seek it in the external world through the gratification of the five senses. They have chosen the world's system. Remember, the world's system can be religious or secular. The world's system is interwoven with the knowledge of good and bad, based on our carnal understanding and judgment. When we seek to determine what is good or bad for us, i.e. what will bring pain and pleasure, independent of light we can't experience the Life of God. Walking in the light and thinking we can use our faith to enjoy life is like eating candy for every meal and believing we will be healthy. No one is punishing you for eating the candy, it is just the way creation works. Whether religious or secular, it is a way of thinking that is not based on God's truth. One of the great deceptions of sin[11] is the fact that it can give us pleasure for a time. But because that which gratifies the physical senses works on the basis of the human body, it always follows the rules of addiction. That which stimulates the brain to cause the release of endorphins (the body's endogenous morphine, pleasure chemicals) always requires more stimulation each time we seek to have the "good feeling." This addictive process leads us to more and more extreme behavior. We think because we felt good for a time, our behavior must surely be the only means to the gratification we were created to enjoy. So we keep pushing the limits, never seeing the warning signs! We mistake and substitute conditioning for heart beliefs.

God is offering every human a quality of life that is better than anything we have ever heard, seen, or personally experienced. It is beyond the grasp of our wildest imagination. The Apostle Paul implied that this offer of life was the embodiment of the Gospel that should be preached to the world. But we have not heard that God was this good. We have not heard that salvation was this good. In many instances, we have heard just the opposite. As such, we have not been highly motivated to make the journey in pursuit of this life. At best, the average believer might hope that it exists in the distant future of the afterlife. But salvation is now! The Kingdom is now! God is the "I Am;" He is not the "I will be," nor the "I Was!" Those who look to the past or to the future negate their capacity to live in the eternal now and experience the Kingdom within!

> GOD IS OFFERING EVERY HUMAN A QUALITY OF LIFE THAT IS BETTER THAN ANYTHING WE HAVE EVER HEARD, SEEN, OR PERSONALLY EXPERIENCED.

In this heart journey we will look exactly where Jesus said to look: within. We will not pray and commune with a God who sits on a throne in Heaven. We will commune with a God who abides in our heart when faith is present. We will facilitate by biblical process that which is within us expressing outwardly until it invades our feelings, thoughts, emotions, and behavior, and touches the outer world.

Endnotes

i. John 10:10

ii. Rom. 8:29-30, For whom He foreknew, He also predestined *to be* conformed to the image of His Son, that He might be the firstborn among many brethren.

iii. Eph. 1:4-5, He chose us in Him before the foundation of the world, that we should be holy and without blame before Him in love, having predestined us to adoption as sons by Jesus Christ

iv. (from Thayer's Greek Lexicon, PC Study Bible formatted Electronic Database. Copyright © 2006 by Biblesoft, Inc. All rights reserved.)

v. (Biblesoft's New Exhaustive Strong's Numbers and Concordance with Expanded Greek-Hebrew Dictionary. Copyright © 1994, 2003, 2006 Biblesoft, Inc. and International Bible Translators, Inc.)

vi. (from Theological Dictionary of the New Testament, abridged edition, Copyright © 1985 by William B. Eerdmans Publishing Company. All rights reserved.)

vii. 1 Cor. 4:20, For the kingdom of God is not in word, but in power.

viii. (from Thayer's Greek Lexicon, PC Study Bible formatted Electronic Database. Copyright © 2006 by Biblesoft, Inc. All rights reserved.)

ix. (from Vine's Expository Dictionary of Biblical Words, Copyright © 1985, Thomas Nelson Publishers.)

x. Biblio – Theological Lexicon of New Testament Greek, Hermann Cremer, D.D., Edinburgh, T. & T. Clark, 38 George Street, 1895

xi. Sin is any thought, feeling, belief, or behavior that causes us to experience ourselves less than God sees us and thereby fail to experience the prize, the goal, i.e. the life of God!

5

THE WAY OF THE DISCIPLE

Like every journey, this heart journey begins with decisions. In fact, it will require the most threatening decisions you have ever made. It is the magnitude of these decisions that prevents most would-be travelers from taking this path. Sadly, this really is the path less taken but most needed for every human, especially for every believer. Freedom of choice is among the most threatening possibilities of life. Choice means we have to be responsible. It means we cannot blame others if we fail. It means PERSONAL RESPONSIBILITY! In the parables of the Kingdom taught by Jesus, there are many consistent themes. It may be that personal responsibility is the one unspoken theme woven through them all! The heart journey is a journey of personal responsibility! Because God gave us authority over our lives, nothing happens without our decisions, whether by intention or default.

> THE QUALITY OF OUR LIFE WILL NEVER BE BETTER THAN OUR CHOICES.

While there are things in life that happen beyond the realm of our control, the one thing that is within our control is the choices we make. The quality of our life will never be better than our choices. In fact, the way we choose to respond to the events that come our way actually affects us more than the event itself! It is always our choice to grow, to follow God, or to make any journey. In order to make the heart journey, it is essential that you know the difference between your part and God's part. Your part starts with reading the Word and knowing God's possibilities for you. The Bible calls this the *renewing of the mind*. You initiate involvement with God and you respond to His drawing. But, more than anything, realize you have to make your own choices. God will never violate that one freedom, responsibility, and innate authority!

Freedom of choice seems to be frightening to humans as a whole. Religion has painted an unscriptural concept of God that implies He makes all of our choices. This concept of sovereignty, which is widely taught today, was integrated into the church by Augustine. Rather than seeing sovereignty as God's right to make choices and then abide by those choices, he presented what has morphed into the idea that God can make any choice He desires, regardless of how it may violate previous choices. But the greatest destruction of fatalistic sovereignty is a perversion of predestination that not only removes man from the right to choose, it takes away from him the responsibility to choose. This twist of doctrine distorts the value of God's true sovereignty, which is the basis of His integrity. God is not a man, that He should lie. He cannot and will not violate His own Word! True sovereignty says that God is the one who made the spiritual and physical laws of the universe. They are always dependable. We can make decisions based on our knowledge of those laws and trust for God's character, and never have to wonder about the outcome!

God's responsibility in this journey is more than I can list and far more than I can know. But I am sure of this: God draws us. He not only draws us to follow Him in a general sense, but He draws us into the biblical wisdom for every problem, goal, dream, or circumstance we face. The compelling desire you have to pray, read the Bible, or do any other spiritual activity is God drawing you to Himself. Be

> HE IS NOT DRAWING YOU TO THE ACTIVITY. HE IS DRAWING YOU TO HIMSELF, TO A PERSONAL ENCOUNTER.

assured, He is not drawing you to the activity. He is drawing you to Himself, to a personal encounter. God teaches us by His Spirit. But as you make this journey, you will discover that He is not so concerned about teaching what a verse in the Bible "really means," as much as He wants to teach you what it means to your life. He wants you to know how to apply truth. By His Spirit He attempts to lead you. If we had no choices, if everything was done by the sovereignty of God, He would have no reason to lead. To be led implies the choice to follow! This is where He shows you the practical application of truth. And then He empowers you to walk in the truth. In the face of challenges, He seeks to comfort and counsel us. In each and every phase of this journey you will discover the need to make choices. Choices belong to you, and only you!

Israel's journey through the wilderness is an example to us to understand aspects of our journey with God. When they left Egypt, every household had to make their own choice to journey into the wilderness or stay in the security of what they knew! Many stayed in Egypt. Every step of the journey and in every battle, everyone had to make choices. When they came to the Promised Land, Joshua reminded and challenged them once again to make a clear choice.[1] Some chose not to live in the Promised Land, even after it was delivered into the hands of the nation of Israel.

> GOD IS ALWAYS OFFERING LIFE. TODAY IS ALWAYS THE DAY OF SALVATION...

Without exception, the most well-known verse about choice is found in Deut. 30:19. Moses tells the people, *I have set before you life and death, blessing and cursing; therefore choose life, that both you and your descendants may live.* God is always offering life. Today is always the day of salvation (being born again, healed, delivered, blessed, prospered, protected, set apart, etc.). Because you are in Christ, all of His promises to you are fulfilled (2 Cor. 1:20). Because you are in Christ, you are delivered from all the curses of the law (Gal. 3:13). Jesus is your only qualification for the inheritance of the Kingdom. I could keep going but by now I hope you get the point. Based on these Scriptures most of what we need or want in life has been provided, but we must make the choice to have them in our life, and that comes inwardly… through the heart!

Religious pride can manifest in two ways: arrogance or false humility. We quickly identify arrogance, but we are not so quick to recognize false humility. False humility is a mask for unbelief, disobedience, and stubbornness. When our beliefs are in disagreement with God's opinion of how something should be done, we are proud. Doubt and unbelief actually have their root in pride. When the Bible says *God resists the proud,* it doesn't mean He is against them personally. But it does mean they are in opposition. The word "resist" means "to set yourself against or in opposition." God cannot agree with that which opposes truth, nor can He agree with that which denies the finished work of Jesus. God is always for us, personally, but in order for us to be in agreement, we must align with Him! This "changing our mind" is what the Bible calls repentance. Repentance is a choice! It is the first choice! It is the most threatening choice! It is the quantum leap! It is the way of the disciple!

The word "repent" has no particular religious meaning. It just means to change our mind or think differently.[2] Every type of human growth or development requires repentance. If you think 2+2=5 and your teacher tells you it equals 4, you have to change your mind to get the equation right. If you think a certain road will get you to a desired location and somewhere along the way you realize it won't, you will change your mind; you will probably turn around to get back to the place where you lost your way. You will probably even regret the time you lost on your journey! In other words, you will repent. Regardless of the associated emotions, repentance only occurs when there is a change of mind.

If you fall on the road beside your car and beg for forgiveness for making a wrong turn, or if you drop into deep sadness, that is a mental issue. It has nothing to do with normal, healthy life. Likewise, contrary to religious teaching, the healthy believer recognizes where he or she is out of sync with God; they change their mind, correct their course, and may have many regrets. But they do not fall into nor does God call them to shame, despair, guilt, and desperation. It is God that is leading them to make the better choice!

Repentance is something that people do toward one another when they have wronged one another. This is why Jesus described what to do if a brother wrongs you but then comes back and repents. [3] The word, in the original, seems to imply some type of afterthought, wherein one realizes what they did and regrets how they did something.[4] This can occur in our relationship with God or people. Part of this realization comes because our teacher, the Holy Spirit, is always convicting us of the truth. The word "convict" is another word that brings forth visions of immense guilt and shame assumed to accompany the process. And if we only considered how this word was used in the common language, we could be left with this assumption. But we know when God deals with us He does it as the child He favors, not the child He hates. We know according to His word we have been delivered from wrath. So we can't interpret anything in a way that violates every other aspect of the revealed knowledge of God. There is, however, a paradox that exists. How God approaches us, and our emotional response cannot be interpreted as one and the same. In other words, if I feel guilty when I realize I am wrong, I cannot create a doctrine that says: God makes people feel guilty when they are wrong.

When Jesus addressed those attempting to trap Him over the issue of the woman caught in adultery, He told the ones who had no sin to cast the first stone. Their internal response gives us some insight about conviction. *Then those who heard it, being convicted by their conscience...* (John 8:9). In another place He asked His accusers: *Which of you convicts Me of sin* (John 8:46)? In John 3:20, we see what I think is very unique. He says, *For everyone practicing evil hates the light and does not come to the light, lest his deeds should be exposed.* You must make a mental note of this: one of the reasons we avoid coming to the truth/light when our behavior is unacceptable is that once we stand in the light the very things we have done will convince us of their inappropriateness. Then in John 16:7-11, He says the Comforter, not the tormenter,[5] will convict the world of sin, righteousness, and judgment. So we see that the word "conviction" is not necessarily a word that has vast spiritual meaning. My own conscience can convince me of the inappropriateness of my actions. Other people can convict me. My very actions will tell me they are wrong if I view them in the light. And the Holy Spirit can convict me.

> WHEN ANYONE OPERATES BY THE PHILOSOPHIES OF THE WORLD'S SYSTEM, THE HOLY SPIRIT WILL ATTEMPT TO CONVICT THEM OR CONVINCE THEM OF THE TRUTH.

When Jesus says the Holy Spirit convicts the world, it is not talking of those outside of the Kingdom. It implies He will convict "the world system." There is room for the possibility that this is a reference to the world's system. In other words, when anyone operates by the philosophies of the world's system, the Holy Spirit will attempt to convict them or convince them of the truth.

John chapter 16 goes on to tell us that the way He will convict is by pointing us to the solution. Jesus is our Shepherd; He is always attempting to lead us in Kingdom living. This means that He will function as a proactive teacher before we make decisions based on the world's system, but it also means He will attempt to point out the godly path when we have made a destructive choice. God, our conscience, our deeds, and the people around us, are all a part of the conviction process. God wired us with a number of warning systems, not to emphasize how wrong we are, but to make us aware that we need to be on another path! Without conviction we would be left with no warning system as we walk the destructive paths of life. Once we have the sense of being redirected we may have regret, we may have momentary guilt or shame, but none of that is the goal of God. God is merciful, patient, and kind in all He does, and it is His *kindness that leads us to repentance.* Don't get hung up on your emotional response if you're headed down the pathway to death; change your course, repent! Shame, sorrow, or any other negative emotion is of no value or determination of how genuine your change of mind is.

Unfortunately, religion has pretty much redefined repentance as penance. Penance is punishment or payment. Penance involves deep sorrow, making sacrifices and any number of religious activities based on your religion of choice. Some groups teach that God brings bad things into their life as punishment for the wrongs they have done. This can come in the form of sickness, financial loss, or the death of a loved one. In these religious philosophies the pain you suffer is a form of penance. But we must place our confidence in the fact that our price has been paid by Jesus. He took the punishment we deserve. We are not called to a life of penance; we are called to a life of repentance. Be assured bad choices bring bad results, but those results are the fruit of our behavior, not the punishment of God!

> WE MUST PLACE OUR CONFIDENCE IN THE FACT THAT OUR PRICE HAS BEEN PAID BY JESUS.

Punishment focuses on the past; correction focuses on the future. God's correction is like child training. Like any loving parent, He doesn't want us to continue in the destructive behavior that brings us pain and suffering. That only happens when we change the way we think and believe. The first step toward believing is to change what we think, surrender our opinions, and renew our mind! But this can never happen in a person who does not have an abiding attitude of repentance.

We all incorporate our past ideologies into our walk with God. When we begin our journey with Jesus, we usually have an opinion about who God is and how He does what He does. Then we are usually immersed into a particular doctrinal perspective that shapes our faith. Unfortunately, most of these ideas are not from the New Covenant teaching about the finished work of Jesus. It is usually a mixture of truth, tradition, and error. It is the clinging to these opinions that puts us into opposition to God's truth, and neutralizes His power to work in our life! These beliefs create the misconception that God has not done a perfect work in us. We think we need to change to become pleasing to God and gain victory over our issues. This is the beginning of a never-ending religious cycle of self-rejection, self-deceit, unbelief, and frustration.

Regardless of your reason for coming to Jesus, God has a greater reason. In the fulfilling of His purposes, all of your legitimate reasons will be fulfilled. But the first thing we must realize is God did not call us to be a Christian. He called us to be a believer, a disciple, and a son in the Lord Jesus. As such, I will spend my entire life learning what I did not know, seeking to turn that information into a heart-belief and, by God's grace (power), I will apply what I have learned to my life.

Jesus said, *A disciple is not above his teacher, but everyone who is perfectly trained will be like his teacher* (Luke 6:40). Those words "perfectly trained" literally mean "suitable, normal or proper."[6] So, by becoming a son and deciding to become a disciple, I have made my first act of repentance. I have decided that I will change my mind about how I live, what I think, how I see God, literally every aspect of life. At every place my opinion and God's opinion cross, I will die to my opinion. This is what the Bible calls dying to self, i.e. life as I know it… me as I know myself!

The word "repentance" doesn't have in its meaning a repentance of things in general, but only specific issues. Therefore, the choice to become a disciple, which is a change of mind, is the entering into a lifelong commitment of continual repentance. I will change my thinking every time I realize my thoughts and opinions are not in harmony with God's word! The repentant attitude is what makes a person teachable. Pride is what makes him unteachable. The Bible calls this surrendering of our opinions *casting down vain imaginations!*[7]

In this new relationship with God, He is our Father, Jesus is our Lord, and the Holy Spirit is our Teacher. If He is the Teacher and I am the disciple I must be teachable, pliable, and ready to make changes in my opinions. A person who is not teachable is a person who will not surrender their opinion. The Bible calls an unteachable person a fool. I have all my students read the book of Proverbs, find all of the references to being a fool or foolish. Then they make a list of how many traits of a fool they have. Then they determine if they intend to keep or surrender those tendencies. Proverbs says *a fool hates knowledge* (1:22). But the best description of a fool is the Amplified translation of Prov. 18:2. *A [self-confident] fool has no delight in understanding but only in revealing his personal opinions and himself.*

> MY CHOICES ARE: DIE TO SELF, BECOME A DISCIPLE, AND ALLOW JESUS TO TEACH ME, OR BE AN OPINIONATED FOOL!

My choices are: die to self, become a disciple and allow Jesus to teach me, or be an opinionated fool! Those are the only two options. How can I become like Him if I do not agree with Him? If I cling to my opinions, I have placed myself above Him and therefore cannot be His disciple and cannot become like Him. I can choose the way of the disciple or the way of the world!

Before moving ahead to the next chapter, make sure you have made the decision and asked God for His help in the journey! You can't do this without Him. It may serve you well to do the previously mentioned homework assignment before attempting to move on to more information. Write down each foolish trait you see in yourself. Do not be condemning or condoning. Don't make excuses. Simply own (confess) the trait. Then decide on the healthy trait you prefer to replace the destructive trait with. Commit it to the Lord, ask Him for His help, and then move forward. You will build on this exercise as you work through this material.

Sons want to be like the Father they love and admire. Disciples want to be like their teacher. The way of the disciple is a life of transformation. When you feel challenged, just remind yourself, *I want to be like Jesus. He showed me the character of God!*

Endnotes

i. Josh. 24:15, …choose for yourselves this day whom you will serve, whether the gods which your fathers served that *were* on the other side of the River, or the gods of the Amorites, in whose land you dwell. But as for me and my house, we will serve the Lord.

ii. (Biblesoft's New Exhaustive Strong's Numbers and Concordance with Expanded Greek-Hebrew Dictionary. Copyright © 1994, 2003, 2006 Biblesoft, Inc. and International Bible Translators, Inc.)

iii. Luke 17:3, Take heed to yourselves. If your brother sins against you, rebuke him; and if he repents, forgive him. NKJV

iv. (from *Theological Dictionary of the New Testament, abridged edition, Copyright © 1985 by William B. Eerdmans Publishing Company. All rights reserved.*)

v. John 16:7-11, It is to your advantage that I go away; for if I do not go away, the Helper will not come to you; but if I depart, I will send Him to you.   And when He has come, He will convict the world of sin, and of righteousness, and of judgment: of sin, because they do not believe in Me; of righteousness, because I go to My Father and you see Me no more; of judgment, because the ruler of this world is judged.

vi. (from Theological Dictionary of the New Testament, abridged edition, Copyright © 1985 by William B. Eerdmans Publishing Company. All rights reserved.)

vii. 2 Cor. 10:1-4

6

THE QUANTUM LEAP: DEATH TO SELF

You have made the decision to live as a disciple. You will seek to do this in the flesh or in the Spirit. Because God is a heart God, this is more than a program of learning information and obeying rules. This is a transformation to become like Jesus in your heart, i.e. your motives, thoughts, and intentions, accompanied by the intention for your behavior to follow. Your source of strength and your source of motivation will either be your flesh, directed by your mind, or your spirit, directed by your heart. To make the conscious decision to be a disciple from your mind and not the heart actually binds you to the sources of all your problems: the flesh! A disciple in the flesh is making a journey of self-deceit, building up and strengthening everything we should be allowing to die. When the focus is external instead of internal, we simply trade old lifestyle addictions for new, more socially accepted, religious addictions.

In Galatians 5:16 Paul says, if we *walk in the Spirit we will not fulfill the lusts of the flesh.* He then lists those lusts. Then he takes the quantum leap in Romans 8:4 and provides what I call a "furthermore" statement about the same topic... *the righteous requirement of the law might be fulfilled in us who do not walk according to the flesh but according to the Spirit.* The "furthermore" is this: when we regulate our lives by the Spirit we not only stop doing the destructive things of the flesh, we also find ourselves fulfilling God's word.

In Galatians 5:25 he says, *If we live in the Spirit let us also walk in the Spirit.* The word for "live" comes from the word "Zoe." The word for "walk" is slightly different than he used earlier. In this instance "walk" means "to line up or proceed in a row." Here you see the person who believes they have the life of God in them. They are not trying to become what God wants them to be. They are yielding to a power already in them activated by belief and awareness. Because they are spiritually minded, their life is regulated by this internal life. This power, which the Bible calls grace, is what gives the believer the ability to effortlessly align his external life with his internal life.

> THIS POWER, WHICH THE BIBLE CALLS GRACE, IS WHAT GIVES THE BELIEVER THE ABILITY TO EFFORTLESSLY ALIGN HIS EXTERNAL LIFE WITH HIS INTERNAL LIFE.

The reason this is a quantum leap is because this is not something that happens by the release of strong will or massive force; this is something that occurs as a change at the smallest level… by simply changing the focus of your attention and then simply yielding to the righteousness that is already in you by the Lord Jesus.

God called us to be disciples by walking in the Spirit. Unless that is the call we responded to, it is unclear where we are going. One thing for sure, if we are not following Him as a disciple, we are not really following Him. Without a commitment to live as a disciple, all appearance of growth is carnal self-deception. Unless this journey is a walk in the Spirit, it will be a walk in the flesh. When our journey is in the flesh, in our strength, it is about us, not about Him; it is about our glory, and not His.

Now you have to make the ultimate decision, the true quantum leap to win over your flesh: die! You cannot experience a new life beyond the degree you die to the old. The old life is based first and foremost on the world's system, i.e. the way you learned to think and perceive yourself and the world around you based on your experience as a sinner.

I heard a popular talk show host interviewing one of the most well-known pastors in America. The host commented that words like "sin" and "sinner" are outdated. The host said that they exclude and insult people. But, in truth, the only thing truly outdated about the word "sinner" is the way religion has used it to pronounce self-righteous judgment on those who need God's help. If people knew God's love for man, the value He has for even the wicked, and a proper definition for sin, it would be an endearing term that always reminded people that God sees them as being far more valuable than they see themselves.[1]

There are nine Greek words for sin. The most common of those words is *hamartia*. This Greek word is normally translated "to miss the mark." This is absolutely correct; however, it is only half the meaning. It is actually "to miss the mark of the prize." The prize is the life of God, the opportunity to know God personally, and life in the Kingdom with all its privileges and benefits. As we discussed previously, sin can only be properly understood when we recognize the following: sin is always a heart issue; it has its roots in faulty beliefs; these beliefs give rise to feelings of fear and inadequacy; fear cannot trust God or His life instructions; inadequacy never feels it is what God wants it to be; therefore, it always leads to destructive behavior, i.e. disobedience. The problem with disobedience is not the simple fact that you disobeyed God. Disobedience means you left the path of life. You missed the mark of the prize!

> SIN IS ALWAYS A HEART ISSUE; IT HAS ITS ROOTS IN FAULTY BELIEFS; THESE BELIEFS GIVE RISE TO FEELINGS OF FEAR AND INADEQUACY; FEAR CANNOT TRUST GOD...

We were all born with a sinful nature. For more reasons than we have space to explain, it seems that the root emotion of the sinful nature is fear. It was the emotional shift that occurred when man gave in to his destructive beliefs. Children come out of the womb not seeking to do evil, but frightened. To soothe their fear they instinctively seek the security of their mother. Fear interprets every uncomfortable or painful experience as a personal attack. So, the interpretation of the world by a child is somewhat skewed! From conception throughout the rest of their life, the way they determine who they are is based on their interpretation of their experiences. This produces an emotional foundation built upon layer after layer of faulty thinking that leads to more flawed judgments. This causes more destructive behavior and more painful experiences which lead to judgments about self, which cycle back through and create new emotional layers with each experience.

By the time we come to Jesus, we have a lifetime of experiences, all of which have been compiled and stored in the cells of our body to create an informational hologram of who we are. And yes, every one of the trillions of cells in your body has this blueprint that creates an informational image of who you believe yourself to be based on faulty, fear-based thinking and irrational personal judgments. Our sense of identity is based on the sum total of all our life's experiences. It does not matter that we cannot consciously recall all of our experiences; they are all recorded as part of the program that runs our life. This program determines how our physical body works. It guides every life decision. It is the relational map moving us down the same road over and over, always expecting a different outcome, but only to experience disappointment.

Empirical observation and emerging biological research reveals that each organ in the body may store different types of emotional experiences. We do know from biblical and scientific research that each organ in the body actually influences specific aspects of thought and emotion. It seems the heart very specifically manages our long-term memory, and thereby in some way becomes the reservoir for storing the thoughts that create our sense of identity. It seems that when the Bible talks about beliefs of the heart, it is more literal than we could have ever realized.

> EMERGING BIOLOGICAL RESEARCH REVEALS THAT EACH ORGAN IN THE BODY MAY STORE DIFFERENT TYPES OF EMOTIONAL EXPERIENCES.

We know that the heart has neurons just like the brain, which means it has the capacity to store memories and generate thoughts. There have actually been medical accounts of heart transplant recipients having the memories of those whose heart they had received, which validates the research. People who have (physical) heart issues often have difficulty maintaining their emotional boundaries. After all, if I do not know where I end and you begin, I will have a tendency to confuse my identity with the people around me. As the seat of love, this becomes a major factor in our ability to maintain harmonious, loving relationships.

The identity I have created through years of life experience can be called the "I," the "ego," the "old man," or the "self." The thing that makes self so deadly is my interpretation of everything I see, hear, or experience. This is the product of my sense of self... who I think I am. We do not see anything as it really is. Everything we see is an interpretation of what is there based on how I see myself. So I cannot see anything as it is until I see it through a new perspective: God's point of view! It is incredibly challenging to give up a point of view when everything in you says, "this is the way it is." Yet, God's word says, "No, <u>this</u> is the way it is."

There is no fixing the "old man." You could get counseling every day for the rest of your life and never come to the end of your convoluted interpretations of all of your experiences and the consequential emotional pain you are suffering. Everything about the "old man" causes you to see yourself as less than God sees you. You will never embrace or experience the "new you" while the "old you" lives and defines the world around you. The only cure for the "old man" is to die.

> YOU WILL NEVER EMBRACE OR EXPERIENCE THE "NEW YOU" WHILE THE "OLD YOU" LIVES AND DEFINES THE WORLD AROUND YOU.

Nothing about Kingdom living actually works as promised until there is a death to self. It is not God restricting what He will do for you; it is just a matter of following His design. The Kingdom has its own laws (of life), and it has a King. We cannot live in one Kingdom but live by the laws of another. This is exactly what a carnal Christian is attempting to do. The "old man" cannot see, perceive, or grasp the realities of the Spirit or the Kingdom. It is not subject to the law of God (law of life), nor can it be.[2]

I have heard every religious, twisted teaching about dying-to-self imaginable. The legalist makes dying-to-self a matter of penance and suffering which is a denial of the suffering of Christ for our sins. The externalist makes dying-to-self an external, behavioral issue with no regard for the heart. But the believer who is seeking to relate to God from the heart realizes that dying-to-self is, more than anything else, the surrender of my identity and all associated thoughts and opinions. This is not pretending to be dead; this is the acceptance of my death in Christ, something that can never be intellectually realized or empowered. *I am crucified with Christ, nevertheless I live,*[3] is one of the great paradoxical realities of living from the heart. How could we have died with Christ and yet still be alive? No matter how much I explain this, the information is useless apart from the experience.

There is nothing I have to do to make this true. Christ died for the sins of the world; yet, not everyone is living in Him. So making the decision to believe this truth does not cause God to do something He has not yet done; instead, it takes us to the place of experiencing what has been done. Somehow, Jesus became my sin… anything that causes me to miss the mark of this high calling. He took all the consequences of that life. Paul said we should just consider it so![4] Until we consider God's reality to be the only reality, this is just information that exists beyond our understanding and experience.

God has a reality! His is eternal and never-changing. He cannot change His reality for us. We have a perceived reality. Ours is temporary and changes with every new experience or judgment. Our sense of reality is based on the interpretation of our life experiences. We can only experience God's reality when we choose it as our own and when we fully persuade our heart. We are not creating it by positive thinking. We are not using mind over matter. We are dying to our false illusion of reality. This cannot be grasped with the natural (carnal) mind. It cannot be explained to the satisfaction of those seeking an intellectual answer;

> WE CAN ONLY EXPERIENCE GOD'S REALITY WHEN WE CHOOSE IT AS OUR OWN…

yet, like all spiritual reality, it can be experienced in a way that is undeniable. Faith is a matter of the heart, not the mind; therefore, Kingdom living is a journey of faith from beginning to end.

Faith is not blind. God is not saying, "Shut your eyes and trust Me." He is saying, "I will tell you My reality. If you trust Me you can choose it as your own. Then I will lead you every step of the way into this reality." The word "faith" simply means, "immovable trust."[5] There is no wavering from one position to another in faith.[6] Hebrews 11:1 says, *Now faith is the substance of things hoped for, the evidence of things not yet seen.* The word "things" is not talking about individual items, trinkets, or toys to be squandered on our lusts. The word "things" refers to things that God has already accomplished. It is not the vague possibility of something He might do should we "believe enough." In the Old Testament faith looked to what God would do in the future. In the New Covenant we have a last will and testament. It is all settled. Religious, Old Testament concepts of faith have no place in the New Covenant believer's walk with God.

When we know what God has accomplished and/or promised through the death, burial, and resurrection of Jesus, our every act of faith is based on whether or not we believe in the cross of Christ! The cross, i.e. death, burial, and resurrection, is the one place we can see what God has ALREADY accomplished. There is nothing we need that has not been provided for in this eternal event. It is what we believe about the finished work that determines whether we are believers living in the Kingdom or Christians living in the world's system. If all of our decisions are made from this perspective, if this

> IT IS WHAT WE BELIEVE ABOUT THE FINISHED WORK THAT DETERMINES WHETHER WE ARE BELIEVERS LIVING IN THE KINGDOM, OR CHRISTIANS LIVING IN THE WORLD'S SYSTEM.

is the foundation for interpreting life, we are, by biblical definition, spiritually-minded, and we live in the law of the Spirit of Life in Christ Jesus.

In several places Paul presents the fact that the struggle of the believer, the actual warfare, is the conflict that is waged in the mind, emotions, and feelings. There is no clear-cut New Covenant reference to any type of spiritual warfare other than that which goes on in our mind, thoughts, emotions, and intellect. Everything in our world-view has been interpreted from the perspective of "self" for our entire life. You can believe your mind will seek to return to old patterns of thinking and interpretation. It has been trained and conditioned to do exactly what it does. This is the believer's spiritual warfare. The outcome of this internal battle is determined by where we focus our attention. Remember, where you focus your attention determines not only what regulates your life, but also what is magnified in your life. What you ignore dies from a lack of attention.

This principle is seen in praise and worship. Psalm 34:3 says, *Oh, magnify the* Lord *with me, And let us exalt His name together.* To "magnify" means "to make bigger." So, can we make God any bigger than He is? No! I never criticize people for their limiting, unscriptural terminology; however, inaccurate terminology causes serious corruption of our faith. I often hear people talking about the presence of God "showing up." They may have felt God's presence in a powerful, simultaneous, corporate experience, but I can assure you God was there all the time. He didn't show up because there was enough fervent prayer and worship. God is omnipresent. The Psalmist asked, *"Where can I go from your Spirit?"* He said, *"Even if I make my bed in hell you are there."* Surely if God's presence is in the grave, He is ever present in church!

These types of unscriptural references and beliefs emerge because of ignorance and rejection of New Covenant reality. He is with us and in us! God doesn't show up after we praise Him enough. God doesn't show His power more after we work ourselves into a "faith frenzy." God is always here, always powerful, and has already given us all we need for life and godliness. So what happens? Simple! We experience the God who is already present as we focus our attention on Him through prayer, praise, worship, or meditation.

The Psalmist said, *Let us exalt His name together.* The word "magnify" can also mean "to make great or important."[8] As I exalt or lift high the name of the Lord by acknowledging how great He is or how important He is in my life, I begin to have an awareness of God. I experience Him because He is the focus of my attention, not because He finally showed up!

The reality of your death is just as sure as the reality that God is always with you and that God raised Jesus from the dead. You can't make it more real, but you can experience it in a more real way. It starts by choosing to believe. When Christ died, the "old me" died with Him.[9] When Jesus was raised up from the dead, I was raised up with Him.[10] I am now with Him at the right hand of God.[11] I am in Him; therefore, I am as He is.[12]

This is the beginning of renewing your mind. Renewing your mind is part of the process of fully persuading your heart. But it all starts with this: all that I was is dead. I will in no way yield to the false realities of my "old man." You may want to write this out on some cards and place them where you can see them. "All that I was, all that I thought I was, is now dead. I died with Jesus. That person is crucified with Christ." Every time you see one of the strategically placed cards, acknowledge this truth. When you find yourself giving in to old patterns, whisper or scream this truth, whatever is appropriate for where you are and how you feel. Then simply say to the temptation, "I am dead to you, you have no power over me." Then choose how you really want to respond to your current challenge.

> RENEWING YOUR MIND IS PART OF THE PROCESS OF FULLY PERSUADING YOUR HEART.

Endnotes

i.   Rom. 5:8, But God demonstrates His own love toward us, in that while we were still sinners, Christ died for us.

ii.   Rom. 8:7-8, Because the carnal mind *is* enmity against God; for it is not subject to the law of God, nor indeed can be. So then, those who are in the flesh cannot please God. NKJV

iii. Gal. 2:20-21, I have been crucified with Christ; it is no longer I who live, but Christ lives in me; and the *life* which I now live in the flesh I live by faith in the Son of God, who loved me and gave Himself for me.

iv.   Rom. 6:11, So you also should consider yourselves to be dead to the power of sin and alive to God through Christ Jesus.
      Holy Bible, New Living Translation ®, copyright © 1996, 2004 by Tyndale Charitable Trust. Used by permission of Tyndale House Publishers. All rights reserved.

v.   (from Thayer's Greek Lexicon, Electronic Database. Copyright © 2000, 2003, 2006 by Biblesoft, Inc. All rights reserved.)

vi.   James 1:6-8, But let him ask in faith, with no doubting, for he who doubts is like a wave of the sea driven and tossed by the wind. For let not that man suppose that he will receive anything from the Lord; *he* is a double-minded man, unstable in all his ways.

vii. Ps. 139:7-8

viii. (from Theological Wordbook of the Old Testament. Copyright © 1980 by The Moody Bible Institute of Chicago. All rights reserved. Used by permission.)

ix.   Gal. 2:20

x.   Col. 2:12-13

xi.   Eph. 2:6

xii. 1 John 4:17

7

RENEWING THE MIND: THE INFORMATION EXCHANGE

Most people use the word "saved" when describing the new birth experience. While there is nothing incorrect about using that terminology, it is a limited concept of the word. It is important to realize that salvation begins at the new birth, but it is also an ongoing experience. We have been saved (in our spirit) and we are being saved (in our body and soul). At the new birth our spirit is born again and made new. Our spirit is made completely righteous by the blood of Jesus. There is nothing we can do to make it more righteous. Our righteousness was a gift from the Lord Jesus and is

> WE HAVE NO NEED TO BECOME MORE RIGHTEOUS. IN OUR SPIRIT WE ARE AS RIGHTEOUS AS WE CAN POSSIBLY BE.

the power at work in us from that day forward. While we cannot become more righteous, we can, however, yield more fully to righteousness. As we renew our mind and influence our heart, the salvation in our spirit expands to our soul, body, and the world around us.

When we yield to sin, we give power to death. When we yield to righteousness, we experience the power of righteousness[1] and life. We have no need to become more righteous. In our spirit we are as righteous as we can possibly be. We have the righteousness of Christ. But the question is this: is the righteousness of Christ permeating and giving life to my thoughts, my health, and the people in my world?

The battle over righteousness has raged since before the conception of the Church. It is the primary issue that causes conflict between religions and denominations. While everyone has their interpretation of righteousness, most are not based on the finished work of Jesus; they do not involve faith, and there are few concepts of the *fruit of righteousness* by either side of the argument. Fruit is something that grows as a result of the root to which it is connected. Righteousness is not earned, it is not forced, and it only comes in season, which means it cannot be demanded. And over time the fruit reveals the true nature of the tree.

Righteousness as a free gift makes no sense to the natural mind. The legalist believes Christ is our Savior but we must earn our righteousness. This is the doctrine of the Judaizers that corrupted the early Church and had to be addressed in nearly every letter written by the Apostle Paul to the churches. Instead of renewing their mind and connecting with God in their heart, they brought their religious past into their faith. Then they interpreted and judged God's Word by their traditions. These people are the overbearing legalists, externalists who based everything on performance, i.e. dead works.

After some time the Church began to distance itself from its Hebrew roots and become more Gentile in culture. Consequently, the Church lost the foundational teaching that helped us understand God, His character, and His covenant. Without a good foundation in the Old Testament, people who had come from various Roman, Greek, and other cults believed in Jesus as Savior; but they, too, interpreted the Word of God from their cult doctrines and cultural traditions. These people took a more liberal or mystical approach to God. They had little value for godliness, especially if it conflicted with their pursuit of personal fulfillment. While Paul addressed some of these, the Apostle John's letters most openly challenged these heresies.

Both of these groups missed a primary factor in this call God was issuing to the world. He was not calling us to be Christians; He was calling us to be sons who became disciples, thereby experiencing Kingdom living. They missed the target, the goal, the mark of the prize. They brought their traditions into the Church with them, and while they may have experienced forgiveness, they never discovered Kingdom Living. They fulfilled the words of Jesus: *You have made the commandment of God of no effect by your tradition* (Matt. 15:6-7).

Faith righteousness, according to Paul, is the STUMBLING STONE of the Gospel.[2] The interpretation of this one issue is what causes more division, strife, and misunderstanding than any other aspect of the Gospel. How you define righteousness determines if you are trying to *become* righteous or if you believe you *are* righteous. If you are trying to become righteous, then you do not truly believe Jesus has made you righteous. If you believe you are righteous, do you believe you should live righteously? Some don't! Yet, that very idea is contradictory to everything we know about God, everything the Scripture teaches, and everything about living an abundant life.

> HOW YOU DEFINE RIGHTEOUSNESS DETERMINES IF YOU ARE TRYING TO BECOME RIGHTEOUS OR IF YOU BELIEVE YOU ARE RIGHTEOUS.

The word "righteous," as previously discussed, seems to be a continuum that begins with what God has done in our spirit all the way through to our behavior: right standing, virtuous character, godly behavior, and many other factors. One very good source translates "righteousness" as: *one who is such as he ought to be*.[3] Because we have all things that pertain unto life and godliness,[4] because our spirit has been made perfect,[5] because all the promises are ours,[6] but mostly because we are *hid[7] with Christ*… we are as we should be! To reject the fact that you are righteous in Jesus is to reject the sacrifice of Jesus. So, the big issue is this: how do I live righteously without getting into legalism and dead works? Having committed to the life of a disciple, having come to the realization that this must be a journey of the heart, I must begin by renewing my mind.

Renewing the mind is more than simply amassing facts and gaining new information. We are disciples. We want to follow our Lord and Master: Jesus.

We want to think like He thought; we want to live like He lived; we want to do what He did; we want to put into practice the limitless possibilities of faith He said were available to us! Renewing the mind is where repentance occurs as we read His Word or follow His leading. This is where, as we discover new truths about who we are, we put off the "old man" and put on the new. Renewing the mind is the prayerful process whereby we die daily[8] to self (opinions) and put on the "new man."

It is important to always remember, I am not *becoming* the "new man;" I am *putting on* the "new man." But before I can put on the "new man," I must put off the "old[9] man"... any sense of me and how I think life should work that is incongruent with righteousness! We are not gathering facts and learning new information so we can give people the right answers. We have a purpose for all we learn; we want to renew our mind to see ourselves as we really are in Jesus, so we can put off the "old man" and put on the "new man."

> I AM NOT BECOMING THE "NEW MAN;" I AM PUTTING ON THE "NEW MAN."

Putting off the "old man" is yielding to death in some aspect of our life. Putting on the "new man" is yielding to resurrection life in a particular area.

Some would argue, "Didn't God give us a new mind when we got saved?" In the Book of Hebrews, the writer describes certain aspects of the New Covenant and says: *I will put My laws in their mind and write them on their hearts...* (Heb. 8:10-11). The word "mind" in this passage is not the word for intellectual mind. This is a word that means "deep thoughts." The language used in the sentence seems to point to the deep thoughts of the heart. We have full control of our conscious mind, what we put in it, and how we think. And it is in the realm of our thoughts and subsequent emotions that a war rages.[10]

God's Word was not written in our conscious, intellectual mind. That is our responsibility. His Word was written on our heart and emerges through the deep thoughts of the heart in the form of intuitive communication. As it emerges to our mind, we put words to what we sense God is saying in our heart! The mind that is not renewed by God's Word interprets the intuitive voice of God to fit his or her opinions, traditions, and cultural concepts.

The conscious, intellectual mind on one level is pretty simple: what you put in determines what you get out of it. Similarly, where we focus our attention determines the kind of emotions we experience. When we seek to walk in faith (immovable trust) in some area of our life, the wavering that leads us to doubt is so very often because of what we think in our intellectual mind. Our intellect is that collection of information we have learned, wherewith we have navigated our life. This information has become part of our survival mechanism. It has kept us alive. We trust it. It makes us feel safe and in control. It is the "known!"

There are at least three different Greek words translated as "mind" and several more translated as "thought" in the English Bible. They each reveal unique insight into the process of transformation. One is our intellect. This is the part of the mind that we feed with information. The other is a word that means "to focus on a particular direction." This is the word Paul uses when he explains spiritual and carnal-mindedness. One or the other is determined by our focus. Paul tells me to *renew my mind* (intellect).[11] But he also tells me to focus my attention, i.e. mind, on the *things of the Spirit*. The third word translated as "mind" refers to the deep thoughts. This could be the thoughts of the heart. Knowing which word is used is crucial to understanding what each verse is discussing when the word "mind" is used.

Paul, the man who pioneered the message of faith righteousness, never suggested, as some imply, that he condoned compromised living. Actually it was just the opposite. Because we have been made righteous, we should walk in righteousness. Yet, Paul never presented the solution to our behavioral struggles as mere behavior modification. Paul's gospel held man in that tension between faith righteousness and personal obedience. The reason people are so conflicted about this issue is they do not approach it as a heart issue. Even in Paul's day, many people twisted his teaching to their own destruction.[12]

Many times Paul would tell people to stop doing certain things and begin doing other things. He was not slack about addressing unacceptable behavior. But when it came down to solving the root problem, Paul always took the believer to the internal world of the heart, soul, and mind. He addressed the way we think, feel, and believe as the cure for all problems. As responsible believers, we should always address and modify our destructive or offensive behavior. But we should never assume behavior modification to be the cure, nor should we equate our efforts for change as our righteousness.

In Romans 12:1, he said; *present your bodies as a living sacrifice, holy, acceptable to God, which is your reasonable service.* This is said in the context of faith righteousness, spiritual mindedness, and determining if we would yield to God or sin. Provided your previous decisions were to follow God's process, he concludes it is only reasonable that you present your living body to God. But He didn't take the plunge into legalistic works righteousness, he addresses the problem internally. *And do not be conformed to this world.* Do not allow yourself to be fashioned after the world. If we are living in the Kingdom in our heart, our life and conduct should be that of the kings and priests.

Then he goes on, *but be transformed by the renewing of your mind.* It is crucial that we recognize the word "transformed." This is the word "metamorphose." This is not the kind of change where you are trying to become something you are not. It is the process whereby what you are changes you. The caterpillar doesn't *become* a butterfly. The caterpillar *is* a butterfly in a different state. When we yield to the righteousness of God already in us, it transmutes us to manifest outwardly what God has already made us to be inwardly.

> THE CATERPILLAR DOESN'T BECOME A BUTTERFLY. THE CATERPILLAR IS A BUTTERFLY IN A DIFFERENT STATE.

But Paul says this happens by the renewing of our mind, i.e. intellect. I must make my intellect new so my conscious thoughts are harmonious with the truth of who I am in Christ. By thinking of myself as God sees me, I put attention on that which is inward, i.e. I am spiritually-minded. As such, the life of the Spirit is what manifests in me. If I think of myself as righteous and believe that I am righteous, I will release within me the power of righteousness.

When addressing corrupt lifestyle issues in the letter to the Ephesians, Paul tells them, *you have not so learned Christ.* Paul had been accused of preaching permissiveness by the legalists who did not understand faith righteousness. And those who sought a permissive lifestyle used faith righteousness as an excuse to live a compromised life. In Eph. 4:21 he goes on to say, *if indeed you have heard Him and have been taught by Him, as the truth is in Jesus: that you put off, concerning your former conduct, the old man which grows corrupt according to the deceitful lusts, and be renewed in the spirit of your mind, and that you put on the new man which was created according to God, in true righteousness and holiness.*

Paul did not tell them they had to become the "new man," but he did tell them that when there is disharmony between the righteousness of God in you and your outward life, you are being deceived by your lusts and you should put off the "old man" and put on the new. The "old man" is the person you were when you operated under the world's system. The new you must live by Kingdom principles or you will find yourself a servant of sin.

Paul said to put off the old and put on the new by this process: *be renewed in the spirit of your mind.* This word for "mind" is the word "intellect." So it cannot be talking about the deep, inward thoughts. We know we do not have the power to make our spirit new. That is the work of the Holy Spirit. This seems to imply that we should renew our mind to be in harmony with what has taken place in our spirit. In other words, we have to consciously see ourselves as God has made us to be. And furthermore, we must choose to put on this "new man."

The person who makes this journey of renewal discovers that they do not have to live in sin to have a great life. In fact, those who make the heart journey discover that life in the Kingdom is better than anything the world has to offer. That's why in Romans chapter 12 he goes on to say: *that you may prove what is that good and acceptable and perfect will of God.* Taking this step is the way to test and see that the will of God is good, acceptable, and perfect. It is never acceptable to test God with our unbelief. But He tells us to test His Word in faith and see how good the benefits are.[13]

At the end of the day, this will be a walk of faith. Do I trust that God has made me righteous, even though I still have struggles? Can I believe what God says about me? Faith is when I am immovable in my trust for what God has said and done, which is really trust for His character. For wavering to occur there must first be conflict between my intellectual mind and the deep thoughts of my heart. The wavering occurs when I shift my conscious attention (mind) from what I believe in my heart to what I think in my mind.

The Bible says when I waver I become double-minded and cannot receive anything from the Lord.[14] This word "receive" is not a passive word that describes a person waiting for God to do His part. God has done His part in Jesus. We must take hold of what He has done! This word for "receive" means "to take hold and bring it unto yourself."[15] There is nothing passive about this word, and furthermore, there is nothing this person is waiting on God to do. The person who thinks they are waiting on God is not taking hold of the finished work of Jesus. This is an action of faith in what God has done. If we believe we have been made righteous, we must take hold of it and bring it unto ourselves by faith. This starts with renewing our mind to see who we are and what we have in Jesus.

When I was first taught about renewing the mind, I was taught this meant I should stop thinking any bad or dirty thoughts. While I fully agree with that idea, in the context of Paul's teaching, renewing the mind is always in the framework of our new identity. He addressed the heart of our sin issues by telling us to change the way we think and see ourselves. Renewing the conscious intellectual mind is just the first step in this process, but is by no means the full process.

The renewing of the mind requires that I see Christ as He is (now, resurrected) and it requires that I subsequently see myself as I am (in Him). This occurs concurrently as we read God's Word, pray, and meditate. The Apostle John tells us we become like Him to the degree we see Him as He is.[16] Transformation occurs on the conscious/intellectual level and the heart level in conjunction, one with the other. In the process they both affect different aspects of your soul. However, when there is absolute harmony between the mind and the heart, transformation will occur. But just like any metamorphosis, it doesn't all happen at once. It

> WHEN THERE IS ABSOLUTE HARMONY BETWEEN THE MIND AND THE HEART, TRANSFORMATION WILL OCCUR.

occurs day by day as we walk with Him. One day we will see Him face to face and the complete transformation, including a resurrection body, will occur. But every step of this transformation is because we grow in the knowledge of Him.[17] This transformation is an experience that begins with intellectually believing the truth, and through the process experiencing it in our total being.

It is essential that you read the Bible, and do so with the attitude of a disciple. This would mean that, first and foremost, every time we open His Word we do so with a disciple's prayerful attitude! "Teach me. Show me what this means to my life. Speak to me through Your Word." Unless you are seeking to apply it to your life, you are just reading a historical account of someone else's life and the teachings of the apostles to other people. This is not an exercise in spiritual voyeurism. You are not merely watching others have intimate spiritual experiences. You are seeking to have one of your own. I recommend my free online "Living Under Lordship Discipleship Program" (http://www.impactministries.com/Ministries/LivingUnderLordship.aspx). It will help you on this journey of lordship and discipleship.

Jesus' life on Earth is not the basis of our faith. All of our faith is based on what was accomplished through His death, burial, and resurrection. But His life provides the opportunity to see how we can live in this world. He modeled what a man filled with grace by God's Spirit can do. The Gospels give us a chance to see who He is, what He taught, and how He dealt with people. He is our model in every way.

> JESUS' LIFE ON EARTH IS NOT THE BASIS OF OUR FAITH. ALL OF OUR FAITH IS BASED ON WHAT WAS ACCOMPLISHED THROUGH HIS DEATH, BURIAL, AND RESURRECTION.

Then, as you read the writings of the apostles, you will see their instructions to the Church. Most of these letters (epistles) were written to correct false doctrine, deal with sin issues, and to help people see the resurrected Jesus as He is now. As you read their writings, you will notice phrases like "in Him, by Him, through Him, or with Him." These are key concepts that are essential for heart transformation into His likeness. The New Covenant not only tells us we can live as He lived, but even more importantly, it tells us we are as He is now, since the resurrection.[18] Since the heart is, more than anything else, the seat of our identity, these identity Scriptures become the source for influencing our heart. I highlighted all of them in my Bible so I could read and meditate on them regularly.

Any way that God sees or relates to Jesus now, anything Jesus has now is yours. If you died with Him, you were raised up with/in/through Him. There is no separating Him from you. I am not saying you *are* Him, I am saying you are *you* in Him. You are one with Him in a way the intellectual mind cannot grasp. It can learn and gather the information, but the understanding will come when you take steps to commune with God in your heart. But the key is this:

We are a new creation IN CHRIST! How easy it is to breeze over the meaning and importance of the phrase "in Christ" or "in Him." We were baptized into the body of Christ at salvation. He is not only in us, we are in Him. As such, all that became His at His resurrection became ours. The Apostle Paul prayed that believers would realize this truth and come to understand that the same Spirit that raised Christ from the dead has raised us up into newness of life. His victories are our victories, His anointing is our anointing, His inheritance is our inheritance, and His position in God is our position in God![19]

For the believer this heart journey is all about putting off any way we see, or experience, or express ourselves that is incongruent with the resurrected Lord, and putting on all that He is. We were predestined to be like Him. This is one of the many reasons He is called the Lord of glory. He will be the focal point for every person throughout all eternity! At first this information will excite you; but unless your goal is transformation, it will become a new doctrine you use to win arguments and prove your intellectual superiority over others. That's when you pretend that talking the talk is the same as walking the walk. Having this knowledge will give you an "ego rush" that you will mistakenly think to be a revelation, or even think it is a transformation. When you find yourself talking about it, arguing about it, or otherwise intellectualizing it more than living it, repent and put your focus back on Him and your commitment to follow Him as a disciple.

> FOR THE BELIEVER THIS HEART JOURNEY IS ALL ABOUT PUTTING OFF ANY WAY WE SEE, OR EXPERIENCE, OR EXPRESS OURSELVES THAT IS INCONGRUENT WITH THE RESURRECTED LORD...

Anything you allow to work in you will eventually influence the world and people around you in a way that far exceeds what you can do arguing the facts. But more importantly, it will do in you that which can come in no other way.

At this point you may want to either order *The Prayer Organizer* or make your own list of identity Scriptures. After using the flash cards to declare your death to sin, quote those identity Scriptures. Acknowledge who you are in Him! But don't do it in an impersonal way, direct all of your communication directly to Him. "Because I am in You, I have life, light, and love. Because I have Your grace, I choose to walk in light, life, and love. By Your stripes I have been healed. I call myself whole, well, and completely healed." As you say these Scriptures, experience them in your own thoughts, mind, and emotions. See yourself living as if they are true and working in your life at this very moment!

Endnotes

i.   Rom. 6:13, Neither yield ye your members as instruments of unrighteousness unto sin: but yield yourselves unto God, as those that are alive from the dead, and your members as instruments of righteousness unto God.

ii.   Rom. 9:30-33

iii.   *The state of him who is such as he ought to be, righteousness,* (from Thayer's Greek Lexicon, Electronic Database. Copyright © 2000, 2003, 2006 by Biblesoft, Inc. All rights reserved.)

iv.   2 Peter 1:3

v.   Heb. 10:14, For by one offering he hath perfected for ever them that are sanctified.

vi.   2 Cor. 1:20

vii. Col. 3:3, For ye are dead, and your life is hid with Christ in God.

viii. 1 Cor. 15:31

ix. Putting off the old man is accepting the death of some part of our life. Putting on the new man is yielding to some aspect of the resurrected life of Christ.

x. Rom. 7:23

xi. Rom. 12:1-2

xii. 2 Peter 3:16, as also in all his epistles, speaking in them of these things, in which are some things hard to understand, which untaught and unstable *people* twist to their own destruction, as *they do* also the rest of the Scriptures.

xiii. 1 Thess. 5:21-22, Test all things; hold fast what is good.[22] Abstain from every form of evil.

xiv. James 1:6-8, But let him ask in faith, nothing wavering. For he that wavereth is like a wave of the sea driven with the wind and tossed. For let not that man think that he shall receive any thing of the Lord. A double minded man is unstable in all his ways.

xv. *to take to oneself, lay hold upon, take possession* (from Thayer's Greek Lexicon, Electronic Database. Copyright © 2000, 2003, 2006 by Biblesoft, Inc. All rights reserved.)

xvi. 1 John 3:2-3, Beloved, now we are children of God; and it has not yet been revealed what we shall be, but we know that when He is revealed, we shall be like Him, for we shall see Him as He is.

xvii. 2 Peter 1:3-4, His divine power has given to us all things that *pertain* to life and godliness, through the knowledge of Him who called us by glory and virtue

xviii. 1 John 4:19

xix. Eph. 1:16-23, do not cease to give thanks for you, making mention of you in my prayers: that the God of our Lord Jesus Christ, the Father of glory, may give to you the spirit of wisdom and revelation in the knowledge of Him, the eyes of your understanding being enlightened; that you may know what is the hope of His calling, what are the riches of the glory of His inheritance in the saints, and what is the exceeding greatness of His power toward us who believe, according to the working of His mighty power which He worked in Christ when He raised Him from the dead and seated *Him* at His right hand in the heavenly *places*, far above all principality and power and might and dominion, and every name that is named, not only in this age but also in that which is to come. And He put all *things* under His feet, and gave Him *to be* head over all *things* to the church, which is His body, the fullness of Him who fills all in all.

8

Spirit, Soul, and Body: A New Look

Before we can move to the next phase of understanding the heart, we need to revisit the spirit, soul, and body and add the dimensions of brain and heart. Remember: the models I set forth in this book are designed primarily for a conceptual grasp of the information. The goal is transformation, not information. When discussing the inner working of man, it is much more important to grasp the workings than the detailed map.

There are things that cannot be precisely explained from a biblical, medical, or scientific model. Interestingly, many of the scientific models which have been used for incredible inventions have known flaws. But the flaws do not keep us from knowing and utilizing what can be known. Unless the Bible gives us precise details, which in some areas it rarely does, these are just conceptual models. At the end of the study, it really doesn't matter if all the details are right as much as it matters that you grasp the concept in a way that you can apply to your life. This is why Jesus so often taught in parables. Parables present concepts. Not all of the details provide accurate parallels of every aspect of their subject matter; they do, however, provide an overall picture that makes it possible to grasp and apply to the heart. In this journey of the heart, we can do things that we can never fully explain.

When we see someone teach about spirit, soul, and body they usually use three concentric circles which represent one valid model. But to add the dimension of the brain and heart, we need to use three circles side-by-side.

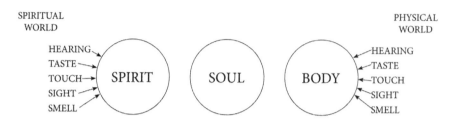

Our body has five senses: taste, touch, smell, sight, and hearing. These five senses are what provide our ability to experience the physical (Newtonian) world. Our spirit has at least five parallel senses. We know this because they are all mentioned in Scripture. For example: *hear the voice of the Lord, if you have ears to hear and eyes to see, taste and see that the Lord is good,* and *smell the sweet aroma,* are just a few general references. There may be more senses, but what matters is that it is our spirit which gives us contact with the spiritual world, while our body gives us contact with the physical world.

Nearly all theologians agree that the soul is the home of our mind, emotions, and, most people would say, will. This is a fairly safe deduction from Scripture. The soul, like the body and spirit, is neither good nor bad. The soul is that part of us where we emotionally experience the input received from the physical or spiritual worlds.

The brain is a processor that overlaps the body and the soul. As you see from the drawing, the brain overlapping the body and soul represents the idea that the brain is both physical and non-physical.

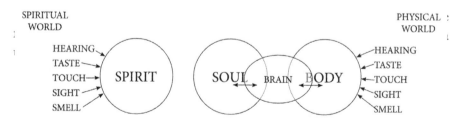

The physical brain takes data from the physical world; it is transmitted via our nervous system to our brain, and at some point that physical data is transformed into non-physical emotions. This occurs at some interface between the brain and the mind. The mind is not the brain. We think with our mind, but our brain processes and, therefore, on some level stores information or at least provides pathways to where the information is stored. The mind is part of the soul. It is in this realm of the soul that information and emotion become one in our experience.

For example, if you touch an apple or some other type of food you enjoy, your mouth may begin to water and you may experience the taste of an apple in your mouth. You could even have certain emotions and memories… all this just by touching an apple. The data received by touch is communicated to the brain, which gathers all associated information, and the mind, in turn, translates that into associated emotions. All of the five senses have the capacity to take in data that can be translated into emotions. The mind then translates the signals from the body into words based on our vocabulary.

Just as the brain takes data from the body and translates it into emotional experience, it can also take thoughts of the mind and turn them into physical feelings or reactions. For example, I can think about bourbon and, in just a few minutes, I begin to feel queasy, a salty taste comes into my mouth, and I come very close to vomiting . These physical reactions are associations that are linked to the one time in my life when I drank bourbon. The experience was not pleasant! From this example we understand how positive thoughts can energize us physically and give a surge of physical energy. Conversely, negative thoughts can cause an instant physiological reaction that strips us of physical energy. When the Bible talks about our thoughts and emotions being able to heal or kill us, it is very true and literal!

The main thing we want to take away from these simple illustrations is the fact that the brain is not a one-way gate. It is the doorkeeper between the body and soul. It controls the flow of information both inward and outward. It causes the physical world to influence the emotional world, and the emotional world to influence the physical world. It seems almost undeniable that the heart has this same two-way capacity. Remember, this is a conceptual model, this is not meant to explain every aspect of the brain and its function, just the parts essential for our understanding of this subject matter.

Now, look at the next three circles that represent the soul and the spirit with the overlapping circle of the heart. Just as the brain is part soul and part body, the heart is part spirit and part soul. Based on its functions, the heart does not seem to be an entity within itself. It contains aspects of both spirit and soul. The world's system would have us intertwine our physical body and how it looks into our identity, i.e. our sense of self. Because the carnal-minded has his or her attention on the outer things, it factors in the external where it does not belong. From a spiritual perspective our identity is inward, involving both spirit and soul.

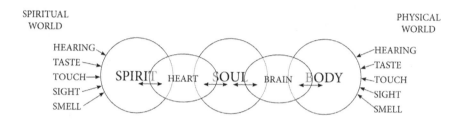

Because the real you is both spirit and soul, the heart must in some way be comprised of both. But for the sake of the illustration, we will use this model. Just like the body takes input from the physical world, our spirit receives information from the spiritual world. When I say spiritual, I am not saying "spirit world." While spirits are in the spiritual world, it is far more than demons and angels. The spiritual world may well be the entire unseen world God created. All that exists was created by the words of God. In the Middle Eastern mindset, the voice is closely connected to the breath. The Hebrew word for "spirit" simply means "breath." That is, however, a conversation too vast for this book. But what is important is to realize that all things created by God's spoken word are, first and foremost, spiritual.

Broadening our understanding of the spiritual world could give us insight into so many mystical things that cannot be explained by our current dualistic, secular, and sacred concepts. This could certainly give us insight into what people consider to be psychic phenomenon. It could be an aspect of our being that we do not understand, and like all things the Church didn't understand, it attributed to the devil.

Man is not just a soul, nor is he just a spirit. I often hear people say we are spirit beings; that is not actually correct. If we were spirit beings, we would have no natural body, or at least we would not be confined to the limitations of a natural body. We are, however, spiritual beings. Before the Fall man was a "living soul." He wasn't just alive physically, and he wasn't just a soul. His soul, the place where we experience natural and spiritual input, was alive to God. The spirit aspect of his being was the main influence on his soul, i.e. thoughts, emotions, and will. But after the Fall man became "flesh." His physical body began to dominate his soul.

After man became a sinner (one who missed the mark of the prize of knowing God, who saw and experienced himself as less than God said), his soul was dominated by the flesh (five physical senses). He now saw and interpreted the world through an intellect that viewed the world from the limitations of the five senses. Just think of what that means. He was now seeking the satisfaction for which his soul craved, that was once experienced with God, through the flesh: taste, touch, smell, sight, and hearing. This is why there are wars, conflicts, competition, and envy. Those who are in the world (believer or non-believer) believe they can amass enough money, power, sex, or fame to meet a need that can only be met by knowing and experiencing God.

This is what the Apostle John warned: don't love the world or the things of the world. To connect with the world you must be in, i.e. aware of, the flesh (five physical senses). If you are carnally-minded, you cannot experience the law of the Spirit of Life in Christ Jesus, and you cannot please God.[1] You also cannot please God without faith,[2] i.e. immovable trust. Faith works by love.[3] The Greek word for "love," more than anything else means "value." So, John is saying that if you have value for the world, you don't really value God: *the love of the Father is not in you.* The only reason one would not value God as much as those things that gratify his flesh is

> UNTIL WE DISCOVER OUR GOD-GIVEN ABILITY TO CONNECT WITH AND EXPERIENCE GOD IN OUR HEART, WE WILL NEVER TRULY KNOW THE LOVE OF GOD.

because he has not known God intimately enough to enjoy the experience. But until we discover our God-given ability to connect with and experience God in our heart, we will never truly know the love of God.

John insightfully told us *we love God because He first loved us.* In other words, you won't just decide to love God and suddenly by faith, fall in love with Him. It is to the degree you experience His love (value for you) that you will, in turn, grow in your value for Him. As you recognize how much He loves you old, legalistic, negative, religious concepts of God vanish. Then, as the writer of Hebrews said, you realize He is the rewarder not the punisher.

The word for "world" is a word that is also used in reference to religion. Religion is many things, not the least of which is carnal, i.e. outward focused. Religion relies on the flesh. Its emphasis is on performance, rituals, and ceremonies. It is all external and just as deadly as any sin. Religion provides the false security that you are experiencing God through the process of outward observances. But in fact, you are only experiencing the stimulation of your senses. Whether religion, sin, philosophy, or success, John described it best: *all that is in the world is the lust of the flesh, the lust of the eyes, and the pride of life.*[4]

However, we will not break our dependency for fulfillment just by intellectualizing the love of God. It must be known, felt, and experienced in every possible capacity. We experience the love of God when we get an answer to prayer. For a brief period we feel something that feels good. We know God came through. But just like human relationships, if we never personally involve ourselves with our benefactor, we will soon lose touch with those positive feelings. Those positive feelings that came from an answered prayer soon fade with memory. Most of what we feel for God is appreciation. Rarely do I meet people who truly value God, hold Him in high regard, and consider Him precious.

Jesus said, *where your treasure is there you heart will be also* (Matt. 6:21). Your heart pursues that which it values. You can tell what a person values by how they manage their life. Would you give up your job if that is what it took to follow God? Would you manage your budget differently so the world can hear the Gospel? We all fail, we all have shortcomings, but over time the accumulation of our decisions (fruit) reveal what we really value. That's why Jesus said: *He who loves his father or mother more than Me is not worthy of Me. And he who loves his son or daughter more than Me is not worthy of Me. And he who does not take his cross and follow after Me is not worthy of Me. He who finds his life will lose it, and he who loses his life for My sake will find it* (Matt. 10:37-39).

He didn't say we could not have our sins forgiven, and He didn't say we could not go to Heaven, He just said we could not follow Him. If we love Him, we will love all of these people, but we will not love (value) them more than we value Him. In fact, I have endeavored to let the people in my life know that they are incredibly precious to me; however, I will never draw back from following God to satisfy any of those I love. But the most important thing they need to know is this: without God in my life, I know I would be a horrible father, husband, friend, and minister. I am better at loving everyone because He is first.

When we are born again, our spirit is made alive to God. In other words, we didn't just get our spirit at the new birth. We've always had a spirit, but our spirit was not always alive to God. I do not claim to know the totality of what this means, but God indwelt us by His Holy Spirit, making our spirit new. We call this the "new birth" because it is a spiritual birth. Our new spirit is where God lives in us. But based on the continual references to the heart in both the Old and New Testaments, we know the heart is the place where God wants to meet us, teach us, and commune with us.

> WHEN WE ARE BORN AGAIN, OUR SPIRIT IS MADE ALIVE TO GOD.

The heart seems to be the Holy of Holies of the New Covenant. The Holy of Holies is where the priest went once a year with a sacrifice to meet with God. Jesus is our sacrifice. Like the priest, we have been sprinkled by His blood. Our sins have been forgiven; therefore, we have access to His throne of grace. It seems that Jesus dwells (abides) in our heart when we are in faith (Eph. 3:17). So, I can only meet Him there and hear His voice when I am in faith, i.e. trust. I have to believe He will honor His Word and meet me. I have to believe He will lead, guide, comfort, and teach me. I have to believe in what was accomplished at His death, burial, and resurrection.

When God speaks in my heart, I will experience deep, subtle feelings and sometimes emotions. Emotions are more a product of the soul, while feelings are more a product of the heart. My capacity to experience either is somewhat related to the soul. Remember, the soul is the place where input, both physical and spiritual, is experienced and intellectually interpreted. So the condition of my heart affects my interpretation of what God speaks. This takes us back to the example of the crooked heart. Light represents truth. When truth passes through a prism, it is bent so that it comes out as a color. Likewise, when truth passes through a crooked heart, it is "bent" or "twisted," which alters the way we understand it. Then we take that understanding and intellectualize it to make it fit into our sense of self.

At some point the truth God spoke clearly into my heart enters my soul, and at that time it is interpreted by my mind. If I have not renewed my mind to agree with, not just God's Word, but His principles, values, and logic, I will twist the Word yet again to agree with my intellect. For example, God could say to you, "Build a white house." Since you have a dislike for white houses, you only hear "Build a house." Maybe your parents had a brick house with white trim. Your intellect could say, "Well, everyone knows that a good house would be made of brick. God would not want me to live in a white wooden house." You have reshaped your understanding of what God said to fit your intellectual preference or culture. Then suppose there is a brick shortage. Before you get your house completed, there are no more bricks. Now you question God. Why did God lead me to build this house if there weren't going to be enough bricks to finish it?

You really do want to please God, but, more than anything else, you don't want to be wrong because you can't imagine that God would want you in a wooden house, and religion has said God will not love you if you're wrong. So you find a way to rationalize your failure. You create a doctrine that says God will lead you into difficult, painful places to make you grow. After all, haven't I grown through this experience? Over time you find other people who have experienced failures they can't reconcile, so you explain your doctrine and you start a church. Then people hear of your wonderful revelation. They hear of how many people got relief from their pain by your doctrine. Pretty soon you have a movement. Since so many people see it the same way, that must be the right way… Get the picture?

The Bible explains the need for a good or clean conscience. In general, the word "conscience" has to do with self-awareness or a consciousness of self. It is critically important that our conscience does not condemn us. The English word for "conscience" has some relevance in the Greek. The English word means "dual knowledge." The Greek word can mean "to know one another"[5] or "for something to be observed by two."

Because we have the Spirit of God in us, He is ever speaking and seeking to lead us into the truth so we can live in the abundant life. Just like the children of Israel; He wanted them to experience the Promised Land and all its benefits so they would recognize His love for them, and in response they would value (love) Him. No matter what God is saying, it can be altered by our heart. Then we have the voice of our mind, i.e. intellect. It is always interjecting its opinion into everything. This opinion is based on your life experience. Both of these sources feed into your soul; therefore, it is possible for two different types of latent emotions to be generated at the same time. The focus of your attention determines which emotion and, subsequently, which voice dominates your experience. To shift back and forth is to waver. This is why a double-minded man is unstable in all his ways. He is constantly tossed back and forth from one opinion and emotion to another. His conscience is not one harmonizing voice; it is two conflicting voices.

This could be why the will is seen as resident within the soul. The will is the ability to make a decision and see it through to completion. When we shift from one thought to another and one emotion to another, it is nearly impossible to make a decision and stick to it. This is why many people give up their faith concerning a particular thing that is not in harmony inwardly.

The religious concepts of faith have not produced what we all know the Bible has promised. But like the children of insecure parents, we are always made to feel that what we don't know is our fault. When formulas don't work, the insecure religious leader only has one answer: you need to do more of something. You need to give more, you need to sacrifice more, you need to get more holy. There is very little, if any, emphasis on developing your heart or addressing faulty beliefs. They will make you feel inadequate, which is

> YOUR UNDERSTANDING WILL GROW BECAUSE OF WHAT YOU PUT INTO PRACTICE THROUGH FAITH...

what got mankind into this mess to start with. Insecure people will always make you feel inadequate to protect their faltering ego, which is deeply attached to their ministry, or title, or position. But more than anything else, their sense of identity and security is established by being right, which is expressed by their need for others to be wrong in any conflict.

Don't be overwhelmed by all this information. Being able to remember this really has nothing to do with whether or not you can escape the limitation of your mind and free your heart. If you have been doing the suggested exercises at the end of the chapters, you are already making the journey. Your understanding will grow because of what you put into practice through faith, not simply learning the information you know.

As we give up our religious traditions and intellectual opinions to follow God's Word, renew our mind, and establish our heart, immovable faith is not as hard as it seems. It is not such a hard thing that we need a specially anointed person to bring it to us. It is not so far away that someone has to get it and bring it to us. It is the word of faith which is (found) in your heart and mouth. *"Do not say in your heart, 'Who will ascend into heaven?'"* (that is, to bring Christ down from above) or, *'Who will descend into the abyss?'"* (that is, to bring Christ up from the dead). But what does it say? *"The word is near you, in your mouth and in your heart"* (that is, the word of faith which we preach): that if you confess with your mouth the Lord Jesus and believe in your heart that God has raised Him from the dead, you will be saved (healed, delivered, blessed, prospered, protected, set apart, made whole) (Rom. 10:6-9).

Endnotes

i.   Rom. 8:5-8, For those who live according to the flesh set their minds on the things of the flesh, but those *who live* according to the Spirit, the things of the Spirit. For to be carnally minded *is* death, but to be spiritually minded *is* life and peace. Because the carnal mind *is* enmity against God; for it is not subject to the law of God, nor indeed can be. So then, those who are in the flesh cannot please God.

ii.   Heb. 11:6, But without faith *it is* impossible to please *Him*, for he who comes to God must believe that He is, and *that* He is a rewarder of those who diligently seek Him.

iii.   Gal. 5:6, For in Christ Jesus neither circumcision nor uncircumcision avails anything, but faith working through love.

iv.   1 John 2:15-17, Do not love the world or the things in the world. If anyone loves the world, the love of the Father is not in him. For all that is in the world — the lust of the flesh, the lust of the eyes, and the pride of life — is not of the Father but is of the world. And the world is passing away, and the lust of it; but he who does the will of God abides forever. NKJV

v.   (from Thayer's Greek Lexicon, Electronic Database. Copyright © 2000, 2003, 2006 by Biblesoft, Inc. All rights reserved.)

9

BELIEVING ON JESUS
IN YOUR HEART

Truth exists as a continuum along the lines of a principle, a string of hard facts, thoughts, feelings, and behavior. Information and truth are not the same. Information is only truth when it is applied from the motive of love; therefore, truth (correct scriptural information) is never true at the deepest level unless it is applied with the proper motive. Two people could believe the same truth and apply it in ways that diametrically oppose one another based on the motive of application. Likewise, truth can be explained in ways that seem contradictory. Thus, you have one of the important heart factors: truth always exists in a paradox. This does not mean truth is not absolute. Truth is always absolute, but application is 100% variable.

Adultery is wrong and in the past was punishable by death, but Jesus did not have the adulteress stoned. Did He break the law? No! He applied a higher law... mercy. He was not approving adultery; in fact, He warned her after the entire ordeal that she should stay out of sin. King David committed adultery and murder. Did God violate His Word by not killing him? No! David appealed to a higher law. In fact, all through the Old Testament, you find people getting better than their behavior deserved. These are people that depended on God's mercy more than their behavior. They perceived Him to be more motivated by love than wrath; therefore, the law was not interpreted from fear. They did not see it as a means to hurt and control. They saw it as a divine prescription for life. One of the greatest paradoxes in Kingdom living is the fact that you have been saved (past tense, it is finished), but you are being saved! Like all paradoxes, the externalist chooses one or the other and develops a doctrine around an extreme concept, totally ignoring the possibilities of what the seemingly opposing truth could mean. Living in the paradox, i.e. staying true to the truth, requires being led by the Spirit. The moment we become static in how truth is applied, we will lose the truth. We will make it a law that kills instead of heals. Truth can be hard while mercy can be totally forgiving. The Psalmist said, *Mercy and truth have met together; Righteousness and peace have kissed* (Ps. 85:10). Until I understood the paradox, it was hard to grasp how these opposing truths could work together.

We should never reject a clear statement in God's Word that opposes another clear statement. What we are seeing is two aspects of the same truth. One of my early study habits that shaped my thinking was the use of my topical Bible. When I wanted to know about any topic, I looked it up in my topical Bible which would give me every reference about any given topic. I would read research and meditate on all of the verses about a topic to give me a broad understanding of its meaning. The thing that forced me to pray and research more than anything was when I discovered what seemed like contradictions concerning a particular subject.

> WE SHOULD NEVER REJECT A CLEAR STATEMENT IN GOD'S WORD THAT OPPOSES ANOTHER CLEAR STATEMENT.

I was, and have always been, fully dedicated to the Word of God; therefore, contradictions never made me doubt, they simply made me ask more questions. My position on all opposing truth was this: all Scripture is true even when it seems to contradict. All contradictions are the result of my not fully understanding this truth. I have noticed that people who tend to be argumentative and dogmatic refuse to consider Scriptures that oppose their position. They simply ignore what doesn't fit into their paradigm and attempt to twist other Scriptures to support their view. A person who does this is usually someone whose security lies in being "right" rather than the safety of a relationship. They are living out of the intellectual mind, not their heart. When our security is in the relationship, we are never threatened by seemingly contradictory information. But when security is in the information, we must fight to defend the information.

In those early days I discovered what I later realized was a heart principle: All truth exists in a paradox. As long as I only see one side of a truth, I don't fully understand that truth, and I will create an extreme interpretation. Based on the previous passage, if I always show mercy I become passive about sin and ignore the truth. If I only spout truth with no mercy, I become a hard legalist. So what's the cure? Simple! Always present even the hardest truth in a merciful manner. Truth in the heart is always about living and being; it is not about knowing (intellectually). Truth in the heart is grasped and experienced; it is not explained. Truth can be lived even when it cannot be intellectually explained. But one thing is for sure: truth is never known until it is experienced in real life application. Jesus taught: *you will know if the doctrine is of God if you will to do His will,* i.e. if you intend to put it into practice.

This whole concept of the paradox is why faith righteousness is the stumbling block of the Gospel. Some who strongly hold to living a godly life say we are only righteous if we live righteously. Some who strongly hold to faith righteousness say that faith righteousness is a gift and it doesn't matter how we live. Because neither side will accept the Scriptures that oppose their position, they are locked into their doctrine. They have closed their eyes. They are blind to any other possibilities because they insist they see! Their real goal is to protect their ego by proving themselves right! Therein they seek the security that cannot be found intellectually.

It is this very issue of righteousness that brings us to the great paradox: I have been saved, I am being saved. Salvation is dependent upon us being righteous. We could not be saved if we were not righteous. We would not qualify for the blessings, promises, and benefits of the Kingdom if we were not righteous. God could not dwell in us if we were not righteous! We know, based on Scripture, that we have been perfected; yet, we find Scriptures that address our need to live righteously. We cannot

> WE KNOW, BASED ON SCRIPTURE, THAT WE HAVE BEEN PERFECTED.

pick and choose that which fits our position. I know people who reject entire books of the Bible simply because they cannot interpret those books to match their doctrine. But if a person's goal is to put it into practice, if they intend to be like their Master and their Father, their goal will be to live as He lives.

So, our spirit has been made perfect, completely righteous, but the goal of God and the goal of the disciple is for that righteousness to manifest in our behavior, in our treatment of others, and in all the dealings of our life. We are, after all, the light of the world and the salt of the Earth. The Apostle John said we are sons of God right now. That word for "sons" is a word that means we are sons with the full inheritance. A common doctrinal error in that day taught that we could be saved, but we were not yet spiritual enough to be heirs. We needed special revelation and ministry from people with special anointing to bring us into our full, rightful position as sons.

But John went on to say it may not yet appear that we are sons of God. In other words, it may not be manifest outwardly. Just because it is not always seen outwardly does not mean it is not an inward reality. Instead of pointing to external works to become more righteous, he says when He is revealed, i.e. made manifest, we will be like Him, for *we shall be like Him when we see Him as He is. Everyone who has this hope purifies himself just as He is pure.* But we can see Jesus as He is now!

John's solution to solving this contradiction between our inner life and our outer life was to sanctify ourselves, i.e. set ourselves apart and contemplate Jesus. He was writing this letter to people who had taken certain truths to an extreme. They had reached such an extreme they didn't believe that godly living was important. There is no place in the Bible where one can prove that ungodly living is acceptable. But legalistic outward behavior modification is not the answer, either.

John, like Paul, Peter, and Jesus never skimmed over sin or its ability to destroy. They addressed the need to adjust our behavior, but they also emphasized the ultimate victory to be resolved in the heart. The heart is the root, we are the tree, and the fruit is the proof of the kind of tree. If we are followers of Jesus, we have to look at Him as He is now and ask, "Do I see Him doing what I am doing as He is seated at the right hand of God?" If the answer is "no," then a disciple will reject that behavior. He will recognize it as part of the "old man." He will put off the unacceptable behavior of the "old man" and put on a new behavior of the "new man." To do this in the heart, we have to start with what we believe. When our beliefs are resolved, our behavior takes care of itself.

We are born again, saved (our spirit made alive), when we believe that God raised Jesus from the dead and confess Him as Lord. Paul takes us through a logical progression of how that happened. Someone felt called to preach, they were sent, they preached the Word, we heard the Word, and based on the Word we heard we exercised faith.[1] In Romans 10 they heard the Gospel of Peace[2]; therefore, faith came because of what they heard. For most of us the message we heard was very limited; therefore, our surrender to Jesus as Lord was only based on what we knew at the time. While our born-again experience was complete, the journey into Lordship has just begun. It is here that the attitude of repentance launches us into a continual life of discovery, development, and growth. The absence of this attitude sets us on a course of struggle, disappointment, and frustration. The attitude of repentance is required for the commitment to Lordship.

> WHILE OUR BORN-AGAIN EXPERIENCE WAS COMPLETE, THE JOURNEY INTO LORDSHIP HAS JUST BEGUN.

As we read the Word, pray, and renew our mind, we will no doubt learn things we never knew about Jesus and how to live, raise kids, manage money, and treat others. Or, we may discover the promises of God that we did not know were part of our salvation. We might recognize some aspect of our life that is in disharmony with God. Or, we may even realize there is something that is lawfully alright to do, but it is not wise.[3] Living from the heart requires love for God, others, and ourselves. Being right doesn't give me rights. Dead people do not exert their rights. If we died in Christ, we are dead to any rights other than those provided in the New Covenant. I now have truth, and I know that love is always the motive behind truth. I have to apply truth in love or it could be as destructive as the most flagrant sin. Any of these scenarios will be opportunities to expand our experience of the salvation of God. It is essential that we not think we are *getting* more of the salvation, but we are *experiencing* more.

Repentance, renewal, and put off – put on are all different expressions that I believe are part of a continuum of the ongoing experience of saving our soul (mind, emotions, intellect, and will). Our spirit has been saved; our soul is continually being saved as we yield to this process of renewal. If your definition of salvation is limited to the new birth, this is not reconcilable. If your definition of salvation is more in line with the meaning of the original word, i.e. healed, delivered, blessed, prospered, protected, made whole, set apart, etc., you can easily understand how it is impossible that we experience all of these in an instant, even though we did receive them in an instant.

Peter told his listeners *receiving the end of your faith — the salvation of your souls* (1 Peter 1:9). I remember a small church that taught a strong message of good works. They were very external. When a person committed a large enough sin, they had to get saved again. You see, the message they heard about salvation, which became the basis for their faith, determined what they were able to experience in their soul. They had so much guilt and condemnation as a result of their behavior that their feelings told them, "I am no longer saved." What I noticed with this group and others who emphasize behavior is they never grow. They never solve their problems. The solution to everything is to get saved again.

Yet, I have noticed those who embrace the paradox. I am saved, I am righteous; yet, my behavior is unacceptable. This person is able to maintain the peace of God while working through the beliefs of their heart and the emotions of their soul. They realize they have problems because of aspects of salvation they have not yet truly experienced in a way that changed their life.

John points out something that I find incredible, *Beloved, I pray that you may prosper in all things and be in health, just as your soul prospers* (3 John 2). It is interesting that he does not say we experience these things as our spirit prospers. Our spirits are prosperous. They are inhabited by God Himself. If that is not enough, there isn't enough. I don't need healing in my spirit. I already have it there. I need healing in my body. Likewise, I have everything that pertains to life (any aspect of the quality of life possessed by God whether peace, joy, prosperity, or victory[4]). But I have to experience these qualities in other parts of my being for it to be of any functional benefit. Peter also says these things are ours through knowledge.

The word "knowledge," first and foremost, is a reference to experiential knowledge. So we have everything that pertains to life and godliness through the experiencing of God and Jesus, our Lord. Remember, Jesus said *This is life, to know God and Jesus whom He has sent.* This isn't the pursuit of knowledge about healing, It is the knowledge that He is in me, I am in Him; He is life and has no death in Him. His name is Jehovah who heals. If I have Him, I have healing. Knowing God means I desire to experience God the Healer, not just God's healing. So the question is, "Am I experiencing Him as healer?" This is all about experiencing what we have because of the One who is already in us. If He is already in us, all He has to offer is already in us!

Knowledge of a person and knowing a person are not the same. One is based on information and one is based on experience. The latter is the developing of a relationship and is something that occurs through time and involvement. It's like the difference between reading a book

> IF HE IS ALREADY IN US, ALL HE HAS TO OFFER IS ALREADY IN US!

about the president and actually spending time with him. There is a tendency to separate God from His attributes. When we know Him as Healer, we can know healing through Him! In fact, when I know Him as Healer, it is much easier to believe for my healing.

A wise man will hear and increase learning (Prov. 1:5). To the wise, learning is a joy, even when that learning means changing what they think. The wise are seeking application, not information. For the wise there is no idea of repentance being a negative ritual; it is a natural celebratory process for the person who loves life. You discover what you have in Him and gladly release any thoughts, opinions, and ideas that are contrary! The moment you release those opinions you can hear the teaching of the Holy Spirit showing you a better way to live, walk, feel, and function.

When you were first born again, someone should have explained, "All that you were has died. In fact, you were living under spiritual death all along. You finally accepted the judgment that way of life deserved, and you allowed it to die. All that you were is dead, and you are now a new creation. You have been given the gift and power of righteousness. The rest of your life is going to be a journey of discovering more about who God really is, following Jesus as your Lord, and discovering your new identity."

Then they would explain that the ceremony of water baptism is only for those who accept the death of their "old man" and commit themselves to living the resurrected life. If you agreed to be baptized it would be explained, "This ceremony really means nothing. It is your faith that matters. When we put you down in that water, I want you to make a decision that at this point all you have been is dead, and the water represents the grave where you leave that 'old man.' When I bring you up out of that water, I want you to determine and fully believe that when Jesus was raised from the dead you were raised up, too. You are in Him, all He has is yours. His every victory is yours."[5]

After the baptism you should have been told, "Now that you are dead, sin has no more power over you. The devil has no power over you. Now we're going to plug you into a discipleship program that will help establish you in your new identity (http://impactministries.com/Resources/FoundationsofFaith.aspx). We will help you understand how to renew your mind until you can't imagine yourself independent of Him!" If that had been the beginning our journey, imagine the pain we would have avoided! Imagine where we would be in our lives today!

Paul said the two criteria for being saved (healed, delivered, blessed, prospered, protected, made whole, and set apart) is that we believe in our heart that God raised Jesus from the dead and that with our mouth we confess Him as Lord. Belief in the resurrection involves all that Jesus had to conquer to be raised from the dead. What occurred from the cross to the throne is the basis for New Covenant faith, yet it may be the least preached information in the Bible.[6] What happened on the cross, in the grave, through the resurrection, and after His ascension gives us the basis for our new identity. As He is now, so are we. It doesn't say as He was when He walked Planet Earth.

> WHAT OCCURRED FROM THE CROSS TO THE THRONE IS THE BASIS FOR NEW COVENANT FAITH...

The heart has to do with our own identity. One of the ways you know when you really believe something in your heart is it changes the way you see, feel, or experience yourself. If I believe in my heart that God raised Jesus from the dead, it will change how I see myself. Ultimately, I will not be able to separate His resurrection from my resurrection. The fact that I confess Him as Lord means I am committed to the journey as a disciple. I will follow Him in my life. I will seek to live as He lives. I will follow His teaching, I will follow His life, and I will follow His Spirit as He leads.

I personally believe we grow in each of these aspects continually; it is a journey. We may get it all at salvation, but according to God's Word we experience more of it through the knowledge (experience) of God! Our belief in the resurrection is as broad as our knowledge of the resurrection. I want to know all that Jesus accomplished through His death, burial, and resurrection. Therefore, the rest of my life, I want to study His Word and listen to the voice of God in my heart. This usually means I have to learn how to get in touch with and recognize my heart. I want to renew my mind and continually repent (change my mind) the moment I recognize thoughts and opinions that are not in harmony with the resurrection life. I want to live a life of transformation, continually manifesting on the outside more of who God has made me to be on the inside. And I do not want any of this because of what is wrong with me. I want it because of what is right about me. I am a new creation. I want to live in this new identity!

When my behavior is a true reflection of my new nature, I will have many incredible benefits. My character will be the testimony to the world around me. My heart will not condemn me when I pray or attempt to walk in faith. I will have confidence before God and man. My life will be free from the chaos of personal corruption. I will live in an outward peace that is a reflection of my inner state. And the longer I walk with God, the more my outer world will change to harmonize with my inner world.

All of this is based on two conflicting realities. We have been saved. We have everything that pertains to life and godliness. Yet, we are being saved, i.e. progressively experiencing the life of God in our soul and body as we renew our mind, put off the old, and put on the new. We are not transforming to become something new. We are transforming because we have been made new. The heart is the key to this whole process. In order for that which is in my spirit to move into my soul and body, I

> WE ARE TRANSFORMING BECAUSE WE HAVE BEEN MADE NEW.

have to believe the truth in my heart and renew my mind. Then as my soul prospers, my physical body and my outer world conform.

After years of working with people, I have realized none of this follows a perfect schematic. You can't predict all the phases. Some things happen out of sequence. But as you will learn about the heart, it will take you through the process in the way you need to experience it. You cannot control the process, you can only yield to the Spirit of God as He leads from your heart! But the absolute starting place is believing that God raised Jesus from the dead and confessing Him as Lord, which is a commitment to follow His life and teaching.

You may want to take a few moments before moving forward and affirm: All that my life is, outside of Jesus, died on the cross. That man is dead. I am raised up with Jesus in resurrection life now! Therefore, sin has no power over me. Because of the incredible price Jesus paid, I know I can trust Him; therefore, Jesus, I surrender every aspect of my life to You as Lord. I choose to be a disciple. I want to live like You lived. As You are right now at the right hand of God, so am I!

Seeing ye have purified your souls in obeying the truth through the Spirit unto unfeigned love of the brethren, see that ye love one another with a pure heart fervently: 1 Peter 1:22.

Endnotes

i. Rom. 10:9-16

ii. The Gospel of Peace, Dr. James B. Richards, Milestones International Publishers, 1990

iii. 1 Cor. 10:23-24, All things are lawful for me, but not all things are helpful; all things are lawful for me, but not all things edify. Let no one seek his own, but each one the other's *well-being*.

iv. 2 Peter 1:2-4.

v. Col. 2:12-15

vi. See my Series, Three Days That Changed The World, www.impactministries.com

10

HEALING
THE BROKEN HEART

Proverbs tells us the heart determines all the boundaries in our life; therefore, the degree of fullness or emptiness, peace or chaos, life or death we are experiencing is the product of our heart. Just as sure as *a merry heart is like medicine,* a heart that does not function as it should is the root of misery and pain.

At this point many ask, "Are you saying that everything that happens in my life is my fault? What about babies who get abused. Is it their fault?" Please don't be too insulted when I say, "If you ask the wrong questions, they will always lead you away from the truth you seek. If you habitually ask the wrong questions, you are not actually open to the truth." It is obvious that a child is helpless in a world of adults. But it is the interaction

GETTING A NEW HEART AND A NEW SPIRIT AT THE NEW BIRTH DOES NOT MEAN YOU GET A DIFFERENT ONE.

with adults, good or bad, that will mold a child's heart and establish boundaries that will be there for a lifetime, unless removed.

As we discovered, getting a new heart and a new spirit at the new birth does not mean you get a different one. It means you get one that has been renewed and made alive to God! We often hear the statement, "We are made new by the Word." That is more literally true than one might think. The Bible teaches that there are at least two initial factors that change our heart: first the blood of Jesus is applied to our heart, which cleanses us from all sin. It purges our conscience concerning our former life, but it also purges our conscience from the need to earn righteousness by dead religious works.[1] The second factor is that the Word of God is written on our heart so it emerges in the form of our deep thoughts. These might well be intuitive in nature. By this we intuitively know what we should or shouldn't do… if we are listening. As He says in Ezekiel,[2] this occurs so we will walk in His statutes and judgments, but it will be from our heart.

The Holy Spirit is at work in us doing so many things. He seeks to guide us into the application of God's Word. He manifests the grace (ability, strength) of God in our heart to empower us to do as God is leading. He comforts and counsels us, and He convinces (convicts) us that God's Word is true and reliable. All of these functions of the Holy Spirit are actually manifestations of His character and nature. It is God being God and expressing it through the person so he can have life at its best.

The believer who is thrown into an external pursuit of God will turn every positive empowering promise of God into a legalistic obligation.[3] Even those who think they have found freedom from the law will find destruction. They will confuse obedience with sacrifice, and law with legalism. They will deceive themselves into defining freedom as lawlessness. They will use their freedom as an opportunity for the flesh.[4] Until we are following God from our heart, we will always err in one direction or the other, legalism or permissiveness.

Jesus quoted Isaiah 61 when He launched into ministry to provide a basis for His mission. He speaks of several conditions which He came to resolve: the needs of the poor, broken-hearted, those taken captive, and those who were bound, and He would do this by proclaiming the year of Jubilee and the Day of God's vengeance. In the Year of Jubilee, all debts were cancelled. It didn't matter if the debt was by no fault of your own or totally your fault. The point is you were in prison, lost your sight, or living in captivity, and the debt you owed had been paid. Jesus became the curse of the law, so we would never have to live under that curse. Jesus was made the propitiation for our sins. The word "propitiation" refers to the satisfying of the wrath of God![5]

It could be that all of these maladies that Jesus came to resolve were actually caused by a broken heart. They certainly fall into the scriptural category of heart symptoms. But it would do little good to heal their heart if the issue of judgment was not settled. A heart cannot be healed if it is filled with fear. Fear is only alleviated by love.[6] Until there is confidence that the debt has been settled for our wrongs, there will

A HEART CANNOT BE HEALED IF IT IS FILLED WITH FEAR.

be an expectation of punishment (condemnation) in our heart. Condemnation is a limiting heart belief that keeps us from ever expecting God's best. We will never believe God can love us. The Apostle John actually said the love of God is manifest in the propitiation, i.e. the fact that God satisfied His wrath for all sin when it was poured out onto Jesus. This is the ultimate reality that will establish our heart in God's love for us!

Religion was, is, and always will be a major factor in alienating man's heart from God. All through the Old Testament, God warned Israel that they should do all He said from their hearts. Neither they nor the Church today seem to understand that which is not done from a heart of love is always turned into obligation and bondage. If the people had obeyed God from the place of trust, they would have experienced the good things He offered. They would have then been able to grasp His love, which would continue to cause trust to abound. But it seems that leaders have a way of turning commandments, which are actually prescriptions for life, into obligations. When they can't move the people with love and inspiration, they tend toward fear and obligation.

The Prophet Isaiah declared that leaders caused the people to go into bondage when they didn't have to; they caused the people to howl and mourn; they even caused God's name to be continually blasphemed. All of this is the product of misrepresenting God. He clearly stated that people would continue to blaspheme God until they saw Him as He really was instead of through the eyes of controlling, unbelieving leaders. This would occur when people heard the Gospel of peace whereby they could see God as He actually is instead of the way religion portrayed Him.[7] In Isaiah 54 God called the covenant He would make in Jesus, "The Covenant of Peace."[8] God made peace with man through the cross of Christ! This should be the Gospel that is preached to the world: the Gospel of peace.

Religion demands change, not transformation. Religion rules through law, not righteousness. Religion focuses on behavior independent of the heart. Religion tells us to earn what Jesus has given freely. Religion controls us through fear. Religion tells us what's wrong with us instead of what has been made right about us. Religion fears freedom more than anything. Religion believes people who are given freedom will run wild… and the truth is they might do just that! So, through fear we recreate the same failure as was shown in Israel, we do not get people serving and connecting to God from their heart. They put their trust in their dead religious works, which makes them feel that God owes them something for their performance.

The freedom God offers is the responsibility to make our own decisions about whether we will or won't serve God. Once having been set free from sin, some choose to go back. Having been set free from religion, some choose to once again become entangled. But we must not facilitate their destruction by preaching works righteousness. It is impossible for a person to stay entangled in religion and ever be healed in their heart and maintain it. All the damage inflicted by religion through fear and condemnation may, in fact, do more damage to our heart, than the actual sins we commit. At least sin does not promote a destructive image of God. We still have a refuge to run to when we are ready to surrender. Religion leaves us nowhere to turn in our time of need. Like it or not, we must offer the same freedom and responsibilities Paul offered to teach them the truth and mentor/disciple them to walk with God from their heart; then it is their choice.

Some would argue that because God gave us a new (renewed) heart, we no longer have to do anything to benefit our heart. Since, however, the New Testament makes statements to believers about managing their heart, correcting the conditions of their heart, and establishing their heart, it becomes apparent that the renewed heart God gave us can still be negatively influenced. Therefore, we must manage our heart. It may not be possible to erase God's Word that has been written on our heart, but we can certainly harden or otherwise influence our heart in a way that brings no benefit.

The following are some of the conditions of the heart I want to address. The Bible's list is much longer than this, but I do not think that each of these conditions is completely distinct, one from another. Many of the terminologies do point to some interesting ways the heart is negatively affected, but some of the terms may be overlapping or even synonymous with other terms. It doesn't really matter if you know whether you have a broken heart or a bruised heart; what matters is if you know how to experience healing in your heart.

> # WHAT MATTERS IS THIS, DO YOU KNOW HOW TO EXPERIENCE HEALING IN YOUR HEART?

Jeremiah 17:9 says, *The heart is deceitful above all things, And desperately wicked; Who can know it?* Based on this Scripture, some have come to believe that you can never trust your own heart. But we must remember that this was before the fulfillment of the promise to write His laws on our heart. Also, an examination of a few of the words used in this passage not only gives us an entirely different understanding of the passage, but a keen insight into how our heart gets so dysfunctional.

In Hebrew the word "deceitful" can mean "showing footprints,"[9] and the words "desperately wicked" would be better translated as "woefully, or incurably sick."[10] Every other time the word is used in the Old Testament, it is translated "incurable." So what is this saying? The heart covered with footprints is a reference to it being covered with wounds that have made it incurably sick. It may be that the phrase, "You walked on my heart," has more validity than we thought. Life's experiences, whether the pain inflicted by others or the consequences of our own sinful action, cover our heart with wounds, i.e. footprints. The idea of footprints could even fit into the category of cellular memories that are imprinted onto the cells of the heart. We must remember, in Jesus the heart is healed. In the Old Covenant they did not have that resource!

The Prophet Isaiah made reference to the broken heart. The word "broken" in Hebrew means "to be shattered, or broken to pieces."[11] Since the heart is the seat of our identity, a person with a broken heart is devastated; they have no sense of self-worth and will most likely not have a healthy sense of boundaries. They will either seek control or allow others to control them. They may lack the emotional capacity to make choices, thus they live as captives… captive to sin, captive to people, captive to the opinions of others, captive to the desires they think will fill the void. They need the ability, the sense of authority, to send away the things that would take them captive. As much as anything, they feel powerless to do anything about their problems. They are, after all, slaves. Any person who feels powerless has footprints on their heart.

The captives referred to in this passage are those people held in slavery who do not feel they have the freedom to make their own decisions. The word "deliverance" more closely means "to send away, to release, or to let go." In Galatians, Paul said we had been given "liberty," more like "an independent self-determination,"[12] as when a slave is set free and can now make his own choices instead of the choices of others being imposed on him. But now that they have been made legally free, their ability to stay free is based on their willingness to make responsible authoritative choices. In Christ you are legally set free from slavery. You now have the right to make your own choices. When Jesus heals your broken heart, you have the power to make your own choices. When your heart is whole, you can send away those thoughts, hurts, desires, powers, or anything else that seeks to keep you captive. You should, in fact, feel confident and empowered to do so.

One truly interesting thing revealed in this passage is the phrase "recover sight to the blind." While Jesus healed the blind on many occasions, it does not seem this passage is referring to the physically blind. The spiritually blind perceive the world through the five senses which are then interpreted by the intellectual mind. They are carnally-minded; they have no other frame of reference. Their eyes dominate their perception of God's resources in relationship to the world they see.

In the story about Jesus feeding the five thousand men, plus women and children, we have someone showing up with just five loaves of bread and two fish. Jesus' natural eyes could have seen as many as 20,000 hungry people. And with His natural eyes, He could only see five loaves of bread and two fish. Since Jesus was a man tempted in every way just as we are,[13] He had to have been tempted to limit God to the resources He could see with His natural eyes.

Remember, sin is connected to the sense of lack that causes us to miss the mark of God's goal. God's goal is to always meet the need. If Jesus had allowed Himself to be overcome with lack, He would have sinned. Instead, however, He modeled what we can do when the resources we see do not seem adequate. Jesus "recovered sight," not natural sight, but spiritual sight. In Mark 6:41 it says, *And when He had taken the five loaves and the two fish, He looked up to heaven, blessed and broke the loaves, and gave them to His disciples to set before them; and the two fish He divided among them all.* The words "looked up" come from the same root word used in Luke where it says "He will recover sight to the blind," which means "to look up and/or recover sight."[14] Before Jesus took action, before He even attempted

> SIN IS CONNECTED TO THE SENSE OF LACK THAT CAUSES US TO MISS THE MARK OF GOD'S GOAL.

to "work faith" for a miracle, He looked to God to recover His sight. He had to see the situation from God's perspective, which is a capacity of the heart. Once His sight was recovered, He spoke blessings on the fish and bread which resulted in thousands being fed.

We see a common thread emerging as the result of a wounded or broken heart. We see the world around us through the lenses of our sense of self. It's like tinted glasses. If the tint is blue, everything you look at appears to have a blue tint. Our interpretation of the world, its threats and its opportunities, are the boundaries our heart imposes, which have little basis in reality. The heart is our seat of understanding and perception. Why? Because understanding and perception is subjective. It is a combination of information and interpretation. That interpretation is based, in part, on how we feel and how we see ourselves.

Another possible reference to perception in this passage is in Isaiah where he says He has come to open the prison doors. The word used for "open prison doors" is only translated as such one time in the whole Bible. All other times, except once where it refers to opening the ears, it is a reference to opening eyes. This word means "to create a new state of awareness, to see things from a new perspective." To be spiritually-minded is to have our awareness or attention on what the Spirit is saying more than what our five senses are saying. We need to perceive and interpret the world through a heart that fully believes the finished work of Jesus and sees itself as one with Him in that work.

Isaiah 42:7 makes another reference to those in spiritual prison: *To open blind eyes, To bring out prisoners from the prison, Those who sit in darkness from the prison house.* Being blind and sitting in darkness is like a doubling of the state of darkness. You notice it says *to bring out the prisoners,* not "open the door," neither here nor in Isaiah 61. You see, the door is already open. But this person with a broken heart feels so powerless to make decisions, they feel so paralyzed by life's pain and disappointment, they are like a blind person sitting in a dungeon with no awareness that the doors stand wide open. They have freedom without the "sight" to implement it!

Let's take one more look at the phrase, *liberty to the captives.* In the KJV it says "*to set at liberty them that are bruised,* which may be a better rendering from the Greek. When a person is struck on the body hard enough, it can create a bruise. A bruise is where the blood has left the vessels and coagulates, making it difficult for blood to flow through the area. This is called stagnation. Stagnation always causes pain. What the bruise needs is the flow of fresh life-carrying blood back through that area. But the problem is the bruise which needs the healing blood flow prevents blood from flowing freely. Thus, the bruise becomes both the cause and the effect.

People with heart issues become their own cause and effect. Their heart gets shattered or bruised, which leads to dysfunctional choices and behaviors. These choices and behaviors are the effects of a broken heart, but they are also the cause of more pain and bruising. Jesus made it very clear in the parable of the sower and the seed that unless we change the beliefs of our heart, we will keep getting more of what we have... good or bad.

> **PEOPLE WITH HEART ISSUES BECOME THEIR OWN CAUSE AND EFFECT.**

People who have enough devastation are like those who have a crooked or froward heart. They reach a place where they have no capacity to find good. Their heart bends the light (truth) in such a way they can no longer hear or see good! They are offended by the truth that would set them free. Teaching feels like criticism. Correction feels like punishment. The God who shows up to deliver them is accused of causing the pain. So they choose the bad that will come closest to giving them some reprieve from their torment. Sadly, the Church, which abandoned nearly all concepts of ministry that heals the heart, has one admonition for these people who have lost their ability to see and perceive the truth which will give them freedom: "live right, trust God!" How can we trust a God who, we believe, caused the problem? Simple! We can't!

God has a reality. The word "glory" addresses the splendor of God that is beyond words and beyond comprehension. But it also implies that this splendor exists in God's reality. Just as people in the Bible had their eyes opened to see angels protecting them against insurmountable opposition, we too can open our eyes to God's reality. We can see our obstacles from God's perspective or ours. As we behold God's reality, the reality we have created by our limited perception loses its grip. We realize we don't need anyone to open the prison door, it has been opened. Now that we can see, we simply walk out.

In order to see this clearly, you may want to think back to a major emotion, pain, or disappointment in your life, then identify the way that pain or the fear of that pain has caused you to make bad decisions. Now identify that original pain and give it a name: embarrassment, failure, shame, or whatever word you would use to describe it. Now get in touch with the event and the original pain. Call the pain by the name you have given it and send it away. Simply say, "Pain, I don't want you. You are not from God. You are bringing no benefit to my life. I will no longer allow you in my heart." Now simply acknowledge Jesus as the Healer of your heart. Thank Him that He is now healing you from this pain and its power to influence your life. Yes, sometimes it is that easy.

Endnotes

i. Heb. 9:14, how much more shall the blood of Christ, who through the eternal Spirit offered Himself without spot to God, cleanse your conscience from dead works to serve the living God?

ii. Ezekiel 36:26-27, I will give you a new heart and put a new spirit within you; I will take the heart of stone out of your flesh and give you a heart of flesh. I will put My Spirit within you and cause you to walk in My statutes, and you will keep My judgments and do *them*.

iii. Gal. 5:1, Stand fast therefore in the liberty wherewith Christ hath made us free, and be not entangled again with the yoke of bondage. KJV

iv. Gal. 5:13-14, For you, brethren, have been called to liberty; only do not use liberty as an opportunity for the flesh, but through love serve one another. For all the law is fulfilled in one word, even in this: *"You shall love your neighbor as yourself."**

v. NT:2434, *an appeasing, propitiating,* (from Thayer's Greek Lexicon, Electronic Database. Copyright © 2000, 2003, 2006 by Biblesoft, Inc. All rights reserved.)

vi. 1 John 4:18-19, There is no fear in love; but perfect love casts out fear, because fear involves torment. But he who fears has not been made perfect in love.

vii. Isaiah 52:5-7, Now therefore, what have I here," says the Lord , "That My people are taken away for nothing? Those who rule over them Make them wail,"* says the Lord, "And My name is blasphemed continually every day. Therefore My people shall know My name; Therefore *they shall know* in that day That I *am* He who speaks: 'Behold, *it is* I.'" How beautiful upon the mountains Are the feet of him who brings good news, Who proclaims peace, Who brings glad tidings of good *things*, Who proclaims salvation, Who says to Zion, "Your God reigns!"

viii. Isaiah 54:9-10, "For this *is* like the waters of Noah to Me; For as I have sworn That the waters of Noah would no longer cover the earth, So have I sworn That I would not be angry with you, nor rebuke you. For the mountains shall depart And the hills be removed, But My kindness shall not depart from you, Nor shall My covenant of peace be removed," Says the Lord, who has mercy on you.

ix. OT:6121, 1676c† OT:6121 bq)u* (±¹qœeb) deceitful; showing footprints. (from Theological Wordbook of the Old Testament. Copyright © 1980 by The Moody Bible Institute of Chicago. All rights reserved. Used by permission.)

x. OT:605
to be weak, to be sick, to be frail
a) (Qal)
    1)   to be incurable
    2)   to be sick
    3)   desperate, incurable, desperately wicked, woeful, very sick
(passive participle)(metaphorical)
b) (Niphal) to be sick

(from The Online Bible Thayer's Greek Lexicon and Brown Driver &
Briggs Hebrew Lexicon, Copyright © 1993, Woodside Bible Fellowship,
Ontario, Canada. Licensed from the Institute for Creation Research.)

xi. OT:7665
to break, to break in pieces
a) (Qal)
    1)   to break, to break in (or down), to rend violently, to wreck, to
crush, to quench
    2)   to break, to rupture (figurative)
b) (Niphal)
    1)   to be broken, to be maimed, to be crippled, to be wrecked
    2)   to be broken, to be crushed (figurative)
    c)   (Piel) to shatter, to break
    d)   (Hiphil) to cause to break out, to bring to the birth
    e)   (Hophal) to be broken, to be shattered
(from The Online Bible Thayer's Greek Lexicon and Brown Driver &
Briggs Hebrew Lexicon, Copyright © 1993, Woodside Bible Fellowship,
Ontario, Canada. Licensed from the Institute for Creation Research.)

xii. NT:1657 The formal sense is the same, but freedom now takes the form
of independent self-determination. To find freedom we must explore
our nature. We cannot control body, family, property, etc., but we do
control the soul. External things seek to impose a false reality on us.
(from Theological Dictionary of the New Testament, abridged edition,
Copyright © 1985 by William B. Eerdmans Publishing Company. All
rights reserved.)

xiii. Heb. 4:15

xiv. NT:308 to look up; by implication, to recover sight:(Biblesoft's New
Exhaustive Strong's Numbers and Concordance with Expanded Greek-
Hebrew Dictionary. Copyright © 1994, 2003, 2006 Biblesoft, Inc. and
International Bible Translators, Inc.)

11

WHERE THE WAR RAGES

If we are to win any war, it will be done by strategy. To develop a winning strategy, we must know certain crucial information. To go to war without the proper intelligence is foolishness, and even with a superior army one could easily lose the battle. We must know our enemy and the terrain where the battle will be fought. After the war in Vietnam it was discovered, much to the surprise of the US Intelligence Agency, that nearly every battle was actually chosen by the enemy. It only appeared that we were searching for and finding the enemy. While we were searching, they were preparing a strategic ambush. They chose the place of the battle so the terrain would give them the needed advantage against superior numbers and massive fire power. Such are the strategies of today's terrorists. And as history has proven, you cannot actually win the battle if you do not understand the enemy and the environment where the battle is fought.

Somehow the Church totally missed the fact that, through the resurrection, satan was completely defeated and stripped of power and authority.[1] Furthermore, the same resurrection power wherewith this strategic battle was won is the power that works in us.[2] Yet, oblivious to the resurrection, we have made the devil the focus of our warfare, which means we have fought the wrong battle on the wrong battleground. We have become like one who *beats the air*, i.e. a shadow boxer who is only fighting an imaginary enemy.[3] And we wonder why we never seem to make permanent, consistent advancement in our life.

The one battle we are called to fight in the New Covenant is the good fight of faith.[4] When we align our thoughts, feelings, and beliefs with the finished work of Jesus, we are resisting the devil. If we put our focus on the devil instead of the promises of God, we have now become devil-conscious instead of Christ-conscious. We are now functioning in the carnal mind, which is in opposition to God and cannot experience the law of the Spirit of life in Christ Jesus. Every Scripture about warfare in the New Testament identifies our battleground as the soul. This is the seat of the struggle because it is the realm of thoughts and emotions.

Remember, the soul is neither good nor bad. The emotions we experience in the soul are merely a reflection of our consciousness, i.e. focus of attention. If the focus of our attention is the Spirit, which is always going to be God expressing His Word, then we will experience life and peace. The life of God in the spiritually-minded floods the soul with healthy, life-giving emotions that permeate our entire being. If our focus is the input our five senses provide concerning our circumstances, we will have death. In our soul that death will be experienced as the emotions of doom, despair, depression, or fear.

> THE LIFE OF GOD IN THE SPIRITUALLY-MINDED FLOODS THE SOUL WITH HEALTHY, LIFE-GIVING EMOTIONS THAT PERMEATE OUR ENTIRE BEING.

When we have renewed our mind with God's Word, we have harmony in our spirit and soul, which means we can stay in faith without wavering. Faith is immovable trust in our heart for God's Word, i.e. His promises. In the New Covenant we are in Christ; therefore, we share in His inheritance, which means any promise God has ever made to anyone is "yes" for us today.[5] Unfortunately, those who are not established in the New Covenant think they should believe on the curses for their life when they fail. It could be that the fulfillment of those curses is actually from our own heart and mind, not the devil.

Because we are in Christ and, in fact, died with Him on the cross, we are delivered from all the curses of the law.[6] The sentence of death has been passed on our "old man" and the full price has been paid. Until this is the way we think about every situation, our mind has not been fully renewed. Thoughts that are not rooted in our new identity in Him become the strongholds that take us captive. They become so predominate that we will not hear God when He tries to lead us into victory through Jesus. However, like the person sitting in the darkness of the dungeon, the gate is open and freedom is ours, but we sit in the darkness because of ignorance or unbelief concerning Jesus' finished work!

The externalist believes one should work to qualify for the promises, which is a rejection of the finished work of Christ. They think the Covenant is an agreement between God and individual men. As such, their extrapolation of the facts leads to an entanglement with the Old Covenant that, for all practical purposes, neutralizes grace (God's power) and puts man right back into his own strength (flesh) in his lame attempt to earn the promises through works. But as Paul so aptly points out, if the inheritance can be obtained by law, it is no longer a promise.[7]

Possibly the greatest misunderstanding of the qualification for the inheritance (promises) is rooted in the fallacy that the Covenant is made to each individual believer. God did not make the Covenant with mankind (seeds, as in many) He made the Covenant with Abraham's <u>seed</u> (as in one: Jesus). And this Covenant was made 430 years before the law. Therefore, the law cannot void this Covenant, nor is it superior.[8] The Covenant was made with Jesus. He lived His part of the Covenant and died.

> THERE IS NO COVENANT BETWEEN GOD AND INDIVIDUAL MEN; THERE IS ONLY A COVENANT BETWEEN GOD AND JESUS.

Therefore, it cannot be changed. But since He rose again, He is also the administrator of the Covenant, which makes it sure. All the stipulations of the Covenant have been met in Him; therefore, in Him we are as qualified as He.[9] So there is no covenant between God and individual men; there is only a Covenant between God and Jesus.

When we believed, we were baptized into Him. Therefore, we enjoy every aspect of His Covenant with God! We are joint heirs with Him; we share in every promise of the Covenant and are delivered from every penalty of the curse. Because we share in His righteousness, we no longer use the law as a means to obtain our righteousness. This doesn't mean the law has no value. It just means the law does not, nor could it ever, make anyone righteous. We, therefore, do not focus on our performance, good or bad, to determine our qualifications. Instead, we focus on Him, His obedience, His death, burial, and resurrection, and the fact that we are in Him. By doing so, our faith is about His works and not ours! This is what it means to believe in your heart that God raised Jesus from the dead. When we take the focus off ourselves, He becomes our everything! And trust me, this type of spiritual-mindedness (awareness) bears the fruit of righteousness. When Jesus really is our focus, sin will not abound!

Sin only has an allure if we feel disqualified (lack). We all have desires. When we have the confidence that our desires can be fulfilled through following the Spirit, we have no need to follow the flesh. This is what Peter meant when he said: *which have been given to us exceedingly great and precious promises, that through these (promises) you may be partakers of the divine nature, having escaped the corruption that is in the world through lust* (desire) (2 Peter 1:4). My immovable trust for Him and the dependability of His promises keeps me free from the snare of the world. It keeps me from using my liberty to make choices that enslave me to the flesh. I don't have to go to the world if God's promises are sure in my heart!

The reason I always insert the word "immovable" into my definition of faith is because we know if there is wavering we are not in faith. So what causes the wavering? The Church has the same tendency to limit God as did the children of Israel because, like them, our *heart is not steadfast in His covenant.*[10] Faith is not blind. Faith is based on clear-cut promises made by God. His Word plainly lays out every aspect of this inheritance and how we qualify. But religion, which is based on the world's system of

IF THERE IS WAVERING WE ARE NOT IN FAITH.

externals, has brainwashed the Church and the world by polluting the Covenant, mixing the old and the new. Sadly, for most their attempts at faith are like closing their eyes and walking down the middle of a freeway, praying they are not struck by a vehicle. Knowing the Covenant is the beginning of faith.

If I do not know and believe the terms of the Covenant, if my mind has been filled with legalistic dead works, there will be intellectual information that will trigger negative, disqualifying emotions in my soul when I consider it, causing all of my awareness to shift away from the promises of God. Thus, I have wavered or shifted from one position to another. I may at some point read the promises concerning my situation, I may hear a rousing sermon, or have a time of inspirational worship, then my focus shifts back to God and His promise; but this is still wavering!

The intellect seeks to preserve the ego, the sense of self based on the life I know. As a believer, the heart is always trying to take me to my new identity in Christ! This is a battle waged in our soul! This is not only the foundation of our faith; it is also the cause of mental and emotional instability among carnal-minded Christians! This struggle puts us into stress mode, i.e. "fight or flight." In this mode we shift to our sympathetic nervous system. Digestion stops or is slowed. Blood that would normally flow to and heal our organs moves out to our limbs in case we have to fight or run. Our immune function is compromised on many levels. Our body begins to produce a steroid hormone called cortisol. In many people this hormone seems to increase later in the day, making it difficult to sleep, producing a tendency toward increased hunger at night, weight gain, and eventually it drains our adrenals. These, plus dozens of other bodily functions that keep us healthy and energetic, are disrupted.

Besides what is happening in our body, there is also something even more deadly happening in our brain. We stop thinking with the part of our brain that considers consequences, sees the big picture, and most of all that takes into account our identity. When we are stressed, we tend to think with a part of our brain that is only focused on survival. Survival means, "I'm not going to consider you, me, or God; I'm going to survive." Tests reveal that most Americans are in some

> MOST AMERICANS ARE IN SOME DEGREE OF STRESS NEARLY ALL THE TIME AND DO NOT EVEN REALIZE IT.

degree of stress nearly all the time and do not even realize it. It's no wonder we have such a rise in sickness, violent crime, divorce, and other destructive behaviors.

Studies indicate that every time our heart beats it sends a signal to the cells of the body which programs the cells to function in a way that fulfills our sense of self. Some feel this signal is blocked from the brain in times of stress. Since God speaks in our heart, this means that even if we were open to hearing God's voice, it would probably not happen. It doesn't mean He is not speaking, and it doesn't mean He is not attempting to lead us to victory and happiness. It means His voice is falling on ears that cannot hear. This could be one aspect of hardness of heart.

Peace is the environment for optimal health, success, happiness, courage, and victory. Peace facilitates the proper working of all bodily functions. In the state of peacefulness, we can face opposition of any kind, yet remain in a state that facilitates hearing the voice of God as He gently leads our heart. Before Jesus began to teach about His departure from Planet Earth by way of crucifixion, He told His disciples: *do not let your heart be troubled, you believe in God believe also in me.* He then talked to them about what would happen and what He would do for them after His departure. He also explained more specifics about the ministry of the Holy Spirit who would come to help them. But all of His teaching about the Holy Spirit started with the importance of living in peace!

He needed them to be at peace so they could receive what He was teaching them. If we are not at peace, if we are focused on what we believe will go wrong, we cannot hear the words being spoken that will strengthen our peace. Peaceful words are pearls before swine when spoken to a person who is focused on the threat. They hear amiss… they refuse to listen or consider. There are nine Greek words for "sin," and they all mean something different. One of the words means "to hear amiss." This means "to hear and not take it seriously, not act on it, not actuate it, not be willing to hear it, or to hear and let it slip from us." Any time we are in trouble we can be assured God spoke to our heart providing answers and direction. He tried to lead us, but our attention was somewhere else. We either blocked His leading or we heard amiss!

This is why it is crucial not to allow ourselves to be troubled. If the news troubles you, stop watching it. It is more important that you hear the voice of God leading you through the trouble than to have an intellectual grasp on current events. At some point we have to cease to hear instruction (words) that causes us to err from the truth.[11] We need God's leading more than we need intellectual input.

> # WE NEED GOD'S LEADING MORE THAN WE NEED INTELLECTUAL INPUT.

The peace that God offers is very interesting. The peace that the world offers is purely circumstantial. If your enemies are destroyed, you feel safe. If your company gets the new contract, you believe you will survive financially. The world can even offer false peace. Since external peace is circumstantial, we can misread the signs and have a peace that has no basis in reality. It is all external, intellectual, perceptional, and circumstantial. But the peace that Jesus offers is just the opposite; it is internal and substantive. It is based on the character of God and His promise of provision. The Greek word for "peace" is more than a state of mind; it involves security, safety, and even prosperity.[12] So it is a tranquil state of mind based on God's provision for every circumstance.

Paul said, *be anxious for nothing,*[13] *instead let your requests be made known to God, with thanksgiving.* Thanksgiving does several things. If I make myself aware of those things for which I am thankful and express that thankfulness to God, it changes the frame of mind I have when approaching God. Also, if I know from the Scripture that a promise is mine, or if I hear God's voice in my heart affirming that promise, I will have thanksgiving at that moment, as if the request is fully manifest. Paul goes on to say that the peace of God that surpasses all intellectual knowledge will keep and guard my heart and my intellectual mind. His peace can overcome the input I have used to saturate my thoughts. Some scholars say the word "keep" means "to referee." The referee will show you what should be observed and what should be let go. The referee declares who wins and who loses!

But it seems there is something more significant than these general, but true, concepts. He says this peace will keep your heart and mind through Jesus. The word "through" should be translated "in." If I can maintain my "in Him" awareness, I will stay in peace. I will take every mental argument and accusation to the finished work of Jesus for evaluation. I will find myself emotionally safe, qualified for the

> IF I CAN MAINTAIN MY "IN HIM" AWARENESS, I WILL STAY IN PEACE.

promises, and unwavering because I know I am in Him and I share His inheritance. When I am conscious of "me in Him," my mind and my heart remain in peace.

There is probably no passage that describes this war for our soul more than 2 Corinthians 10:3-6. Paul explains that the weapons we use for warfare demolish (pull down) strongholds. These strongholds are not demonic strongholds in the heavens. That concept is merely religious interjection that ignores what the passage says. These are the strongholds in our own mind. Paul identifies them as imaginations, intellectual arguments, anything on which we would rely to prove our point or win our argument. These imaginations are actually a way of reasoning that is contrary to the finished work of Jesus.

In the issue of warfare, we use an Old Testament model, we ignore the finished work of Jesus, and we string together unrelated Scriptures to create an image of the devil that does not exist. Then, using our false conclusion, we extrapolate this felonious concept of New Covenant warfare that does little more than appeal to a mystical mindset. It gives the mind something with which to occupy itself and seem in control of the situation, but it is actually little more than doubt and unbelief concerning His finished work!

Any thought, idea, inspiration, doctrine, or fear that would refute what the Bible tells us about the victorious death, burial, and resurrection of Jesus and how we share in it, is a stronghold. The only cure for this is to subjugate that thought/argument/imagination to the obedience of Christ. In other words, I need to obliterate that stronghold by reminding myself of all that Jesus obtained though His obedience to God. A renewed mind will not entertain that which opposes the finished work of Jesus. A carnal mind will always seek to compare the circumstance to the promise, attempting to reach an intellectual understanding that "makes sense."

> A RENEWED MIND WILL NOT ENTERTAIN THAT WHICH OPPOSES THE FINISHED WORK OF JESUS.

Then Paul says: *and being ready to punish all disobedience when your obedience is fulfilled.* First, being ready, i.e. alert… this is reminiscent of the admonition in Proverbs *to guard your heart with all vigilance.* Don't hesitate, don't entertain it for a moment; don't let anything slip by that undermines your confidence of yourself in Christ. This is more of a literal rendering of this verse. Paul is saying, be on your toes ready to punish (bring to justice) all disobedience (hearing amiss or refusing to hear) in your obedience (at the time your belief and obedience to the truth is brought to fulfillment). The thing that put this person in a compromised state where they found themselves as a Christian opposing the message of the cross was all because they were hearing amiss. They may have refused to hear the message Paul was preaching, but even worse, they refused to hear the Holy Spirit. Because they needed to preserve their opinion, they could not hear the Word of God attempting to emerge from their heart to lead them into victory over any and all opposition. They didn't diligently guard their heart. But if they renew their mind, they can bring to justice (punish) their failure to hear by repenting and believing the truth.

This battle rages in our soul, our intellect, and our emotions. Our mind seeks to run our life in a way that preserves our ego by limiting our life to our intellectual knowledge. But the deep thoughts of our heart are always expressing the voice of God. When one has not developed a listening ear, their only sense of safety is found in listening to their intellect. Sadly, most believers I have ever worked with did not know the difference between the voice of their mind and the voice of God in their heart. But after spending time in *Heart Physics,* the difference became more than obvious.

Becoming aware of Christ in you, attuning your inner ear to hear and recognize the voice of God in your heart is the ultimate key to consistent victory. Knowing the difference between your mind and your heart ends the war. It stops the wavering. It anchors your soul in peace... the peace that doesn't even make sense!

Heart Physics is a tool that I developed to help people make a journey in about thirty days that took me years to make. You don't need *Heart Physics* to do this; you simply have to make it a way of life to spend time in reflective, meditative thought on a regular basis. In a physically relaxed state, our brainwaves slow down, making our intellectual mind less dominant. It is in this state of peace that we start recognizing the still, small voice of God! Make time to spend with God in a worshipful, relaxed, meditative state regularly. Learn to recognize the difference between the voice of your mind and the voice of your heart!

Endnotes

i.   Col. 2:15, Having disarmed principalities and powers, He made a public spectacle of them, triumphing over them in it.

ii.   Eph. 1:19-23, and *what is* the exceeding greatness of His power toward us who believe, according to the working of His mighty power which He worked in Christ when He raised Him from the dead and seated *Him* at His right hand in the heavenly *places,* far above all principality and power and might and dominion, and every name that is named, not only in this age but also in that which is to come. And He put all *things* under His feet, and gave Him *to be* head over all *things* to the church, which is His body, the fullness of Him who fills all in all.

iii. 1 Cor. 9:26-27, Therefore I run thus: not with uncertainty. Thus I fight: not as *one who* beats the air. But I discipline my body and bring *it* into subjection, lest, when I have preached to others, I myself should become disqualified.

iv.   1 Tim. 6:11-12, But you, O man of God, flee these things and pursue righteousness, godliness, faith, love, patience, gentleness. Fight the good fight of faith, lay hold on eternal life, to which you were also called and have confessed the good confession in the presence of many witnesses.

v.   2 Cor. 1:20-21, No matter how many promises God has made, they are "Yes" in Christ. And so through him the "Amen" is spoken by us to the glory of God (NIV)

vi. Gal. 3:13-14, Christ has redeemed us from the curse of the law, having become a curse for us (for it is written, *"Cursed is everyone who hangs on a tree"**), that the blessing of Abraham might come upon the Gentiles in Christ Jesus, that we might receive the promise of the Spirit through faith.

vii. Gal. 3:18, For if the inheritance *is* of the law, *it is* no longer of promise; but God gave *it* to Abraham by promise.

viii. Gal. 3:16-18, Now to Abraham and his Seed were the promises made. He does not say, "And to seeds," as of many, but as of one, *"And to your Seed,"** who is Christ. And this I say, *that* the law, which was four hundred and thirty years later, cannot annul the covenant that was confirmed before by God in Christ,* that it should make the promise of no effect

ix. Col. 1:12

x. Psalm 78:37, For their heart was not steadfast with Him, Nor were they faithful in His covenant.

xi. Psalm 78:41, And limited the Holy One of Israel.

xii. Prov. 19:27, Cease, my son, to hear the instruction that causeth to err from the words of knowledge. KJV

xiii. (from Thayer's Greek Lexicon, Electronic Database. Copyright © 2000, 2003, 2006 by Biblesoft, Inc. All rights reserved.)

xiv. Phil. 4:6-7

123

12

WHY I REALLY HATE BEING WRONG

Jesus concluded many of His sermons with this phrase: *He who has ears to hear, let him hear.* This, of course, was a reference to hearing with the inner ear of the heart. In a broader sense it refers to a heart that is teachable, that is not threatened by change. Jesus ministered from a very different perspective than the typical western idea of ministry. He knew not everyone would "get it!" In fact, He knew that because of the attitude of their heart not everyone had the capacity to "get it," nor did they want to "get it." So He ministered the Word in a way that, if you had the heart to "get it," you did. If you didn't have a heart for it, you probably thought it just foolishness.

Not having a heart for it was not because your heart had been broken. Those who had been wounded and oppressed, i.e. the poor in spirit, readily received the Word with joy. They had no false hope in power or affluence. They had no affluence and very little resources, and sadly had little hope of ever having them. The people who couldn't "get it" were those who refused to surrender their own opinion. They were not open; they were not teachable. They had no willingness to change their mind (repent). Being right was their god! They hated being wrong!

What every person needs to see and perceive the truth is a revelation, an unveiling. Religious externalists have wrongly taught us that revelation is something wherein God rewards us when we have paid a great enough price through long enough prayer, fasting, suffering, or some other form of sacrifice. They make us feel that God somehow treasures the insight we so desperately need more than He values His children.

Since Jesus came to show us God, we can look at His life and see the truth any time we truly desire it. We have the Holy Spirit who is always attempting to lead us into the truth anytime we are willing to hear it. Any teachable person who will humble himself and surrender his opinion to God can get any needed revelation anytime he or she needs and desires it. The day of salvation (healed, delivered, blessed, prospered, protected, made whole, set apart) is always today.[1] We are never waiting on God.

The externalist uses the Old Testament believer as his model for the Christian life. We should use Jesus as our model. In the Old Testament, there was much about God that was not yet revealed. Man did not have the Holy Spirit dwelling in him as his teacher. But after the resurrection and the outpouring of the Holy Spirit, we have all we need, but we have to listen to God in our heart to perceive the truth that we do not yet grasp. Unfortunately, most of our struggle with truth is the pursuit of intellectual understanding instead of establishing our heart beliefs. *Knowledge puffs up; love builds up.* Getting the information feeds my ego but still does not set me free. Experiencing the truth in my heart as an expression of God's love sets me free.

A person who does not see, know, or have what they need to experience life to the fullest (keep in mind what we think we need and what we really need can be worlds apart), is not limited by a reluctant, stingy God. He or she is limited by their own opinions or beliefs. They are like a person who longs to peer into the Promised Land, but there is a hill between them and what they long to see. The person doesn't need to use their faith to move the hill. They just need to stand in a different place so the hill is no

> THE THING BLOCKING OUR ABILITY TO SEE THE TRUTH, THE THING WE'RE STANDING BEHIND, IS OUR OPINION.

longer an obstacle. The thing blocking our ability to see the truth, the thing we're standing behind, is our opinion. If we change our vantage point, we can see past our opinion and have the revelation we need.

Paul explained that, like the children of Israel, hardness of heart is a veil that blinds us. A veil does not completely hide the truth, it merely distorts the truth. So, the veil doesn't make me reject God or Jesus; it just causes me to see Him as something other than He really is. We all have a tendency to create an image of God that facilitates our personal preferences. If we are hard and judgmental, we find Scriptures that make God appear hard and judgmental. We want to believe in a God that validates our predisposition. Idolatry in the New Covenant is not an image that has been hewn from a tree trunk. It is the image of God we have shaped in our own imagination. And the image of God I create justifies me staying just the way I am. It makes me feel right. And I can even find the Scriptures to support my position.

Paul explained in the passage[2] that the veil, the thing that is distorting the way we see God, is taken away IN CHRIST! This is more than just getting born again. It is just as he says, IN CHRIST. In Christ is where we give up our identity, die to self, follow Him as disciples, and find this new life. But remember, this requires that I die to self. In 2 Corinthians 3:18, Paul explains that with the removal of the veil we not only see Him clearly, but because we see Him clearly we are transformed into that same image. Possibly we have this innate knowledge that seeing God brings change. Sadly, change is something we resist because it is a form of death.

It may be that the primary reason I am clinging to my opinions is because they are so related to who I see myself to be. The old idea of who I am and how I will find fulfillment is an identity/life/way of thinking I know. To put on new ideas and opinions, I must release the old. On some level that is death to self. It is a quantum leap toward accepting and embracing death in Him! It is the launching point for all true growth and development.

TO PUT ON NEW IDEAS AND OPINIONS, I MUST RELEASE THE OLD.

Considering that death is man's ultimate fear, this death to "self" touches on our most deeply rooted fear. Man always resists what he fears. He has plenty of resistance mechanisms to justify his lack of adaptability. "I'll pray about that. I need to study that some more. God is not leading me that way. I'm just not ready. I need a revelation!" Then probably the most common is, "I don't understand." But all of these are simply forms of resistance!

"I don't understand" is probably the most used and least legitimate resistance tactic. In light of God's Word, it seems the need to intellectually understand as the precursor for following God is a serious issue of the heart. At its core it falls into the category of pride. *Trust in the LORD with all your heart,* ***And lean not on your own understanding*** (Prov. 3:5). While we claim to be seeking God out one side of our mouth, out the other side we are in absolute defiance as we insist, "I need to understand before I will follow You." Possibly people do not realize their need to understand intellectually is a declaration that says, "I trust me more than I trust You!" Verse 6 goes on to say: *In all your ways acknowledge Him, And He shall direct your paths.* The Hebrew word "acknowledge" is translated as "know" nearly every other time it is used in Scripture. So it is saying *know Him in all of our ways.* If we know Him, He will direct and make our path straight, smooth, pleasant, and upright![3] The only other option besides trusting the Lord is to be *wise in your own eyes.*

Man is wired in such a way that he seeks and is drawn to what he believes will bring him pleasure. Conversely, he will avoid or run away from that which he believes will cause pain. That's why our body has both a sympathetic and parasympathetic nervous system. One governs the function of our body when situations are safe, peaceful, and normal. But when we feel threatened, we shift into what is called the "fight or flight" mode, i.e. the sympathetic nervous system. In other words, we are so designed to avoid pain it is hardwired into our physical body! When we feel fear, we even think with a different part of our brain.

Our opinions, which are deeply intertwined with our sense of self, were formed in our life experiences. Over time our opinions become so intertwined with our life experience that, to some degree, they represent who we are (our identity). Since opinions come from what we know, they give a feeling of being in control. This feeling of control creates the illusion of safety. When my opinion is challenged it touches on my ego. My ego is my sense of self, independent of Christ. Giving up this thing that makes me feel strong (stronghold) is seen as threatening and painful; therefore, I resist.

The part of us that must die, however, is the part that is causing all the pain. It is the "I," i.e. the "self" Jesus said must die, if I have any desire to follow

Him as a disciple. My need to be right when challenged shakes my false sense of security. This produces fear. Then I attempt to find rationalization to justify disobedience. I resist what I fear because it represents pain, and I will give myself fully to what I know because it represents safety or pleasure.

Fear of dying-to-self invokes my primal need to survive. I begin to think with a part of my brain that doesn't consider who I am. It doesn't even consider the consequences of my actions. All factors other than survival are non-essential. Often that fear is expressed through anger. Anger can be expressed by projecting false strength, arguing, and any number of defense mechanisms. Usually people do not even understand why they are reacting in such an irrational manner. They are seeking to preserve the self, ego, and I ... they are seeking to survive, which means they cannot grow beyond their current state. They are seeking the thing that made them feel safe in the past. They are attempting to stay within the invisible boundaries created by the beliefs of their heart.

All of these dysfunctional beliefs and behaviors that are destroying us today were at some earlier time used to help us survive. They were the mechanisms we learned to survive our family, our neighborhood, the school bully, and all the things in our young life that threatened us. These thoughts, opinions, and behaviors are "right." They have worked for me in the past. I will be vulnerable if I give them up. I will not know how to survive. No one holds to their ways because they think they

COUNSEL BRINGS US BACK TO THE NEED TO BE TEACHABLE...

are wrong. From their perspective their ways are right! But as the Scripture tells us, *all of our ways seems right in our own eyes, but the end of that way is death*. And there is only one solution to thinking we are right: heed counsel either from people, God's Word, or God's Spirit.[4] But counsel brings us back to the need to be teachable, to have an attitude of repentance, and to be ready to consider things from a different point of view, which is an unknown, and therefore provokes fear.

The wisdom (ability to apply truth in real-life situations) we so desperately need to survive and be happy doesn't require that we blindly surrender our opinion, but it requires that we be willing. That basic teachable attitude of repentance is the never-ending path to wisdom. If we are not teachable, we are fools. Our defense against learning is to always express, defend, or prove our opinion. Finding fault with the one who opposes our opinion is a common defense mechanism. Criticism of the teacher falsely hides a rebellious attitude, resistant to change. Carnal logic makes more sense than the counsel of those who are succeeding at life.[5]

We have all heard that to do the same thing over and over expecting a different outcome is the definition of insanity. Proverbs explains it like this: *As a dog returns to his own vomit, So a fool repeats his folly.* Verse 12 explains why the unteachable fool keeps doing the same thing over and over: *Do you see a man wise in his own eyes? There is more hope for a fool than for him* (Prov. 26:11-12). He is wise in his own eyes. He thinks his ways (opinions) are right, even if they don't work. According to this verse he is worse than the average fool because he is wise in his own eyes; he thinks he's right even when it is killing him. There is little hope for the one who trusts in his own wisdom; all he has left is the pain of consequences. But even then, instead of accepting his responsibility for the pain in his life, he blames God. *The foolishness of a man twists his way, And his heart frets against the LORD* (Prov. 19:3).

In Matthew 13 the disciples asked Jesus why He spoke in parables. At first glance the answer seems rather negative: *Because it has been given to you to know the mysteries of the kingdom of heaven, but to them it has not been given.*[6] This sounds like predestination, but Jesus brings this into perspective as He explains: *For whoever has, to him more will be given, and he will have abundance; but whoever does not have, even what he has will be taken away from him.*

These words were spoken immediately after the teaching of the parable of the sower and the seed. In Mark's account of this, he explains how they are able to draw life from the Word they hear by the degree of thought, study, pondering, and meditation they give to it. As James later echoed, *don't be a forgetful hearer of the Word.* The Word must be taken into our heart or it is lost by all the circumstances. Those who hear the Word and do not follow

> THE WORD MUST BE TAKEN INTO OUR HEART OR IT IS LOST BY ALL THE CIRCUMSTANCES.

Jesus' prescription to establish it in their heart will let it slip from them. They hear amiss! The result is they will spend the rest of their life getting more of what they have. Whatever they have... more is given, i.e. more poverty or more prosperity, more sickness or more health, more happiness or more sorrow. When it says "more will be given," that word means, "to cause to happen;" for example, the sky gives the rain.[7] But this doesn't mean God is giving and taking the rain. The Scriptures reflect this giving and taking to be the product of the beliefs of our heart. After all, in the parable it was all about how the heart that receives the seed determines the harvest.

Jesus goes on in verses 13-15 to explain, *they hear and do not understand, they see and do not perceive, their eyes THEY HAVE CLOSED!* Why would people close their eyes to a message that would bring them life, peace, and joy? If they were willing to see, hear, and understand, they would have to "turn around." They would rather live in their pain and have the false sense of security than to die to self's opinion, self's wisdom, and self's survival. The unteachable, unrepentant attitude of the heart must live in a state of willful confusion.[8] Thus, the ultimate resistance, "I don't understand." But the truth is, I hate being wrong because it threatens my sense of self. It represents pain. If I am wrong, I will have to repent... die to my opinion.

Jesus told the disciples, "you see, you hear, and you are blessed." But the key is this: they were disciples. It doesn't say He told the crowd; it certainly doesn't say He told the Christians... no! He told the disciples. They had made the choice to follow Him at all cost. In America we don't have to live in threat of losing our life to

THE DISCIPLE HAS NO DREAD OF BEING WRONG!

follow Jesus as do believers in countries all around the world. We won't have our property and assets confiscated. We just run the risk of giving up this life that has come to define us.

The disciple has so come to terms with the death of self that he is eager to learn. He loves instruction. He values correction. Being wrong is no threat to the disciple; it presents an opportunity for growth. He knows he is loved by God even if he is wrong. He knows God will not punish him, but will correct him gently as the child He loves. When the disciple hears the words of correction, the voice of God in his heart says, "This is truth." While there is always a momentary "sting" of embarrassment, the negative feelings are soon replaced by the comfort of the Holy Spirit. The defensiveness and arguments give way to peace. He seeks to know God in his heart (acknowledge Him) and God makes the way of correction even, straight, easy, prosperous, and pleasant. But the capacity to hear and feel these wonderful inner expressions of love, peace, and power are only known by those who listen to God in their heart. The disciple has no dread of being wrong!

It might be interesting to sit and quietly reflect on your conflicts with others. Are you really open to the view of others, or are you more anxious to prove your point of view? Do you feel that listening to others means you agree with them? Do you feel embarrassed or blessed when you discover an area that you previously misunderstood? It could be interesting to go to people around you and ask for their input. "I promise I will not argue or become disagreeable, but I need to know, am I generally open to your input? Do I argue when I am challenged?" But keep in mind, if you are a dominator, no one will tell you the truth.

Get alone with God, repent, and change your mind about your need to be right. Then give yourself permission to be wrong. Over time as you develop your heart, you will identify the reasons you are argumentative and unteachable.

Above all, do not make the most crucial of self-deceptive mistakes. Don't think you are closed to people but open to God. I promise you, as you are with people, so are you with God!

Endnotes

i. 2 Cor. 6:2, *"In an acceptable time I have heard you, And in the day of salvation I have helped you."** Behold, now is the accepted time; behold, now is the day of salvation.

ii. 2 Cor. 3:14-18, But their minds were blinded. For until this day the same veil remains unlifted in the reading of the Old Testament, because the *veil* is taken away in Christ. But even to this day, when Moses is read, a veil lies on their heart. Nevertheless when one turns to the Lord, the veil is taken away. Now the Lord is the Spirit; and where the Spirit of the Lord *is*, there *is* liberty. But we all, with unveiled face, beholding as in a mirror the glory of the Lord, are being transformed into the same image from glory to glory, just as by the Spirit of the Lord.

iii.   OT:3474, yashar —to be right, to be straight, to be level, to be upright, to be just, to be lawful, to be smooth
    a) (Qal)
       1)   to go straight
       2)   to be pleasing, to be agreeable, to be right (figurative)
       3)   to be straightforward, to be upright
    b) (Piel)
(from The Online Bible Thayer's Greek Lexicon and Brown Driver & Briggs Hebrew Lexicon, Copyright © 1993, Woodside Bible Fellowship, Ontario, Canada. Licensed from the Institute for Creation Research.)

iv.   Prov. 12:15, The way of a fool *is* right in his own eyes, But he who heeds counsel *is* wise.

Prov. 14:12, There is a way *that seems* right to a man, But its end *is* the way of death.

Prov. 21:2-3, Every way of a man *is* right in his own eyes, But the Lord weighs the hearts. To do righteousness and justice

v.   Prov. 26:16, The sluggard is wiser in his own eyes *and* conceit than seven men who can render a reason *and* answer discreetly. AMP

vi.   Matt. 13:10-17

vii.   to cause to happen, used particularly in relationship to physical events - 'to make, to cause, to give, to produce.'[157] kai\ o(ou)rano\ 'and the sky produces rain' James 5:18; 'I will produce omens in the sky above' Acts 2:19; kai\ h 'and the moon will not produce its light' Matt 24:29. (from Greek-English Lexicon Based on Semantic Domain. Copyright © 1988 United Bible Societies, New York. Used by permission.)

viii.   James 3:16, For where you have envy and selfish ambition, there you find disorder and every evil practice. NIV

13

KNOWING GOD
IN YOUR HEART

Adjusting our priorities to be in harmony with God's is a natural, healthy, never-ending journey for the disciple. For the externalist this about discovering they are wrong, penance (in some form), and then changing their behavior in a legalistic attempt to recover what they feel they have lost with God. For the disciple making the heart journey, it is another natural step which results in a richer, more experiential relationship with the Father and a process which leads to a better quality of life! Every new challenge of life is approached with our heart opened to God's wisdom. Living in the eternal now requires us to be alive to the Spirit daily; we can never live from past encounters or experiences with God. They can encourage us and provide insight, but they can never provide wisdom for today!

For those who believe the finished wok of Jesus and realize this is a metamorphosis, there is never any sense of getting more of God, trying to please God, trying to get Him to do something for us, or attempting to get what we lack. Harmonizing is not the climb up a ladder in some type of spiritual hierarchy in our standing with God. Harmonizing with Him, adjusting our values and priorities is simply the journey of transferring that which is in our spirit into the rest of our being, via faith in our heart.

Almost all the reasons we come to Jesus in the beginning are somewhat selfish: we are tired of our destructive life, we are in trouble, we are sick, or we need help. Essentially, we are in pain, and we are hardwired to avoid pain, so we open ourselves to new options. Hearing the Gospel is a viable option for a life of pain. Thankfully, God is not an insecure idealist. As a loving Father He longs for the missing relationship, regardless of what compels us to come home. He wants to deliver His children from their pain. *The LORD is near to those who have a broken heart, And saves such as have a contrite spirit.* (Ps. 34:18). You are not required to have a broken heart for God to be near. This verse is an assurance to those who are in pain that God is still there to deliver them when they turn their hearts to Him. He is a loving Father. His reason for wanting us to follow Him is because it is through the development of that relationship that we experience life at its best…. on every plane! As Jesus said, *This is eternal life, that they may know You, the only true God, and Jesus Christ whom You have sent* (John 17:3).

As we experience His goodness, we are naturally drawn, led, and accompanied to the place of repentance.[1] The goodness of God that accompanies, draws, and leads us to repentance is such a wonderful picture of our journey with God.[2] This word "goodness" means "mild, or gentle," but it also means "useful." We start this journey from the place of need. In the beginning we only know Him as Savior. If we do not grow to know God in any other form, we will have codependent, and probably turbulent, involvement with God. If we only know Him as Savior, He is only useful when we are in trouble. But, like all codependent involvement, it never evolves into a truly, healthy, loving relationship.

> AS WE EXPERIENCE HIS GOODNESS, WE ARE NATURALLY DRAWN… TO THE PLACE OF REPENTANCE.

The highest form of love is "agape," a word that means "to value, hold in high regard, and consider precious." This is the type of love God has for us. When this quality of love inspires our actions, we will never wrong anyone, we will obey all of God's Word, and our faith will work perfectly. God values us. To Him we are precious, and to all religious consternation He holds us in high regard. Amazingly, this was how He viewed and related to us before we came to Jesus. Imagine how much more now that we have [3] been justified by His blood and reconciled to Him! The word "justified" means "to be rendered righteous,"

136

i.e. as we should be.[4] The word "reconciled" means "to exchange coins of equal value." So we have been made righteous and we have been reconciled. A price equal to our value was paid for us; therefore, we have been purchased for God.[5] Since Jesus was the price paid, this means we are as precious to Him as Jesus. This is the love God has for us.

John said, *we love Him because He first loved us.* We don't get saved because we love God. How can we love Him? We don't even know Him. Unless corrupted by external religious legalism or religious philosophies, every day we follow God with our whole heart we will experience more of the goodness and love of God, i.e. how valuable and precious we are to Him. Based on the meaning of the word "goodness," that will also be a discovery of how useful God and His truth are in our life. As we see how our life improves, how His Word gives us insight and understanding, or how following His voice delivers us from danger, we have more and more value (love) for God. This is why spiritual leaders for centuries have all loved (valued) the Word of God and considered it more precious than silver, gold, or anything one could own. They saw that it was useful for life!

Over the course of 30+ years of pastoring, I have had people born again in nearly every service. The last time research was done, over 80% of the unsaved people who attended one of my services made a decision to follow Jesus the first time they attended. The most interesting thing about this phenomenon is that I never preached the typical salvation message. I preached messages about the application of God's Word and how He would personally empower us. The two most consistent reasons people felt moved to make the decision are: first, they discovered how much God loved them; second, they realized this would work in real life, in practical ways. Since

> WHEN WE DISCOVER THAT SOMEONE IS CONSISTENTLY GOOD, WE GROW IN OUR TRUST (FAITH) FOR THEM.

the number one reason people do not attend church is lack of relevance, it is obvious that the messages being preached do not reflect the usefulness of God in daily life.

As these believers walked with God, renewed their mind, and applied His truth to their life, they experienced the goodness of God. This moved them to be more willing to die to self (repent). This made putting on the "new man" far more appealing and much less fearful. By continuing this process the focus was moved from "what am I giving up?" to "what am I benefitting?" Staying the same no longer looked appealing, and yielding to transformation no longer appeared threatening. When we discover that someone is consistently good, we grow in our trust (faith) for them. But when fear is the motivation used for obedience, a person may alter their behavior, but they will not love God; therefore, they will not trust Him.[6]

This "knowing God" is an experience with God as an individual, yet it is also the experience of His attributes, especially love. Looking at the root word of knowledge, "gnosis," provides an amazing scope of what this entails, but we have to begin by explaining, "this is not just intellectual knowledge. This suggests the act of knowing. This act embraces every organ and mode of knowledge."[7]

Science is discovering that our past ideas about knowledge, memories, thought, and even learning, are not only limiting but, in many cases, in stark contradiction to how our mind and body actually work. We have more sensory perception than we ever imagined. Every organ in our body actually plays a specific role in influencing certain aspects of thought, emotion, and memory. We have the molecules of emotion all over our body, not just the brain. This type of knowing God involves all we are... literally!

Because God's Word has been written on our heart, there is also intuitive knowledge—that knowledge we possess but don't know how to explain. This knowledge does not emerge as words but as impressions, concepts, or intuition. Therefore, every true experience with God and His attributes is a progression in recognizing this type of knowledge. It brings a perception and understanding that is beyond the scope of human explanation. When the experience with God harmonizes with our inner truth, we have the sense of a "witness" or verification. When the mind has been renewed, there is no internal conflict or confusion.

This "knowing" is of an extremely intimate nature. It is used of a man and woman making love, sharing that which they should share with no one else, discovering what should only be known between a husband and wife. If love-making is to be what it has the potential to be, there has to be vulnerability among both parties, which involves the willingness to be known in a very intimate and private manner. The word used for "knowing God" carries with it the implication of being known, as well. And just like the marriage bed, this is a knowing that only comes through intimacy. That's why the Apostle John rebuked the Gnostics' error of special revelation knowledge, and instead called the deceived believers back to intimate fellowship, sharing in the death, burial, and resurrection of Jesus, which could be seen by all if they were in the light (truth). This knowledge is neither observation nor mystical vision; it comes to expression in acts. Observing the commandments is a criterion of knowledge (1 John 2:3ff.). Also involved is an awareness of being loved as the basis of loving others (John 15:9; 13:34). This requires the recognition and reception of love, i.e. faith. It is not direct knowledge of God, but knowledge through the revelation in Christ.[8] Obedience and the way we treat others becomes a part of the witness to our heart that we are "in Him."

This knowing is like an infusion, intertwining, or becoming one experientially! This is the place where we see Him as He is. It's not theory, it's not information… but then again, it is. Remember, in all issues of the heart there is always a paradox. Light is the word that God chose to use for us to understand truth. Light is a particle, but if you look at it from another perspective it is a wave. If you slow it down, it is sound; if it is slowed enough, it is matter. Life, light, and truth are one and the same. Like energy, it is a continuum capable of manifesting and expressing itself

> YOU CAN'T EXPERIENCE THE LIFE OF GOD AND WALK IN DEFIANCE OF HIS WORD.

in many different ways. So while life is based on information, it is not just information, and information does not equal life. This infusion of intuitive information manifests along a broad spectrum of identity, obedience, belief, understanding, obedience, giving and receiving love, trusting God, and an infinite number of other possibilities. For example, you can't experience the life of God and walk in defiance of His Word. You can't be experiencing the love of God and hate your brother. Yet, obeying His Word does not equate to having life or love.

It is here, in this type of fellowship where an interchange occurs of seeing Him as He is and seeing ourselves as we are in Him, that the heart experiences identity in a way that supersedes simply hearing the message of identity. For most Christians identity in Christ is just another batch of informational doctrine that makes us feel good when we think about it, but has never actually become a belief of our heart; thus, no effortless transformation to be more like Him! The writers of the New Testament speak of having this kind of knowing based on accurate and precise knowledge of the truth. One of the most powerful Scriptures that presents this concept is Philemon 6: *That the communication of thy faith may become effectual by the acknowledging of every good thing which is in you in Christ Jesus.*

The word "communication" is actually the Greek word "koinoonia," from which we get the word "fellowship." The word would more accurately convey "something people have in common." This is not a reference to believers having fellowship with one another as much as it refers to what believers have in common with Christ. Our fellowship with Christ, i.e. what we share in common, is the resurrected life which He now shares with us because we are in Him.

This Scripture is giving us the primary key to actuating the "life of God" which is already in us, but we may not be experiencing. After all, we ALL have everything we need for life and godliness (2 Peter 1:3), but as Peter and Paul both say, it has to be activated, initiated, or actualized, or it is just a dormant unrealized potential. Any believer that is having problems has simply not died to self or put off the "old man" in that area of life and put on, activated, engaged, or embraced the "new man." THERE ARE NO OTHER PROBLEMS, AND THERE ARE NO OTHER SOLUTIONS for the believer!

> ANY BELIEVER THAT IS HAVING PROBLEMS HAS SIMPLY NOT DIED TO SELF, OR PUT OFF THE "OLD MAN"...

Paul then goes on to say, *this life that I share with Jesus is activated by the acknowledgement of every good thing which is in you in Christ!* That word "acknowledge," based on every language resource I have, should have been translated "precise and correct knowledge." When Paul corrected those who were living a compromised life and justifying it by the forgiveness they had in Christ, he said, *you have not so learned Christ, if indeed you have heard Him and have been taught by Him, as the truth is in Jesus* (Eph. 4:20-21). Then he tells them to put off the "old man" and put on the "new man." But they could only take this step if they heard, believed, and knew (experienced) the accurate and precise truth about the life they share (fellowship) with Jesus!

He doesn't tell them they need to become something they are not. He reminds them that they are righteous; they simply need to put that righteousness on, and they may have to adjust what they believe. But he made it clear that unacceptable behavior is never justified by the grace or love of God. All the Epistles address these kinds of problems. They do not do it, however, by manipulating a believer into mere behavior modification or works righteousness. They do it by encouraging them to connect with their true identity, the "new man," created in His likeness, found only in intimate knowledge of God through the Lord Jesus.

In both of these passages, Paul makes the contingency for putting on this "new man" two-fold: First, you must have heard and believed the precise and accurate truth in Christ. Second, you must put off the "old man," and die to self. He explained to the believers at Colosse that the message of grace was only bringing forth fruit in those who had the precise and accurate knowledge of the Gospel, i.e. in truth. ...*which you heard before... in the word of the truth the gospel... in all the world, is bringing forth fruit, as it is also among you since the day you heard and knew the grace of God in truth* (Col. 1:6). If the Gospel we heard is not bringing forth fruit unto godliness, we either did not hear the truth or we have not actuated it with precise and accurate knowledge of all the good things in us in Christ.

If we have fellowship with Him, i.e. share the same life He now has, then His life will be mirrored in our life. That's why John and Paul both tell us that we become like Him to the degree we see Him as He is. If my life is not being continually transformed, it means that at some point I have stopped looking at Jesus. I started looking at the Church, other Christians, my doctrine, or the world... but one thing is for sure: I am not beholding Him. This seems to be what happened to the believers John addresses in his first Epistle. They were seduced into Gnostic doctrines and left the light that only comes by fellowship (sharing in the resurrection reality) with Jesus. They stopped fellowshipping with God and started looking for a personal divine revelation. They were branches that were losing their life-giving connection to the Vine, and it became evident in their lives. One of the laws of transformation is this: you become what you behold. Beholding doctrine has no power to transform you. Beholding Jesus is where the power that is in you comes alive.

If I see Him as righteous and I acknowledge the very reality that His righteousness is in me, it will cause righteousness to come alive in me. If I acknowledge that I share in healing because together we rose from the dead, conquering sickness and disease, I can actuate healing. We never have to "get" these things. We *have* these things. But the question is, "Am I experiencing them?" My faith comes alive as I commune around the truth of all that we share through His death, burial, and resurrection with the clear and accurate knowledge that these good things are already in me, in Christ. In fellowship I see this in Him, but I also see it in me; *I know as I am known.*

When Peter said we already have everything that pertained to life and godliness, he used the same words as Paul to explain: it is experienced through the knowledge of Him that has called us to glory and virtue. At the end of the process, this is a knowledge that uses all the inner senses to experience the truth, and the mind that has been renewed by the Word of God acknowledges the accurate and precise truth of what we share in common. All of this harmonizes to create an intimate experience in the heart with our Father, an experience that goes beyond words, but has the power to bring alive every word God has ever spoken concerning us, and the truth to embrace the life we share with Jesus, i.e. our true identity in Christ.

This type of knowledge can only be grasped, known, and experienced in the heart, the true facility of understanding. It is the heart that grasps what cannot be put into words, and experiences what cannot be explained; and it is where our weakness puts on His strength, His identity becomes our own, His inheritance is shared with us, His calling becomes our calling, and the power that works in Him explodes in us. The exchange that took place on the cross is experienced in a heart that is knowing, experiencing, and feeling empowered by coming to the precise and accurate experiential, transformational knowledge of God!

> IT IS THE HEART THAT GRASPS WHAT CANNOT BE PUT INTO WORDS...

Write down as many identity Scriptures as you can find. Any Scripture that says "in Him, through Him, by Him, or with Him" is a good starting place. Then, on a regular basis, worship God by acknowledging all of these attributes are in you. Thank God for righteousness, healing, peace, and joy. Involve your thoughts, emotions, and imagination! All prayer is a meditative process. As these attributes of Christ become real to you, they will begin to manifest. If you don't have time to do this yourself, you can order *The Prayer Organizer* that links hundreds of identity Scriptures to the names of God for use in prayer and worship.

Endnotes

i. *to bring, to lead by laying hold of, to lead by accompanying* to (into) any place, *to lead with oneself,* attach to oneself as an attendant (from Thayer's Greek Lexicon, Electronic Database. Copyright © 2000, 2003, 2006 by Biblesoft, Inc. All rights reserved.)

ii. properly, *fit for use, useful; virtuous, good, manageable, i. e. mild, pleasant* (from Thayer's Greek Lexicon, Electronic Database. Copyright © 2000, 2003, 2006 by Biblesoft, Inc. All rights reserved.)

iii. Rom. 5:9-11, Much more then, having now been justified by His blood, we shall be saved from wrath through Him. For if when we were enemies we were reconciled to God through the death of His Son, much more, having been reconciled, we shall be saved by His life. And not only *that,* but we also rejoice in God through our Lord Jesus Christ, through whom we have now received the reconciliation.

iv. Justified: properly, *to make to render righteous or such as he ought to be Thayers*

v. Reconciled: properly *to change, exchange,* as coins for others of equal value; hence *to reconcile*
(from Thayer's Greek Lexicon, Electronic Database. Copyright © 2000, 2003, 2006 by Biblesoft, Inc. All rights reserved.)

vi. 1 John 4:18, There is no fear in love; but perfect love casts out fear, because fear involves torment. But he who fears has not been made perfect in love.

vii. (from Theological Dictionary of the New Testament, abridged edition, Copyright © 1985 by William B. Eerdmans Publishing Company. All rights reserved.)

viii. (from Theological Dictionary of the New Testament, abridged edition, Copyright © 1985 by William B. Eerdmans Publishing Company. All rights reserved.)

14

LAWS OF THE HEART

After forty years of working with people, there are two things that seem to be universal: everyone wants a better life, but nearly no one wants to change. The Church's emphasis to use your faith to change things "out there," combined with the humanistic socialism imposed by society, says everyone else needs to change for me to be happy. It has subverted God's plan for happiness. Our focus for change should always begin internally. People want

> **EVERYONE WANTS A BETTER LIFE, BUT NEARLY NO ONE WANTS TO CHANGE.**

things to be different, but few people know how to bring about an internal heart transformation that moves from the inside to the world around us. Everyone wants everything different; they just want to find a way for that to happen without having to change. This mentality creates a codependent, irresponsible lifestyle filled with disappointment. Even those who understand that the change needs to begin with them try so hard to change, but they usually do so by grit, willpower, determination, and behavioral modification. They, too, usually find bitter disappointment at the end of their efforts.

Behavioral modification has its merits. In fact, conditioning to the basic rules of society is part of the normal process of child-raising. You even find it in man's instinctive attraction to pleasure and avoidance of pain. But like anything that benefits us, when it becomes a substitute for God's best we end up with the worst! Behavioral modification is nothing more than animal training. It emerged from studies with animals by those who deny God, reject man as created in the image of God, and think man evolved from some prehistoric primate. They see man as another species of animal. Behavioral modification, therefore, is based on providing the proper stimuli, either positive or negative, to condition a person to prefer or avoid a particular behavior. This is not totally wrong unless it is seen as a permanent solution.

When people try to change through willpower or sheer effort, this is what the Bible calls "being in the flesh." The only other option is transformation, which depends on God's strength at work in your heart. This is often called "being in the Spirit!" God's power that works in us to bring about painless, permanent, positive, and effortless transformation is called grace. Grace is God's strength, capacity, ability, and power which comes by unmerited favor, but here is the key… it works in our heart! So we are either in the flesh conditioning our brain, depending on our ability, or in the Spirit developing our heart, experiencing God's ability.

Life in the Spirit occurs when we experience the life and power of the Spirit as it flows from our spirit, through our heart, into the rest of our being… that's grace! God's power, to be and do anything that He says we can be, do, or have in Jesus works by very clear-cut heart laws. These laws (governing principles) always work; they are sure and dependable. The problem is, even though they are obvious, easily found, and easily understood, they don't fit into how we have been conditioned to live our life.

We lack the power, strength, and ability to change our lives permanently. No matter how many self-help books we read or faith classes we attend, until we know how to connect with God in our heart we are basically alienated from the life of God which is in us. Some of this is caused by conditions of the heart (which we will discuss), some is ignorance, but so much is simply resistance to that which we do not know and understand.

Each chapter has given you exercises or steps you can take to begin this journey. This chapter begins to take us deeper into practical application. I will now begin to introduce heart issues described in the Bible. Likewise, I will explain more exercises you can employ to deal with these issues. Not every exercise will work for you. The key, however, is to find what works by implementation not by passing intellectual judgment. When you find yourself judging or criticizing what you have not attempted, you should take this as a red flag of resistance. Your mind seeks to preserve your ego by doing things the way you have always done them. This proves you are right and makes you feel secure! This resistance is an attempt to override your heart, which seeks to confirm your identity. The problem is, your identity in Christ is completely different from your identity determined by your life experience, so this is a form of death to self.

At this point you will serve yourself well to remember that much of what I, or anyone, can say about the heart, unless clearly expressed in Scripture, is conceptual. It cannot always be understood in precise measurements or external behaviors. And we must remember, if what we have learned in biology, psychology, or any other arena of study contradicts Scripture, there are three possibilities: the science is inaccurate; the research is accurate but the conclusions are wrong, or we misunderstand the Scripture. Sometimes we misunderstand the Scripture, sometimes we misunderstand the science, and sometimes we misunderstand both! But the Bible must be our basis of interpreting all data. For 40 years I have seen science reverse its absolute assertion of proven "facts" in favor of something far more biblically consistent. But there is never an announcement in the news that says, "Science agrees with the Bible." There isn't even a statement that says, "Science has been wrong all these years."

> THE BIBLE MUST BE OUR BASIS OF INTERPRETING ALL DATA.

There are more differences between ministry to the heart and external religious behavior modification than even I have discovered in my 40 years of making this journey. But I can tell you the top two real reasons people resist putting these exercises into practice: first, they really do not want to change. The excuses will range from, "I don't understand," all the way to, "That's of the devil." But Jesus said the real reason people didn't see and perceive, hear and understand was because they did not want to change. The second reason is Heart Work requires internal application. We love to talk about the Bible; we just don't really like to put it into practice. Why? It might require change of thought, change of behavior, or change of direction…death to self!

There are reasons we are not comfortable putting truth into application. Our Western left brain culture is all about information. We equate knowledge (intellectualism) for knowing (experiencing). It is foreign to our culture, and culture (tradition) is one of the things Jesus said would cause the *Word of God to be of no effect* in our lives. But I think one of the greatest factors is that few, if any, are actually making disciples… I mean leading by example. We hear preachers talk about prayer, but rarely do we ever have the opportunity to pray with them. We hear them talk about winning the lost, but seldom do we see it put into practice in their personal life.

The Western culture has segued back into the Catholic concept of clergy and laity. The ministers are so distant to the common man (laity) that it is impossible to follow their way of life. In some circles leaders claim to avoid contact with people to protect their anointing, which I find interesting considering Jesus was surrounded by people who argued, antagonists who were attacking Him, and children playing, but somehow managed to maintain His anointing. It is reasonable that you cannot actually spend time with the pastor of a mega-church. But when the pastor of a two hundred member congregation tries to imitate the demanding life of a mega-pastor as a means of isolation… it's just imitation on the part of an insecure leader.

People need to see the Word put into application for everyday life issues. They need models, real mentors. The Holy Spirit is the Teacher. No one can really teach you to know God, but we can show people what it looks like in our life by application. I had a pastor invite me into his church to teach the congregation how to pray. So every morning we would have about 20 minutes of teaching, then my wife and I would pray and invite them to join us. Nearly every person in the congregation just sat and watched as we prayed and worshipped. At the end of the meeting, the pastor told me how disappointed he was. As it turned out, he really didn't want his church to learn how to pray, he wanted them to learn about prayer. Conversely, there were many churches that exploded with a new life of prayer by the same type of meetings.

In Heart Physics[1] we put it into practice. It is not an information-based program, although it includes wonderful information. It is a Bible-based, experience-driven program. You are given the opportunity to put the truth into practice, which is a road seldom traveled by the modern believer. One of the laws of *Heart Physics* is: any inspiration of God you do not actuate, you lose. And as you will discover, you may lose it within a few seconds but will almost never have more than about 12 hours before it evaporates.

Jesus really didn't say the truth would set you free! Let's get it in context. He was speaking to people who believed on Him but had not yet made the decision to be a disciple. The person who has not made the decision to model his life on the life, teaching, and power of the resurrected Lord is still a slave to sin (a life of missing the mark of God's promise for him).

HEART PHYSICS... IS A BIBLE-BASED, EXPERIENCE-DRIVEN PROGRAM.

He then explained, [2] *If you abide in My word, you are My disciples indeed.* A disciple abides, continues in, and puts into practice from the heart the teachings of Jesus. But it doesn't stop there, that is the beginning. This abiding, living in, putting into practice, and continuing in His Word from the heart (not from an external-legalistic approach), will bring us to this place of knowing and experiencing the power of His Word. It is the experiential knowing that sets us free.

Then He introduces a concept that Paul echoes in the Book of Romans. *Whoever commits sin is a slave of sin.* The phrase "commits sin" has a similar idea of continuing in something much the same as continuing in His Word. But there is a difference; continuing in His Word is a choice we make, it is a lifestyle choice. This word for "commits" means "to make fruit."[3] If the fruit that grows in your life is sin--living, believing, feeling, or thinking in a way that causes you to miss the target of what God has for you--you are still a slave to sin… even though you are born again. Fruit grows as a result of the root, your heart. The only way to truly know the condition of the heart is the fruit. The new birth set you free legally; experiencing the power of the living Word by God's grace sets you free in real life experience. Besides the aforementioned factors, the uniqueness of every person's life experience introduces certain variables in exactly how they will apply the truth. Everyone has a unique set of life experiences that "shaped" their heart (beliefs). Those experiences forged their current sense of identity (self). Therefore, how they hear, perceive, and understand is mixed in with the perfect work of God, all manner of personal beliefs and cellular memories (which make up the subconscious mind); and thus requires a path that can only be found following the Spirit as He leads.

Many who are ready to put it into practice (believers) desire a detailed blueprint so precise that it allows no room for the Holy Spirit's involvement. But at the end of the day, the person who requires a blueprint will get overwhelmed by all the details it demands. So the truth is that wanting to know every detail is a form of resistance, which we will address. Which brings me to another heart law. There is no map for where you want to go, but there are signposts you will see as you follow Him. Every day the world around you changes, the people involved in your life change, people make different choices; therefore, being led by the Holy Spirit is dynamic, day by day. God wants to give you the wisdom to walk in victory the way things are today, not how they were yesterday. Any blueprint would be outdated in a matter of hours.

> THERE IS NO MAP FOR WHERE YOU WANT TO GO, BUT THERE ARE SIGNPOSTS YOU WILL SEE AS YOU FOLLOW HIM.

On this journey you will be learning many laws of the heart. These are biblically-based "principles" that help us understand how to minister to, govern, guard, write on, or develop our heart. When it comes to helping others and yourself, one has to work within the biblical prescriptions for the heart, or you will find yourself defaulting to religious formulas, outward actions, or something that worked for you in the past but is no longer applicable today. Jesus didn't perform many healings the same way twice. He didn't spit in the mud and rub it in the eyes of every blind person to heal them; He didn't have everyone go to the priests and make an offering. To some people He spoke one word, but there were others He ministered to first with the Word, and then there were the ones upon whom He personally laid His hands, and some He just spoke the Word without them even present. And what we rarely realize is there were some He simply let walk away. But He didn't set up a formula factory to churn out shallow, temporary results.

The process whereby people were healed was based on truth… that was not variable; it was the one fixed piece of the puzzle. But the application of that truth depended on how He was led by the Spirit. And the Spirit would have led in the way that best addressed the need of the person. Had He simply attempted the same formula (process/application) on everyone, many would not have been healed.

Scripture is clear that the majority of individual healings in the Gospels occurred because of the faith of the recipient. Faith is an issue of the heart. Therefore, He ministered to them in a way that would be most effective for their heart beliefs. Thus, another law of the heart: truth is absolute, but the application of truth is 100% variable. The Word of God is absolute. The promises of God are for everyone who is in Christ. The one variable between the absolute promise and what should be a predictable outcome is the heart. Rather than deal with the variable of a wounded heart, in our foolish self-righteousness we question the validity of God's Word. Then, to avoid dealing with the possibility that the problem could be in us, we create religious formulas that complicate or neutralize the truth.

The functions of the heart are not theoretical, yet many of the ways we explain them are theoretical, and many of the ways we understand them are conceptual. Through His Word God has graciously revealed everything we need to know about developing, managing, and ministering to our own heart, which we shall address in future chapters. But all that wisdom will be lost if, while reading conceptual explanations, you attempt to apply left brain, hard-and-fast intellectual definitions. Can you imagine how foolish Jesus' parables seemed to the Pharisees, whose only mode of listening and interpreting the Word was based on left brain intellect and external observation? They heard the greatest sermons in the world taught by our Lord and Teacher, yet it benefitted them nothing!

> THROUGH HIS WORD GOD HAS GRACIOUSLY REVEALED EVERYTHING WE NEED TO KNOW ABOUT DEVELOPING… OUR OWN HEART…

As we will discuss in a future chapter, the laws of the heart are based in the Word of God and mirrored in the natural laws God used to create the universe. So the more perfectly we come to understand true science (physics), the more perfectly we understand some of the workings of God.[4] Nature itself, when properly understood, testifies to the greatness and glory of God. That is why so much of the secular world vehemently opposes the slightest hint of intelligent design. The politically correct way one is forced to interpret the facts of science requires that any possibility of an intelligent creation be handled with reproach, scorn, condescension, and even censoring. Even though they could know God through His works, they reject Him. As Paul said,[5] *professing to be wise they became fools.* The pagans of old became slaves to the gods of their imaginations. The pagans of intellect become slaves to their own ego!

Scientists do make wonderful, insightful, and valuable discoveries. Sadly, the Church has tended, in violation of Scripture, to reject discoveries (knowledge) that come from any outside source. That seems to be done from what appears to be three primary motives: first, if the Church acknowledged that science accurately knew something the Church didn't know, it would diminish its control over the people. Throughout history many wonderful scientists have been killed, tortured, or as it is in this generation, scandalized for discoveries that could have moved the world into a much better place. Second, because scientists used accurate information to reach inaccurate conclusions, the Church rejected the information. We have the Bible as our basis of absolute truth. That does not, however, mean our interpretation of the Bible is correct. Using the Bible independently of religious dogma and inaccurate bias provides a basis for reaching accurate, revealing, and relevant conclusions using the world's research.

"Scientific" conclusions are very rarely based on objective observation of facts. As someone said, "Don't be fooled into thinking science is scientific."[6] Scientists very often want the conclusion to be something they have already determined. Or, in many cases their bias causes them to interpret the facts in a predetermined manner. And in this modern politically correct insanity, there is pressure to interpret the facts to support the latest political agendas.

Third, and probably the greatest, shows gross ignorance on the part of the Christian community. If the discovery does not come from within the Church's accepted culture, the information is vilified to be "of the devil!" The devil did not create any part of the world or anything that is in it! Science is observing the natural world (God's creation) and gathering information. Physics is the study of the natural world and the laws that govern. Quantum physics looks at the laws that govern at the sub-atomic level. These laws of quantum physics are so in sync with God's Word that they seem at times to be taken from the pages of the Bible. The more science advances, the more it catches up with the Bible. Due to ignorance and bias, neither the Church nor the scientists seem to understand or admit this wonderful phenomenon!

Nothing natural can be of the devil! While anyone's conclusions may be demonic, worldly wisdom,[7] the natural facts are not. To reject the wisdom that comes from science (observation and knowledge of God's creation), is to reject God's revealed wisdom. We should know the Word of God well enough to reach better conclusions than they reach. Our conclusions will cause us to see and glorify God regardless of what conclusions they reach. Refusing to accept the facts because they were discovered

NOTHING NATURAL CAN BE OF THE DEVIL!

by an atheist or a pagan would be like Balaam refusing to repent because the warning came through a donkey. It was still a message from God, no matter the source! It is only when we use information to deny the Bible, deny God, or deny His creation that we are using that information in an evil way.

As you learn what I call "laws of the heart," you may want to highlight them and ponder them. You may see ways that you already use them for good or bad. The more you ponder on what you read, the greater the opportunity the Holy Spirit has to show you how it is relevant to your life.

You may want to read this entire book through once, to just get the concepts. When you don't understand, ask the Holy Spirit to teach you. Then let it go; just keep reading. Then read it again and consider trying some of the exercises. To find out more about *Heart Physics®* programs you can begin to apply to your life, go to www.heartphysics.com.

Endnotes

i. Heart Physics® is a registered trademark. This is the name I have given to the programs I have developed to help people learn to live from their heart. You can learn more at www.HeartPhysics.com

ii. John 8:31-36

iii. NT:4160, NT:4160† poie/w karpo/n^b (an idiom, literally 'to make fruit'); karpofore/w^b: to cause results to exist - 'to produce results, to cause results. (from Greek-English Lexicon Based on Semantic Domain. Copyright © 1988 United Bible Societies, New York. Used by permission.)

iv. Rom. 1:20, or since the creation of the world His invisible *attributes* are clearly seen, being understood by the things that are made, *even* His eternal power and Godhead, so that they are without excuse.

v. Rom. 1:21-22, Although they knew God, they did not glorify *Him* as God, nor were thankful, but became futile in their thoughts, and their foolish hearts were darkened.²² Professing to be wise, they became fools,

vi. Source unknown

vii. James 3:13-18, Who *is* wise and understanding among you? Let him show by good conduct *that* his works *are done* in the meekness of wisdom. But if you have bitter envy and self-seeking in your hearts, do not boast and lie against the truth. This wisdom does not descend from above, but *is* earthly, sensual, demonic. For where envy and self-seeking *exist*, confusion and every evil thing *are* there. But the wisdom that is from above is first pure, then peaceable, gentle, willing to yield, full of mercy and good fruits, without partiality and without hypocrisy. Now the fruit of righteousness is sown in peace by those who make peace.

15

GROWING THE WORD IN YOUR HEART

Heart Physics® is based on God's consistent emphasis on His desire for us to know and experience Him in our hearts. The concept of using physics as a means to understand spiritual laws is based primarily on Romans 1:20, *For since the creation of the world His invisible attributes are clearly seen, being understood by the things that are made, even His eternal power and Godhead.* As explained earlier, the study of the natural world is physics. Because God is completely consistent in everything He does, this Scripture tells us we can understand invisible things about God through what He has created. Those same laws that govern all of physical creation are harmonious with God's nature, wisdom, and logic, as well as the laws of the heart.

It is important to realize and trust how consistent God is. His ways are only foreign to the one who does not see and perceive

> IT IS IMPORTANT TO REALIZE AND TRUST HOW CONSISTENT GOD IS.

what God has provided. Jesus is referred to as the Word of God, the "Logos." This Greek word is very rich and very inclusive. Just the fact that this is a terminology describing Jesus should give us some realization that it is more than a mere spoken word. The Word (logos) of God is as much about what is behind the word as it is about the word itself. After all, it is the integrity and consistency of God that makes His Word of value. His Word is filled with life because He is filled with life. His Word is a verbal expression of Himself. There is no chaos or contradiction in God, so there is no contradiction in His Word or any aspect of His creation.

Through reductionist thinking we have made the same error with God's Word as doctors have with health and as scientists have with observing the world. We zero in on a doctrine without considering the whole of who God is, His character, and His Name. The end result is a contradiction of the bigger picture. The parts, when interpreted separately, do not align with the whole. All things God created follow the same laws of creation because they all represent God to Him. Sadly, the Church has banished all value of nature to scientists or the New Age Movement, resulting in a huge deficiency in our understanding of God!

Until Jesus came, we had no unifying factor around which to organize all that was revealed about God. We knew He was all-powerful, but we were not sure if He would use that power to heal or hurt. We knew He could be merciful, but would He forgive every sin? We knew Him as Lord and Master, but not as Father.

> NO ONE COULD CLAIM TO UNDERSTAND GOD PRIOR TO JESUS.

No one could claim to understand God prior to Jesus. But Jesus came because God wants to be known by His children. He does not desire to be a mystery. Jesus is the revelation or unveiling of God that makes God understandable. He is the "Logos" of God because He embodies everything God has ever spoken or thought! That's why without Jesus we have no basis for interpreting any part of the Bible or nature.

After the fall of man, oral traditions were passed down from generation to generation as a testimony of God. Nature revealed God. And there was God's direct interaction with those who would hear. In time, the oral tradition became perverted and thus came about the birth of religion. Nature was interpreted subjectively, so man soon lost the value of seeing God in nature. Those who interacted with God could share their experience, but that could be easily refuted by the naysayers. God, because of His love, progressively revealed Himself to mankind through His actions, His names, and His Word. But the matrix, around which all that could be known and accurately understood concerning God, came together in the person of Jesus. He is the revelation of God… the "Logos."

Recognizing this consistency in God, His Word, His character, and His creation is essential in order to transpose the written Word in practical application. Jesus utilized parables about nature (physics), or things in nature, to reveal the "logos" of God and show how to apply it to life. Because so many of His teachings were conceptual, their meanings are lost to those who do not take them to heart. It seems that one parable provides the consistent logic to understand all parables. We call it the parable of the sower and the seed. I call it the *Heart Physics Parable*.[1]

This parable is pretty basic. These are the key points: you have the seed which represents the Word and the soil which represents the heart. You have the things that prevent the Word from getting into and taking root in your heart. Then you have instructions about how to get the Word into your heart in a way that will bear fruit. In Jesus' introduction to this parable, you have a bonus that is usually totally missed because the answer does not come until after His explanation of the parable. You have the key to how you will understand all parables and, I believe it would be safe to say, all things pertaining to God!

Our first misunderstanding about this parable is the seed sown by the wayside. It was never sown in the heart. The translators complicated this even more by inserting a word that is not in the original text. Satan did not steal the Word from someone's heart. The word "heart" is not in the original text, and obviously the Word was never sown in their heart. When it says, "Satan came immediately" that could literally read, "he found a place of influence."[2] Satan came to Jesus after He had been fasting for 40 days. He did not enter Jesus' heart; he simply found a place of opportunity through His hunger from fasting, through His calling, and through His identity. These are the three areas Jesus was challenged. He was challenged in those areas because that was the only opportunity provided by what God had showed Him up to that point. This first group heard, but it never entered their heart.

The second group had the Word sown on stony ground. The fact that it could not find a root would indicate, once again, that even though the Word was received it really had no access to their heart. The KJV says, *when persecution arose for the Word's sake,* but the original text says, *"pressure arose through* the

Word and they became offended." This brings us to another *Heart Physics®* law: The truth that has the most potential to set you free has the most potential to offend.

Remember, we all believe we are right and the way we do things is right. But if how I do something is "right," then it should be working and the fruit should be good. When the Word is in opposition to my opinion, it means I am wrong.

> ## WHEN THE WORD IS IN OPPOSITION TO MY OPINION, IT MEANS I AM WRONG.

I don't like being wrong! But the words that I have heard present me with two options: reject God's Word or surrender my opinion, i.e. die to self (ego) and come alive to God, or save my (self) life and die to God's truth. If we are not willing to repent (change our mind), we become stuck where we are with what we have and as with most syndromes the problems escalate.

The third group heard the Word, but their heart was filled with other things. There was no place for God's Word in their heart. This group of people typify what Jesus meant when He said, *where your treasure (what you value) is there your heart will be also* (Matt. 6:21). The place they looked for hope, security, and fulfillment was the thorns that choked out the Word and made it unfruitful. They loved (valued) the world; therefore, the love of (value for) God was not in them.

If we become too fixated on trying to analyze every aspect of these who did not receive the Word, we could miss the main point of this parable. The primary point of this parable is the instructions He gave about how to make the Word bear fruit.

The final group of people received the Word in a heart that was not full of the cares of this life. But something different happened in these people! Why did the Word bring forth fruit in them and not the others? All the other groups committed one of the nine Greek words that results in sin; they heard amiss. They all had their own reason for not pursuing or developing God's Word in their heart. They heard the Word that would have set them free, but for lack of attention, ego, or trust in other things, they let the Word slip from them. And after 40 years of ministry I can assure you they all had an excuse that made wonderful sense! But as we all know, an excuse has never set anyone free, no matter how good the excuse may be. This brings us to another law of *Heart Physics*®: As long as I have an excuse, I have not confessed or repented.

The one thing all of these people had in common was they all heard the Word, but only this group got the Word into their heart in a way that allowed it to take root and bear fruit! Why? How? You see, they took the next step…. They accepted it, which means: to receive, to admit, or to take upon oneself! If we stopped here, we would answer the question, "what happened?", but we would not know how it happened. Thankfully, Jesus did not leave us in the dark. After all, the primary point of this parable is to teach us how to get the Word to bear fruit in our lives.

It seems in verses 21-25 He has totally changed subjects, but, actually, He is answering the very question He posed to the disciples in the beginning. *How will you understand any parable?* Then He makes what I consider to be one of the most hope-filled statements in the New Testament. He tells us that God desires to reveal everything to us. God doesn't light a lamp and put it under a basket. No! He puts it on a candle stand to light the entire room. But the key is: do you have ears to hear? Then His next words tell us how to have "hearing ears."

GOD DESIRES TO REVEAL EVERYTHING TO US.

Take heed what you hear. With the same measure you use, it will be measured to you; and to you who hear, more will be given. Take heed… this is what you do with what you hear. Look at it until you perceive it. Take note, handle it with care. This is done by pondering, considering, thinking about, and meditating on the Word. This is cultivating the seed just as you would in any garden. Those that did not bear fruit were what the Bible calls "forgetful hearers." They did nothing to cultivate the Word. The group that heard and received the Word is what the Bible calls "doers" of the Word. This concept is essential to understanding how to develop your heart. It will be discussed in a future chapter.

So God wants you to have revelation. But as we have already discussed that revelation is dependent on me, not God. I have to prayerfully look at and ponder the Word of God with an open, teachable attitude and a repentant mindset until my heart has the capacity to see and perceive what the great Teacher is attempting to show me. So He gives us the process. With the measure you meet it will be measured to you. One way to understand this is, what I put into this is what I'll get back. The Amplified Bible says, *The measure [of thought and study] you give [to the truth you hear] will be the measure [of virtue and knowledge] that comes back to you…* This is where I actuate the Word by meditation, prayer, pondering, and considering what this means to my life or what this would look like in my life. The disciple is always more concerned about application than intellectual interpretation. He is seeking not just to know what the Teacher knows; he desires to live as the Teacher lives. He or she wants to see what this would look like in their life!

Then the last phrase in the KJV says, *and to you who hear, more will be given.* The second use of the word "hear" is another insertion by the translators; it is not in the original. He is not saying those who heard the Word will get more; He is saying those who actuated the Word, those who considered, pondered, studied, or meditated got more back. And they are getting back in direct proportion to what they put into it.

Verse 25 introduces the sad reality of those who have no knowledge of, or otherwise resist, heart-work. *For whoever has, to him more will be given; but whoever does not have, even what he has will be taken away from him.* The word "given" has a wide possibility of meaning. One is "by his own accord," which is what the context seems to imply. This is not something God gives him as a reward for his efforts; this is the fruit of his efforts. Just as exercising builds muscle, what we invest into incubating the Word in our heart bears fruit.

> WHATEVER YOU HAVE, GOOD OR BAD, YOU KEEP GETTING MORE OF IT…

Then it says to the one *who has not,* even what little he has will be taken away, lost, or destroyed. The idea here is you keep getting more of what you have. Whatever you have, good or bad, you keep getting more of, and the only way to break the cycle is based on what you do with the Word you hear.

We have been programmed to be hearers of the Word only. We hear a sermon on Sunday morning, go out to eat, take a nap, and before we have given it a second thought, we are in another service hearing another sermon that we will never actuate. After being in church all day, we rush home, get the kids ready for school, do everything that we didn't get done by being gone all day, go to sleep, and once again we "heard amiss!" Whatever God may have been attempting to say to us was lost to our busy schedule.

Everything about Western culture is based on externals. More activity means you are committed to God. Sitting through a sermon equates "hearing" a sermon. If a little helps, a lot really helps. If going to church once in a week is good, let's do it several times in a week. But the truth is, no matter how many sermons we hear, how "anointed" they are, or how sincere the person is who speaks them, unless we are incubating the Word so it takes root in our heart, we are doomed to keep getting more of what we've got. Too many wonderful, insightful sermons are lost on people too busy to ever incubate the Word in their heart.

But the person who will hear the Word, receive it, ponder it, and incubate it, will see fruit grow in his or her life that is beyond explanation or understanding. He or she will come to understanding and insights that make life's greatest challenges simple. They see God's Word work. With every victory, faith and immovable trust for God becomes more and more resolute.

When listening to a sermon, reading your Bible, or whenever an idea comes, immediately write it somewhere. If you can't stop at that time to take any other action, just pray: "Father, I receive this inspiration and I thank You that I will retain this until we can be together alone. I trust the Holy Spirit to teach me what this means to my life." Then as the day passes, until you can get alone with God, allow your mind to consider this as opportunity comes. Write any thoughts or ideas that come to you. As soon as you have the opportunity, get alone with God, meditate, and see yourself applying whatever you saw or heard in your heart. Look up Scriptures about that topic. Discover what God is saying to you about that thought. Don't try to force a theological interpretation, just seek to understand how to apply it to your life.

Endnotes

i.   Mark 4:13-25

ii. comes: NT:2064'; *come forth, show itself, find place or influence*: (from Thayer's Greek Lexicon, Electronic Database. Copyright © 2000, 2003, 2006 by Biblesoft, Inc. All rights reserved.)

16

LIVING IN HARMONY

One of the laws of physics says, "for every action there is an equal and opposite reaction." This law of the heart inflicts as much damage among serious, devoted believers as any other. Most of what we have been taught about prayer and confession invokes this law in a way that works against our faith. Each time I ask God to give me what He has already given me in Jesus, I am at the same time making a statement that God has not given it to me in Christ. The more passionately I seek to get what I already have, the more deeply I persuade my heart that I do not, in fact, possess it. Even my so-called confessions or affirmations of Scripture, if not believed in my heart, work against my faith.

Confession is crucial to the continuum of faith. Sadly, most of what we have come to believe about confession is external, formula-based, dead works. If I confess it, I will convince God that I believe it. If I confess it long enough, loud enough, and passionately enough, it will somehow cause it to come to pass more quickly. The more I follow this formula, the more I convince myself of the complete opposite. This type of confession is similar to

> **CONFESSION IS CRUCIAL TO THE CONTINUUM OF FAITH.**

positive affirmations. I have no problem with being positive, and actually feel that we should always strive to speak and think with the most positive attitude possible. And I am a huge supporter of confessing Scripture, but maybe not the way we have been exposed to in the past. Studies show that positive affirmations only work for about 15% of the population. One source states that they only work for those who already believe they will work.[1] This fact, discovered by secular research, when examined in light of Scripture is absolutely correct.

The word "confess" means "to say the same thing, to agree, or to confirm."[2] So, a confession or affirmation is when we confirm something, not when we try to bring it into being. The truth is, positive confessions and affirmations have been shown in some instances to cause higher levels of stress in the participants. Why? When people "try" to confess or affirm that which they do not believe, they have the deep inner sense that they are lying... and they are! There is no agreement between what they say and what they believe. Therefore, the key to confession is never found in an attempt to make something come to pass by saying it. It has to be based on something that is already done and believed.

The message of the finished work of Jesus is based entirely on what has been accomplished through the death, burial, and resurrection of Jesus. Hebrews 11:1 tells us ...*faith is the substance of things hoped for...* The word "things" refers to things that have been accomplished.[3] Faith, which is rooted in the heart, is never an attempt to make something come to pass or come into being. It is always based on accomplished facts. Likewise, confession is an agreement with what Jesus has accomplished on the cross, what you believe in your heart, and what you are saying with your mouth. Unless there is harmony in all three places, your "faith" will not be faith at all. If you speak it but don't believe it, you will waver. Remember, faith is when you are fully persuaded, no wavering, no wondering.

> FAITH IS WHEN YOU ARE FULLY PERSUADED: NO WAVERING, NO WONDERING.

When the mind has been renewed to an *accurate and precise* knowledge of what Jesus has accomplished through His death, burial, and resurrection; when our heart has been fully persuaded with the facts, confession, i.e. saying or acknowledging this truth will be a harmonious, natural expression of truth. It

164

will not cause stress or any other negative reaction. It will instead bring peace and a sense of power. It will be conversational, not contrived. It will be done more in the presence of God than in the presence of people. It is not a frantic effort to get what you don't have; it's more of an overflowing from the heart of what you do have. *Of the abundance of the heart the mouth speaks…* effortlessly! (I added effortlessly.)

While still walking with the disciples, Jesus taught this truth about "things that have been accomplished," in the famously misused Scripture about binding and loosing. I'm sure the disciples didn't grasp its meaning or immense value until after the resurrection. The Amplified Bible provides a very accurate rendering of this passage: *Truly I tell you, whatever you forbid and declare to be improper and unlawful on earth must be what is already forbidden in heaven, and whatever you permit and declare proper and lawful on earth must be what is already permitted in heaven* (Matt. 18:18, AMP).

Binding and loosing is when we declare something to be lawful or unlawful in our life, or our world, based on what has previously been accomplished in Heaven. On this side of the cross, we have to make that determination based on the death, burial, and resurrection. Doing it in faith is when there is harmony between that which has been accomplished in heaven, what is in our heart, and what is in our mouth. The issue of harmony becomes clear in the next verse: *Again I tell you, if two of you on earth agree (harmonize together, make a symphony together) about whatever [anything and everything] they may ask, it will come to pass and be done for them by My Father in heaven* (Matt. 18:18, AMP). As made clear by the Amplified translation, the word "agree" is actually the word "harmonize." It is the word from which we get the English word for "symphony." A symphony is when different instruments are all tuned together, playing the same song, with different notes, yet in harmony.

There is an interesting anomaly in the translation where it says, *if two of you agree.* The word *"you"* is not in the original language. This is most probably saying, "if two agree on Earth, as concerning anything in Heaven, the Father will do it." So the emphasis is not on two people agreeing, it may be referring to the need for Heaven and Earth to be in agreement. If from Earth, we agree with what has been accomplished in Heaven… it will be done. Or, it could be, if two agree, Heaven and heart, you can ask of your Father and it will be done. Or, it could be when heart and mind agree on Earth about what has been declared lawful or unlawful in Heaven, it shall be done. Any way you look at it, Heaven and Earth only come into harmony when someone on Earth agrees and harmonizes with what Jesus has accomplished.

But then the word "ask" in the original presents such a radical departure from religious thinking that it cannot be calculated in the mind of the carnal believer who is following the Old Covenant model of prayer and faith. That person is praying and seeking to discover what God will do in the future based on their righteousness and faith. They have no basis for being sure in their heart because their prayers were not based on a finished work. It was all based on a conditional covenant. In our Covenant all the conditions have been met by Jesus. After all, the covenant was not made with individual believers, it was made with Him. He did His part in the Covenant and all its provisions are sure! Since we are in Him, we share in His inheritance from that Covenant. Faith in the heart has to be sure! In Him everything is sure!

> HEAVEN AND EARTH... COME INTO HARMONY WHEN SOMEONE ON EARTH AGREES AND HARMONIZES WITH WHAT JESUS HAS ACCOMPLISHED.

The word for "ask" is really more along the lines of "demand!"[4] We are certainly not demanding God to do anything. But this is obviously not the typically passive idea of faith where one asks because they don't know the answer. This is a faith that is akin to the Greek word for "receive" which, in our mind, is passive. But in the mind of God, a heart that is *steadfast in the Covenant* is assertive and proactive. Faith is sure of the promises. Faith is sure of the answer. Faith receives: it takes hold of something and brings it unto ourselves. Faith in the heart is so sure of what it speaks or requests that it is never asking from a perspective of waiting for an answer. It is taking hold of the promise because we have the "deed," the proof of ownership. We ask because we know it has been given. We know this is all about Jesus and not about us. This faith in the heart is based on the written Word of God; it is supported by the Word written on the heart and the witness of the Holy Spirit. There is harmony within; there is harmony between heaven (God) and earth (man); the promise is sure! There is harmony in my renewed mind and my heart!

Interestingly, most of the time the word "ask" is used in the New Testament it is with the expectation to receive. This concept of demanding is an assurance that is so sure, based on the finished work, that we will not be refused by the world, by the devil, or by nature. If it was settled at the cross, it is settled in Heaven. We must settle it in our heart. Instead, the believer that is not fully persuaded concerning the Covenant will ask God to do the things that are already done. They refuse to make a choice based on God's Word. Their prayer is not a prayer of faith, but the proof of wavering.

The Scripture continues by saying in English *it shall be done for them by My Father in heaven.* This isn't really how it reads in the original. It should say something like, "it shall come into existence[5] with, alongside, or in the opinion of My Father."[6] Instead of presenting the idea that when we take the appropriate steps God takes action, which is the Old Covenant model, this presents a different idea: once we align or harmonize with the steps God has taken, we experience, bring into

> IF IT WAS SETTLED AT THE CROSS, IT IS SETTLED IN HEAVEN.

physical existence, make manifest, or take hold of that which was already given from the Father. The heart of faith knows these things intuitively, even when it can't explain why or how. Faith in the heart knows. However, if we only know about faith as a doctrine, we waver!

Faith is the substance of things hoped for. The word "faith" could be translated as "being sure of deed," i.e. proof of ownership. This Greek word is used for a property deed. So when we are in real faith in our heart, we are immovable, we have all the evidence we need. It is in God's Word, it is real to me; it is based on the finished work of Jesus… I am immovable! I have the deed; of course, it's mine! The Word of God, my mind, my heart, and my words are unified; they are in harmony, fully agree, and are, therefore, immovable. *Heart Physics*® is a meditative process based on the Word of God that moves a person to the place where they are immovable because they are in harmony. Remember, you don't need a *Heart Physics*® module to do this. You can develop this in your life, just as I did. These modules were developed to help others make the journey more effectively and quickly.

Once we learn to connect with our heart, we have access to all that God is on an intuitive level. We have access to His Word in us, and we have access to the power to do whatever needs to be done. Connecting with God in our heart gives us what information has never, and will never, provide! This kind of confidence is not far away from you. No one has to get it for you, and no one has to explain it to you. It is the word of faith which is in your heart and in your mouth.

Be sure to always be honest with yourself when seeking to believe the truth. Otherwise, self-deceit and failure will surely come. Always ask yourself, "Am I really immovable on this, or am I still wavering? Are my emotions and feelings in conflict? Have I already experienced this promise as mine?" By evaluating where you are in the journey, you can determine if your confession is a harmonious statement about which you are sure, or if it is a statement you are using to persuade your heart so you can become immovable. There is no shame in recognizing where you are. In fact, owning where you are in the process is one of the keys to consistent victory.

Endnotes

i. http://generallythinking.com/positive-affirmations-dont-work/

ii. NT:3670 "to say the same thing." We thus get the senses a. "to agree to something" (an affirmation, a charge, etc.), b. "to confirm receipt," c. "to agree or submit to a proposal," and d. "to agree to a wish," "to promise." (from Theological Dictionary of the New Testament, abridged edition, Copyright © 1985 by William B. Eerdmans Publishing Company. All rights reserved.)

iii. NT:4229, NT:4229* pragma, pragmatos, to
   a. *that which has been done, a deed, an accomplished fact:* Luke 1:1
   b. *what is doing or being accomplished:* James 3:16
   c. *a matter* (in question), *affair:* Matt 18:19
   d. *that which is or exists, a thing:* Heb 10:1
   (from Thayer's Greek Lexicon, Electronic Database. Copyright © 2000, 2003, 2006 by Biblesoft, Inc. All rights reserved.)

iv. NT:154, The basic meaning, *ask for or demand*, (from Exegetical Dictionary of the New Testament © 1990 by William B. Eerdmans Publishing Company. All rights reserved.)

v. NT:1096, *come into existence*. In the NT the following meanings are found: (1) *happen, occur;* (2) *become, originate;* (3) *attain to or arrive at* (something); (4) *be made, be created.* (from Exegetical Dictionary of the New Testament © 1990 by William B. Eerdmans Publishing Company. All rights reserved.)
   NT:3844

vi. with gen.: of, from; with dat.: at, by, in the opinion of; with acc.: at, along, alongside of, (from Exegetical Dictionary of the New Testament © 1990 by William B. Eerdmans Publishing Company. All rights reserved.)

17

HARDNESS OF HEART

In light of what we now know about the heart, one of the most legitimate questions we ask is, "What is the condition of my heart now that I am a believer?" Before the new birth, Jeremiah 17:9 says it was covered in footprints. Jesus said it could be broken, but He would heal that. When I was born again, the blood of Jesus purged my conscience and God's laws were written on my heart (Heb. 8:10-12). If this is true, why do I have to do anything for my heart? It should be completely fixed!

While it is true that God's law is written on our heart, this does not make everything as automatic as it might seem. If our heart was as it should be (righteous), we would be completely healed of all diseases; we would be prosperous, and nothing would be impossible to us. We would be experiencing all the promises of God! If the heart is, as we discussed, some combination of spirit and soul, this would account for how one part of our heart could be made completely whole, yet the part of our heart that we manage could still have issues. This may explain why Scriptures make reference to loving God with "all of our heart" or our "whole heart," indicating that we could love or trust Him with "part of our heart." It falls to us as independent individuals to align our whole heart with what God has written on the spirit part of our heart.

The word "righteousness" addresses more than behavior alone. In the Old Testament behavior was pretty much the only concept of righteousness. That concept is still held by the externalists. But righteousness in the New Covenant, like all truth that applies to the beliefs of the heart, is a continuum. In the broadest sense, righteousness is "the state of a person who is as he should be."[1] Along the lines of the continuum we have been made righteous (as we should be) in our spirit, and we believe unto righteousness (as we should be) in our heart. When the belief of being as we should be is settled in our heart, we experience salvation (being saved, healed, delivered, blessed, prospered, protected, made whole, set apart… as we should be) in other aspects of our being.

Along the lines of a continuum in our spirit, righteousness could manifest as our perfect, complete, and whole "new man" who is in perfect, unbroken communication with God. This would also mean that all of the life of God is in us because He is in us. The reality of this finished work, which must be established in the renewed mind, is the only basis for New Covenant heart development. Any hint of attempting to *become* is a constant signal to your heart that you are not. Any effort to *get* tells your heart that you do not have. Renewing the mind is about *being*.

> THE REALITY OF THIS FINISHED WORK... IS THE ONLY BASIS FOR NEW COVENANT HEART DEVELOPMENT.

In the heart righteousness manifests as a belief. Beliefs of the heart manifest through our feelings. Feelings, as opposed to emotions, are long-term and subtle. Beliefs determine our self-perception, which shapes our world paradigm and, to some degree, shapes the world around us. They become the "automatic-pilot" that moves us into specific action or choices when we are not using willpower to do otherwise. Then our thoughts, when we consider ourselves righteous in our renewed mind, manifest in our emotions (short-term and more acute than feelings) and conscious choices. Then, as we make choices based on the sense that we are as we should be, righteousness manifests in the individual areas of our life. These areas include integrity, character, finances, relationship, and physical health. Righteousness manifests, making those areas as they should be (righteous). None of these individual manifestations are righteousness; they are all the fruit of righteousness.

Righteousness in the heart is not an automatic state of being; it is the result of believing.[2] If you recall, the word "repentance" does not mean, "one repentance covers everything!" We change our mind one issue at a time. Every time we change our mind about any issue and choose God's truth based on the finished work of Jesus, we experience how it should be (righteousness) in that area. So we have the paradox: we are completely righteous, but we are experiencing righteousness one area and one decision at a time. Therefore, the willingness to minister to, guard, and develop our own heart is a lifetime journey wherein we deal with each individual issue as it arises.

When we were first saved, most of us had a deep, profound sense of a change. If that was not how it occurred for you, it doesn't mean you didn't have a genuine experience. It probably means no one explained that, as a new creation, you could let go of the past. One can only surrender to Lordship to the degree they relinquish control of their own life. Likewise, our new life is experienced as we release our old life. For everyone that is incremental, one area at a time. But, the more complete the surrender of your life in the beginning, the more profound the initial experience.

Many who had a phenomenal experience in the beginning unfortunately did not sustain that level of certainty, confidence, peace, and joy. Why? There are a number of reasons people lose the joy of their new birth experience, and they all relate to the heart. There are those mentioned in the parable of the sower who allow the desire for other things to choke out the Word. But for so many who have a very genuine experience, it's a different journey. Sometimes what chokes out the Word is not the desire for other things; among the truly serious, it is usually religion. Religion doesn't renew your mind to a finished work. Religion convinces you that you must finish the work. The attempt to find righteousness through performance neutralizes grace (Gal. 2:21). In religion you don't get to enjoy *being* the new you, you are burdened with the labor of *becoming* the new you!

The externalists insist that sin (behavioral) is the real cause of people losing their joy, and it can be. However, it is my observation that (behavioral) sin is the fruit of the problem, not the root. The root problem is ALWAYS THE BELIEFS OF THE HEART! Fruit does not go away permanently until it is dealt with at the root.

As much as it grieves me to say this, most heart problems for the new believer start at church. The joy of the Lord, the confidence to always get your prayers answered... all these wonderful aspects of new life seem to slowly fade as indoctrination to works righteousness corrupts the mind. Instead of renewing

THE ROOT PROBLEM IS ALWAYS THE BELIEFS OF THE HEART!

the mind, works righteousness corrupts the mind. The more the person attempts to earn righteousness, the more they convince their heart that they are not righteous. Religious formulas replace the simplicity of living out of your new heart. Church attendance replaces intimacy with God! (Thank God for pastors who do not equate attending church with closeness to God!)

If God's laws are written on my heart, how can this be? If the heart is part soul and part spirit, we have the ability to influence the part that is of the soul. If it is not part soul or part spirit, the Bible still tells us ways we can harden our heart. Even if the part soul, part spirit model is incorrect, it still proves a conceptual basis for the two sources of input that converge in the heart: the external and the internal!

The Bible speaks of our conscience. The underlying concept behind this word in the Greek is "a shared knowledge."[3] We know from the conscience we get our sense of good and bad, right and wrong. This is probably why this English word was chosen. The English word for "conscience" is similar; it means dual knowledge, i.e. two sources of information.

We have the knowledge of our inner man that is based on God's laws. This particular word for "law" includes the commandments, anything God ever said or implied, and the teachings of Jesus. In other words, the "logos" of God is written on our heart and it seeks to emerge from the deep thoughts of the heart. This is why listening to a pure heart is the same as listening to the voice of God. But remember, the other source of knowledge is our mind. This source is only in harmony with God's law to the degree we have renewed our mind. When these two are in conflict, there is not harmony, the agreement is lost, and Heaven and Earth are not in symphony. We have, but cannot experience, what Jesus provided!

The wisdom of God says to guard your heart above all else. This management of the heart is the determining factor for all of our future growth development and the fulfillment of all of life's dreams! The breastplate mentioned by Paul in Ephesians is a piece of armor that guards the heart. Our breastplate is *the breastplate of righteousness!*

> # THE WISDOM OF GOD SAYS TO GUARD YOUR HEART ABOVE ALL ELSE.

The moment we depart from faith righteousness we have departed from the Gospel. When we depart from the Gospel, we are limited to our own strength. When we are limited to our own strength, we have the same problems we had before we got saved, but we feel much worse about them. This begins a syndrome of hardening from which few recover.

One of the most powerful influences over any person is that of their peers. Our friends and peers form a subculture. Cultures produce a shared consciousness, which becomes an incredible pressure. Even in psychology there is an understanding: without re-socialization an individual can seldom sustain his or her choices for a different life. The influence of the group is often too pervasive. We so closely identify with the group that it is part of our personal identity.

One of the problems with groups is they tend to function by an order that has never been verbalized but is firmly fixed! Each member of the group fits into a specific place and function. When we begin to change, we upset the unity and order of the group. The group on a conscious, or sometimes subconscious, level attempts to force us back into our place in the group. There is massive emotional pressure to go back to seeing yourself the way you and the group have always seen you. Then there is the added loss of identity that results from separation from the group, which is a form of death to self.

New believers who never separate themselves from destructive associations seldom, if ever, go far in their journey of personal transformation. They cling to the old image of themselves as part of their group. They are reminded of it in every social interaction with the group. Paul gave this somber warning, *Do not be deceived: Evil company corrupts good habits.* If we remain in the company that seeks to hold us in our earlier patterns of dysfunction, we fall prey to the power of our culture. Jesus made this astonishing statement about culture: *Through your traditions you make the word of God of no effect.*

The word "tradition" is the act of giving up or giving over. The Jews gave over to the religious customs that had become a part of their culture, even though they were really not in God's Word. The traditions of the group are comprised of the views and behaviors that have been accepted within the group! But make no mistake, these social and familial pressures and expectations have the power to neutralize the Word of God in our life, primarily because they hold us captive to a world that only sees us as "the old man."

Paul's solution for those who are involved in bad company and bad behavior is not to "become righteous!" His prescription is: *Awake to righteousness, and do not sin; for some do not have the knowledge of God* (1 Cor. 15:34). This word for "awake" is more like "sober up." When we perceive ourselves as anything other than our new identity in Christ, we are like a drunken introvert who suddenly becomes the life of the party, or the little guy who wants to fight the biggest man in the room. Our drunken state alters our sense of identity.

It is easy to miss the last phrase, *some do not have the knowledge of God.* Remember, Peter said it was through the knowledge of God that we partake of all the things we already have in Christ. It is through "knowing Him" that we experience the Life of God. Anything that distracts or obsesses us causes us to turn our focus away from Him and that life-sustaining awareness. The things that seem to be the most destructive are those things that cause us to see and perceive ourselves as being the person we used to be. The beliefs of the heart create the invisible barriers that hold us within the social, physical, emotional, financial, and relational boundaries of our sense of self!

> THE BELIEFS OF THE HEART CREATE THE INVISIBLE BARRIERS THAT HOLD US WITHIN THE SOCIAL, PHYSICAL, EMOTIONAL, FINANCIAL, AND RELATIONAL BOUNDARIES OF OUR SENSE OF SELF!

The whole issue of sinful behavior is possibly locked up in the after-effects on our heart, more than anything else. The writer of Hebrews warns of a little-realized effect of sin. ... *Lest any of you be hardened through the deceitfulness of sin* (Heb. 3:13). Anything that causes us to miss the mark of the prize, whether it be thoughts, beliefs, words, or actions, has a residual deceitful (unexpected, unforeseen) effect… it hardens the heart. This is one of the many places where Christians who had their heart renewed by the new birth are warned about our ability to damage that which God had restored!

Hardness refers to callousness, stubbornness, and insensitivity. A callous is something that is developed over time. When we use our hands repeatedly in a manner we shouldn't, it forms a blister. If we continue working with our hands, the blister causes pain. That pain is a signal that says, "You need to stop what you are doing!" But if we persist, that blister which is alerting us to destructive behavior becomes a callous. Once it becomes a callous, it is *past feeling*. This is the deceitful process of sin; it creates an inability to feel, sense, or perceive God as He gently leads or instructs. We are left to the devices of our intellectual mind. Our conscience is defiled. We only hear one voice, that of our five senses interpreted by the unrenewed mind. The voice of God in our heart is past feeling!

In Ephesians 4:17-19, Paul admonishes the believers at Ephesus that they should no longer live as the Gentiles; interestingly, he addresses the root problem before he addresses the behavioral problem. The problem is they live *in the futility* (nothingness or vanity), *of their intellect.* He explains to these believers that living in sin of any kind is the result of being in darkness. This darkness is the same issue John pointed out when he wrote a letter to believers who were getting involved in Gnosticism; he called them to come back to the light. The light is the truth, the word that God wrote on your heart at the new birth. But you can only get in the light when you reconnect to God in your heart and give up the vanity of trying to connect in your mind (intellect).

When our understanding is darkened, we are alienated from the life of God. We didn't lose it; but we no longer sense or feel it. Interestingly, the cause of all of this is hardness of heart. Although the English uses the word "blindness," in the original it is the word "callous," obtuseness of mental judgment, dulled perception, or hardness of heart. This hardness renders them *past feeling.* The callous has formed a covering over their heart that makes it impossible to feel, perceive, or understand what God is saying or doing! They are no longer in touch with their "new man."

This is where the syndrome picks up incredible momentum. He says that once we are past feeling *we give ourselves over to lewdness, to work all uncleanness with greediness.* So our sinful thoughts, feelings, or behavior, according to

Hebrews, hardens our heart. We are now in darkness, and our understanding is darkened. In other words, it is now easier to justify our unacceptable, destructive behavior. It is harder to see and perceive the truth. Since we are alienated from (have no fellowship or intimacy with) the life of God that is in us, we are now feeling lack. When we feel lack, we look for ways to feel satisfied. In this state of darkness and our inability to feel God, we give ourselves over to more destructive behavior which once again hardens our heart even more.

> WHEN WE FEEL LACK, WE LOOK FOR WAYS TO FEEL SATISFIED.

Any believer who is able to live in a consistently compromised life has some degree of a hardened heart. Any believer who cannot understand what God would have them do, i.e. they lack understanding, is to some degree experiencing a hardened heart. I am always astounded when someone makes a statement like, "I know he's living a horrible life, but he's got a good heart!" This kind of thinking is a testament to how far we are removed from God's Word and God's realities. If the fruit of your life is not good, you have a heart issue!

In the bigger picture, sin (any behavior that causes us to miss the mark of the prize, i.e. causes us to live, think, feel, or behave less than our true identity in Jesus), condemns our heart. It challenges the fact that we are a new creation. It challenges who we really are in Christ. If I am not in fellowship (sharing the resurrection life I have in common with Jesus), I am in darkness. If I am not sharing in the resurrected life, I am attempting to live out of the identity of my old life. This means there is already some degree of hardness of heart. Now I resort to living out of my intellect, which has no power to sustain my new identity. As I live more and more from my mind, I conform more and more to the sense of self defined by my mind. It is a vicious, ever-downward spiraling life more and more devoid of a present tense experience with the life of God!

Thankfully, God does not leave us without a solution. Paul explains how to get out of this drunken state and come alive to the righteousness that is in us by Christ Jesus. No matter what the problem, we must put off the "old man," which is a deliberate choice, renew our mind, specifically about what we have in the resurrected life, and put on the "new man." Make the choice to take hold of that identity.

This may be a good place for personal examination without condemnation. Are there areas of compromise that have gone on in your life so long you no longer feel remorse, regret, or compromised when you participate? You may want to write these areas on a list and then determine characteristics with which you will replace them. Before you move forward acknowledge that this behavior is not from God; it is not godly and it is not consistent with who I am in Jesus. Acknowledge that you have God's forgiveness; therefore, you are free from condemnation. Then express to God your intention to put on these new characteristics!

Endnotes

i.   NT:1343

NT:1343* dikaiosunee, dikaiosunees, hee
he virtue or quality or state of one who is dikaios;
1.   in the broad sense, *the state of him who is such as he ought to be, righteousness*
       a.   universally: the doctrine concerning the way in which man may attain to a state approved of God, Heb 5:13
       b.   *integrity, virtue, purity of life, uprightness, correctness in thinking, feeling, and acting: Matt 3:15*
       c.   in the writings of Paul *hee dikaiosunee* has a peculiar meaning, opposed to the views of the Jews and Judaizing Christians.
2.   in a closer sense, *justice, or the virtue which gives each one his due* 2 Peter 1:1
(from Thayer's Greek Lexicon, Electronic Database. Copyright © 2000, 2003, 2006 by Biblesoft, Inc. All rights reserved.)

ii.   Rom. 10:10, For with the heart one believes unto righteousness

iii.   NT:4893, [to be aware, share knowledge], syneíd¢sis [consciousness, conscience]
       a. *sýnoida* is first of all knowing something with someone.
       b. *sýnoida emautœį* combines in one the person who knows and the person who shares the knowledge.

18

ENTERING THE WAR ZONE

So why are we even fighting these battles? I thought this was a *finished work?* These kinds of questions point to a basic flaw in our understanding of what God accomplished in Jesus, as well as a fundamental misunderstanding of how we were created. We were created in the *likeness and image of God.* We were given authority over our life and our world. God had provided all we needed to have a perfect life. This would inspire love and trust, out of which would grow a relationship. At the fall man did not lose authority or independence, but he chose to reject God's leadership. It would be contrary to how we were created, and actually not possible, because of the way we were created for God to make our choices!

> WE WANT GOD TO DO FOR US WHAT WE WERE DESIGNED TO DO FOR OURSELVES.

We want God to do for us what we were designed to do for ourselves. Fear causes us to avoid responsibility as much as possible. That could be why one of the primary themes woven through the parables of the Kingdom was personal responsibility! Responsibility feels too much like the possibility of failure and pain. And remember, at the core of what drives us, we are created to avoid pain and pursue pleasure. This tension between wanting to be independent, yet desiring to avoid responsibility, is one of the many emotional conflicts that factor into most of our inner battles.

We are a new creation, but we still have choices. We can make the world as it is experienced through our five senses the focus of our attention, or we can make the world as experienced through our inner man our focus. This does, of course, require us to spend time connecting with God in our heart. The absence of an intimate, active connection with God leaves us nothing but the information we hold in our intellect which is woven into the fabric of the information received by our senses. Where we place our attention and whether or not we develop the connection to our inner man… these are all choices… responsibilities that we, and we alone, must assume! Choices are an aspect of the continuum between the finished work and our free will! There is nothing left for God to do; His part is finished, yet we must make all of our own choices.

The *finished work* refers to God's part of the arrangement. God has done everything there is to be done to provide life at its best. Jesus will not come and die again if another person decides to get saved. He died once for all. Neither will there be deliberation concerning God's will to save the one who awakens to God today, tomorrow, or fifty years from now. Those who desire to participate in this finished work can enter in through a heart of faith. In the same fashion, by faith we share in joint participation (fellowship) with the death, burial, and resurrection; we become one with Him in His victories. Likewise, when we desire to participate in any of those victories through the resurrected life of Jesus, it is done through faith in the heart. By faith, we share His victory in the area of our need. God will lead us, teach us, talk to us, and empower us. He will comfort us. But as far as His provisions, they have all been given freely, deposited in our heart at the new birth! Jesus will not return to the cross the next time a believer decides to fellowship around the resurrected life!

> BY FAITH WE SHARE HIS VICTORY IN THE AREA OF OUR NEED.

In attempting to call believers back to a life of grace and righteousness, John reminded them, *if we walk in the light as He is in the light, we have fellowship one with another and the blood of Jesus cleanses us from all sin* (1John 1:7). Fellowship is where I engage in joint participation, i.e. share in Jesus' resurrected life. If I am struggling with victory in any area, it means I am missing the mark of the prize of the resurrected life (experiencing some aspect of sin). But to grasp this without condemnation, we have to stop thinking of sin as merely "something I have done wrong." Our corrupt definitions and linear thinking makes it all but impossible for the natural (carnal) mind to grasp the realities that exist in the continuum of truth. Thankfully, even when they can't be defined by the intellectual mind, they can be experienced by the heart.

Some argue that a believer, having been washed in the blood of Jesus, has no need to be cleansed from sin. This external concept of sin coupled with a partial and inadequate definition of sin is more focused on what one has done wrong rather than on missing the mark of the prize! In Matthew 8:2, a leper came to Jesus and said, *if you are willing you can make me clean!* This person was unclean in two ways. First, he was ceremonially unclean. As a leper, he could not go to the temple to worship, nor was he allowed to be involved with people. But he also had a physical uncleanness, i.e. his disease. Likewise, our need for cleansing is also two-fold!

We have been made clean spiritually at the new birth. We can appear in the presence of God. But as we make this journey of the heart, following Jesus and daily yielding to the process of transformation, we realize physical or emotional areas that are not as they should be (unrighteous); therefore, in that area of life we experience missing the mark/goal of the prize. That's exactly what the Apostle John is referring to when he calls believers who are moving into deceptive doctrine which will eventually lead to a corrupt lifestyle "wretched/miserable/ blind." He is saying that once we come back to the light, to the sharing in the death, burial, and resurrection of Jesus, the blood of Jesus will cleanse that root problem, the destructive belief that causes us to *miss the mark of the prize!* It is actually the departure from that fellowship that gives rise to any aspect of life less than He has provided. He was calling them back to the life wrapped around the reality of the resurrection.

This struggle between *having* the life of God and *experiencing* the life of God (fellowship) is the battle that rages between our mind and our heart. We feel pain in our body, yet we have the inner witness that *by His stripes I am healed!* We are struggling to pay the bills, yet the Scripture says *God shall supply all your needs according to His riches in glory.* The conflict between the inner witness (deep thoughts) and what we experience with our five senses is a battle and the war zone is the soul.[1] Our conscience (dual sources of knowledge) is incongruent. This disharmony is the source of negative conflicting emotions. When we return to the light by entering into fellowship and heightening our awareness in our joint participation in His death, burial, and resurrection, our conscience is again purged (cleansed) by the blood of Jesus and there is internal harmony! The blood of Jesus cleanses, and thereby harmonizes our conscience every time we revisit the truth (return to the light) and restore fellowship!

Paul explained this conflict to be the result of a hardened or darkened heart that has become insensitive to the inner witness of God; the understanding is darkened, and our reasoning is twisted. Remember, a crooked or twisted heart alters our perception of truth. In these states of stress and crisis we become consumed with lying vanities, i.e. thoughts, arguments, and reasoning that seek to exalt themselves above the experiential knowledge of God found in His finished work. In Corinthians Paul says these must be cast down and our thoughts must be focused on what Jesus accomplished by His obedience. John said we had to return to the light and experience fellowship, and in Ephesians Paul said we have to put off the "old man." All of these expressions and many more are either synonymous, or at the least, overlapping. We have to renew our mind based on what has been done in our spirit. We must return to the joint participation in the finished work of Jesus. We must experience the resurrected life again so it becomes more real than the imaginations and intellectual arguments we have entertained. However, few people have developed their ability to connect with God in their heart in such a way that creates a stronger emotional experience than what is occurring from their five senses.

> THE BLOOD OF JESUS CLEANSES, AND THEREBY HARMONIZES OUR CONSCIENCE EVERY TIME WE REVISIT THE TRUTH...AND RESTORE FELLOWSHIP!

We now know that as we focus our mental attention on anything, neuropathways are created and/or strengthened that make it easier for us to experience the focus of our attention. We create a heightened awareness of our fixation. As we focus on the pain in our body, it seems to get worse. But what is happening in many cases is by our constant attention given to the pain, we have become much better at feeling it. We have magnified the problem above the promise of healing. By focusing our attention on the problem, we have chosen to experience the pain instead of the healing. The amount of attention we have given to anything magnifies it in our experience, including the life we share with Jesus. This is how mental arguments become bigger than our experience with God. As my experience grows, my soul (thoughts/emotions/will) is shifted to believe this more than I believe in the reality that Jesus conquered sickness. I have left fellowship. I am no longer sharing in His resurrection victories. The war is raging!

Remember, the mind has the ability to create emotions which have a very quick onset and are very overwhelming, but emotions can be changed by simply refocusing. As we focus our attention on the situation that contradicts our identity, that contradicts righteousness (as it should be), or contradicts the promises of God, it grows in intensity. Our capacity to experience these emotions is magnified in our neuro-pathways. These ever-growing emotions convince us they are, in fact, true. If our heart has become hard we cannot hear the still, small voice of God in our heart attempting to draw us back to fellowship around the finished work. If we do not magnify the truth more than we magnify the problem, the truth will not prevail.

Religious externalists look to outside sources as the problem. They fight the devil, totally ignoring Jesus' absolute victory over the devil. They focus on personal opposition as they create a martyr's complex. In stereotypical, codependent fashion, they always look outside themselves to meet a need that can only be met by God in their own heart. Rather than accept responsibility, they always look for some place to lay blame. After all, their legalistic teaching

> RELIGIOUS EXTERNALISTS LOOK TO OUTSIDE SOURCES AS THE PROBLEM.

has no place for accepting responsibility without placing blame. Then they cry out to God who is "out there" somewhere, and pray a prayer that negates the cross of Christ. All the while they are managing their insecurity by convincing themselves that the devil is attacking them, or even worse that God is testing them. The end of all this is condemnation, fear, more doubt, and an expanded capacity to experience negative thoughts and emotions.

The believer in the finished work of Jesus realizes the battle is within! The Holy Spirit is within! The "new man" is within! The Kingdom is within! The solution is within! I am not being attacked from the outside. I am being carnally (five senses) minded. I am more aware of what my five senses say than I am aware of what Christ in me is saying! I am magnifying the problem! The solution is to magnify God through connecting to the resurrection life we share with Jesus.

Paul offers a three-phase solution. *Put off the old man. Renew your mind! Put on the new man which was created according to God in true righteousness and holiness* (Eph. 4:22-24). He didn't say *repent*, because repentance is implied by the fact that you need to renew your mind. He didn't tell you to *confess* because that is implied by the fact that you acknowledge your need to renew your mind. He didn't say God needed to *do something* on your behalf; that would deny the finished work of Jesus. He didn't tell you to *seek deliverance*, although this process would facilitate any needed deliverance. He did not tell you there is something you lack which you need to get from God. This would deny the reality that we are complete in Christ! The solution to these behavioral issues would all be solved by taking these three internal steps. Presumably, these steps would solve the problems of hardness of heart, walking in darkness, corrupt understanding, and carnal logic, and would reconnect you to the life of God that is in you, the resurrection life you share with Jesus!

This is where the rubber meets the road and where theory and application part ways. This is about as far as the intellectual (carnally-minded) Christian ventures. This is the place where massive self-deception and personal disempowerment escalates on a massive scale. This is where the struggle between heart and mind takes on a new dimension. You must never forget, the mind seeks to preserve the ego. It resists any possibility of change unless the change in some way confirms that you are right. Therefore, it intellectualizes the issue. You somehow reach the conclusion that you need to hear a sermon or read a book about the problem. Or, the extreme intellectual, ego-driven resistance: you think because you know the information that you have solved the problem.

> YOU MUST NEVER FORGET, THE MIND SEEKS TO PRESERVE THE EGO.

The mind is seeking security through a false sense of control. To yield to the Spirit of God, to consider putting off the "old man" or putting on the "new man" is death to self, and death is man's greatest fear. It is through the fear of death that we spend our lives in bondage. Read these incredibly insightful words from the writer of Hebrews about the mission of Jesus to ... *release those who through fear of death were all their lifetime subject to bondage* (Heb. 2:15). If we are confident in the quality of life we have in Him, there is no fear of giving up our life in the flesh or ultimately giving up our life in this physical body! It is our attempt to hold to life as we know it that keeps us in perpetual bondage, for which we must create doctrine that justifies our position. Just as God pointed out to Job through this piercing question, "Would you condemn me that you may be justified?" (Job 40:8) Yes! Yes! Yes! Religion will create doctrine that disannuls God's Word to preserve its own sense of being right! Otherwise I might have to change, and change is death.

Jesus faced death on a cross. Our cross is to follow Him in death... death to self. If we seek to preserve this self life, we face ultimate death. If we accept the judgment and death of this self life, we save our life. We don't have to die for our sins, He did that! But in order to have fellowship (joint participation) with His resurrected life, we must have fellowship (joint participation) in His death. There are few places this idea of sharing in the death, suffering, and resurrected life is made clear more than when Paul, after years of life experience, made the most incredible statement concerning his passion to stay in fellowship with His Lord and Savior.

After compelling the Philippian believers to have the *mind of Christ* and follow His example as a servant who lays down His life, he explains his position toward outward expressions of religion. His words are warnings against those who taught Jesus was Lord, trust Him as your Savior, yet earn righteousness through performance. They required the observance of the Sabbath, circumcision, and obedience to the law as the means of earning righteousness. He said, *For we are the circumcision, who worship God in the Spirit, rejoice in Christ Jesus, and have no confidence in the flesh* (Phil. 3:3). He then lists all of his external religious qualifications, which he says were nothing to him. He literally referred to them as dung! He was not interested in what he could gain by his life's efforts. His focus was on what Jesus had obtained and the fact that he could share in that inheritance.

Paul's life was founded on the "in Him" realities. I am as He is because I am in Him; because I share in His death, burial, and resurrection. We only share this identity when, by active faith, we abide in fellowship. He wanted to be *found in Him, not having my own righteousness, which is from the law, but that which is through faith in Christ, the righteousness which is from God by faith.*

> ## THE HEART CAN ONLY FUNCTION WITHIN THE BOUNDARY OF WHO YOU ARE, NOT WHO YOU WANT TO BECOME.

The issue of faith righteousness must be settled and absolute if you have any intention of making this heart journey or entering into fellowship with Him. The heart can only function within the boundary of who you are, not who you want to become.

Then Paul goes into some of the most insightful teaching about fellowship (joint participation) with Christ. *...that I may know (experience) Him and the power of His resurrection, and the fellowship of His sufferings, being conformed to His death, if, by any means, I may attain to the resurrection from the dead* (Phil. 3:7-12). Paul knew that experiencing the resurrected life was not possible without experiencing His death. When he says he wants to "attain" to the resurrection, this word means "to arrive at."[2] It is not something earned; it is the destination at which we arrive if we have shared in His death on the cross.

When we share in His victories, the battle within us is over. The war zone becomes a place of peace and joy. We move into the place of rest. Effortless living replaces striving! Trying to get is replaced by "in Him, I have." Trying to become is eradicated by "in Him, I am!" This transition from being controlled by the five senses through the carnal mind to yielding to Christ in you ends the struggle. We move from carnal to spiritual! The crooked path is made straight. The way becomes easy and light!

I encourage you to have a prayerful conversation with Jesus where you talk to Him about all the things you share with Him through His death burial and resurrection. Acknowledge the complete surrender of your righteousness for His. Use your mind, thoughts, imagination, or any capacity you have to experience yourself in Him, sharing all that He now has at the right hand of God! You will soon realize that fellowshipping with Him replaces the mundane Old Testament prayer of trying to get things and attempting to think of things to say. Learn to fellowship with Him... share what we have in common!

Endnotes

i. 1 Peter 2:11-12, abstain from fleshly lusts which war against the soul, having your conduct honorable among the Gentiles, that when they speak against you as evildoers, they may, by *your* good works which they observe, glorify God in the day of visitation.

ii. NT:2658 *arrive at* (from Thayer's Greek Lexicon, Electronic Database. Copyright © 2000, 2003, 2006 by Biblesoft, Inc. All rights reserved.)

19

ENTERING THE HEARTZONE

The HeartZone is a terminology I created to describe the realm we enter wherein we can accomplish many functions described in the Bible without attempting to over-define. The HeartZone is a realm we can enter wherein we escape the dominance of the intellectual mind (ego/self), influence the beliefs of the heart, and renew our intellectual mind, as well as the subconscious mind.

Any attempt to over-define these inner workings is not only a vanity, but a distraction to the biblical message! While we may not have a clear blueprint, we do, however, have clear directives about our interaction with the heart in both the Old and New Testaments. The Bible tells us to direct our heart, write on our heart, establish our heart, guard our heart, incline our heart, sing and worship in our heart, love God with our heart, and many other such instructions. All of

> WE HAVE THE SOLE RESPONSIBILITY AND AUTHORITY TO MINISTER TO OUR HEART.

these indicate a level of personal responsibility and personal influence we have over our own heart, and even over our subconscious mind. It is my understanding from the Scriptures that neither God nor the world can influence our heart. We have the sole responsibility and authority to minister to our heart. We do so from our choices, beliefs, judgments, and meditations. Regardless of what God says or what happens to us, it does not affect our whole heart until we move through one of these specific internal processes.

In the HeartZone we internalize input. We give it significance by attaching our education, cultural concepts, assumptions, or judgments! Nothing anyone does means anything to us until we attach significance.[1] The significance we attach, combined with how we see ourselves (our self-worth), determine which emotions we feel in response to any input. This significance is the beginning of a process that influences our subconscious mind and has the ability to eventually influence the beliefs of our heart. Make no mistake, we have the ability to twist what God says or what people say. Our experience is not based on what actually happens; it is based on our interpretation of what happens.

God created us in such a way that we have the power and the authority (right) to allow (cause) anything to which we are exposed to affect us at a very deep level, for good or bad. Because of ignorance, most of us influence our heart by default rather than by faith-filled intentions. The intention of the other person is not the true factor that determines the effect of their input. Likewise, whether from God or the world, we determine the effect of the input. When there is information plus emotion, those things to which we are exposed have a far greater influence. For example, you ask your wife, "Would you bring my coffee?" What you fail to realize is she did not hear you. So instead of bringing your coffee which is sitting on the counter beside her, she simply turns, looks at you and walks past you….without the coffee and without a word.

One of the primary elements of judgment is when we assume to know why anyone does what they do. God warns that when you judge *the measure you meet is measured unto you* (Matt. 7:2). In other words, the way you measure it out is how it comes back to you. The moment we assume to know why someone does something (assume good or evil intent), we are affected by that judgment, independent of the real intention. This capacity to judge was exactly what God warned would happen if we gained the knowledge of good and evil!

So, what if after asking your wife to bring your coffee and she doesn't, you pass a judgment: "She just does that to tick me off!" That is the information. But two factors are needed to affect you at a very deep level. As inaccurate as it may be, you have information. Keep in mind the information may not be the facts;

it is simply your perception or interpretation of the facts. Maybe your wife's hearing has gotten worse, little by little, over a period of time. She would have no way of knowing she is missing requests, questions, and conversations. But the more this happens, the more it negatively affects you because you judge it to be for some negative reason.

In addition to your corrupt knowledge, you have the emotions that arise from your inaccurate judgment. Neither the facts are true nor the emotions warranted, but as far as your experience is concerned, you have a major marriage issue. You now have an offense, i.e. something that can cause you to stumble. Information plus emotion has the ability to affect your subconscious mind and eventually your heart... and neither the information nor the emotion has to have its basis in reality. Because our paradigm is shaped by the beliefs of our heart, this is an important law of Heart Physics®, which is essential for guarding your heart: how I see it

> INFORMATION PLUS EMOTION HAS THE ABILITY TO AFFECT YOUR SUBCONSCIOUS MIND AND EVENTUALLY YOUR HEART

is not how it is; it's just how I see it! Living by this knowledge will prevent you from endless pain as well as irreparable damage to your heart.

The brain is a processor of information. We do not think with our brain; we think with our mind. If thought was generated in the brain when we died, we would have no capacity for eternal life, personal identity, or experiencing God. The brain is a place of overlap between the physical and non-physical. It translates thoughts into feelings or emotions that can be experienced physically by the production of hormones and other biological factors. It is part of the continuum that manifests in our spirit and ends with our influence on the world outside of ourselves, and contains everything in between.

The brain is divided into two hemispheres, left and right brain. The left brain is the more analytical processor and the right is the emotional processor. When information (left brain) is accompanied by emotions (right brain), we reach a deep determination based on joint information and everything involved in the entire experience. This results in the conclusion and associated emotions being stored in the cells of our body. Based on the latest cutting-edge science, we have every reason to now believe the information stored in these cells is what we know as the subconscious mind.

As Candice Pert points out so masterfully in her book, *Molecules of Emotion*, the molecules needed to create emotions are found all over the body. Attributes that were once relegated to the brain are now known to be everywhere in the body. This scientific data supports what has been known by empirical observation for thousands of years: every organ in the body is affected by our emotions, and likewise every organ in the body influences specific aspects of our thoughts and emotions. We don't just think with our brain, we think with our entire body, which gives new insight into Jesus telling us to love God with our entire being.

In Luke 10:27 Jesus acknowledged the accuracy of this statement, *You shall love the LORD your God with all your heart, with all your soul, with all your strength, and with all your mind...* The word "strength" comes from a root word that means "physical strength." Commentators and translators generally discount this as being nonsensical. After all, how could our physical body or physical strength have anything to do with our capacity to love? Like translators down through history, instead of allowing the Bible to speak for itself and accept that their logic was faulty, they attempted to interpret based on the science of their day. This explains how we can know God with every capacity our being has to experience something.... Knowing or experiencing God is something that happens at every level of our being: spirit, soul, and body... and literally every organ in our body, and every cell in every organ!

> EXPERIENCING GOD IS SOMETHING THAT HAPPENS AT EVERY LEVEL OF OUR BEING: SPIRIT, SOUL, AND BODY...

Today cutting-edge science is starting to make a connection between emotions, the physical body, and illness, which verifies what the Bible has taught and we have misunderstood for thousands of years. The science of psychoneuroimmunology attempts to identify the correlations between emotions and physical illness. This is a great tool in healing people with physical issues that have their roots in emotional experiences. When properly coupled with a biblical foundation and a proper understanding of the heart this can be an incredible tool.

It seems the subconscious mind stores negative experiences in cells of the body causing disruption in their ability to function as they should. This disharmony may be the cause of all sickness. Even those illnesses that are considered genetic could be the result of generations of disharmonious cellular imprinting that ultimately affects the genes. Proverbs talks extensively about the effects of words and emotions on the body. Time and time again we are warned that our physical health is dramatically influenced by these factors, yet it has been somehow dismissed. We are even warned about the damage that can be done to our bodies by others' hurtful words.[2] We ignore these warnings because, truthfully, they were so advanced beyond our understanding that we discounted them as mere analogies or superstitious sayings.

Cellular imprints exist in the form of a sub-(beneath) conscious memory, which can be recalled in an instant. But the catch is, it is not just the information that is recalled, it is also the feelings. While there are many ways this recall can happen, the most common may be by association. An association occurs when something we are doing today is similar to something that occurred in the past. For example, let's say your father had certain mannerisms that were very threatening to you. Years later as an adult, you go into a meeting with a new client that has some of these same mannerisms. For no logical reason you are instantly uncomfortable with the new client. You have bad feelings about doing business with him, and you "blow up" the deal. You have no reason for what you did, other than feelings. Those feelings were subconscious (cellular) memories emerging because of the association. Because these feelings arose slowly and subtly, they redirected your thoughts before you recognized what was actually happening.

> CELLULAR IMPRINTS EXIST IN THE FORM OF A SUB...CONSCIOUS MEMORY...

It is important to remind ourselves that conscious thought evokes emotions, which are short-term and come on very rapidly. But the key factor with emotions brought on by thought is they can be changed by simply changing what you're thinking, i.e. refocusing! Subconscious memories, beliefs of the heart, or cellular memories, however, evoke feelings, not emotions. Feelings are very subtle. They come on so subtly that we seldom recognize when it is happening. These feelings drive our thoughts. Even when we attempt to change our thoughts, they may not immediately change!

Most teaching about the thought life tells us if we change what we think, our negative feelings and emotions will change. I have made that partially correct statement hundreds of times. The problem is twofold: feelings and emotions are not the same, and we manage thoughts and subconscious memories two different ways. I am using the term "subconscious" to describe both cellular memories and thoughts of the heart because both occur beneath our conscious awareness, but there is a distinct and important difference.

Emotions come because of thought. Thought is conscious. It is the result of where we place our focus. All of this is done by choice. Therefore, emotions follow thoughts. So, it is completely correct and viable to change our emotions by simply changing our focus.... think about something else. All of this is done by conscious choice! However, with feelings it is just the opposite. Subconscious thoughts (cellular memories or heart beliefs), on the other hand, emerge after the presence of feelings. In the continuum of thought and emotions, the emotions come after the thoughts. But in the feelings subconscious continuum, thoughts come after the feelings.

So in the realm of the subconscious, a feeling begins to slowly and subtly emerge, usually without my conscious awareness. The feelings that follow seem so logical because they are based on something I am feeling. But here is the catch: no matter what I try to consciously think about, I find that in the absence of effort, my thoughts end up drifting back to that which has been provoked by the feelings. In other words, these thoughts don't go away just because of my attempt (willpower) to change my focus.

There are many protocols that teach us how to recondition ourselves to deal with these repetitive feelings and thoughts. Reconditioning works very effectively with thoughts and emotions. And there is a degree of limited success that comes from reconditioning with feelings and thoughts. Reconditioning, which is a technique I have taught and utilized both personally and clinically for years, is based on interrupting the pattern. If I catch a feeling early enough, instead of following the feeling to destructive thoughts, I interrupt the feeling. Then I will experience a temporary reprieve. If I do this enough times, I will train my brain to react differently to this feeling. This is a form of behavior modification.

It is important to replace the negative, destructive thought with a positive, productive thought. The key to this is, however, to create as much emotion as possible to the new thought. This emotion can create a new neuro-pathway that gives your sub-subconscious mind a new track to run. Unless you can create enough positive emotion about the new thinking, it is doubtful you will overcome the

> THE KEY...IS...TO CREATE AS MUCH EMOTION AS POSSIBLE TO THE NEW THOUGHT.

deep power of feelings. In other words, it will come back! But this is a great exercise that I have utilized hundreds of times.

This is what people experience when they have a bad thought and scream at the devil. We know, biblically, that the devil cannot put a thought in your mind. You put the thought there in response to whatever spiritual tactic was used to entice you. When you screamed at the devil, you interrupted the pattern. The feelings were interrupted. You put your attention in another place. You got relief. So, you assume it must have been the devil in your mind! The next phase of this scenario is one of the ways we know the period of relief was not actually the devil leaving: the feeling comes back. In order to justify what is happening, we have created a doctrine that says, "I rebuked the devil, then he came against me stronger." It sounds good when you're preaching. It makes sense in your experience. It even justifies your experience, but it nullifies God's Word. It denies Scripture. The Bible says, when you *rebuke the devil he flees from you* (James 4:7). It does not say he comes against you stronger!

The problem with reconditioning is it does nothing to remove these cellular memories from your physical body and bring an end to their health-destroying power working in your cells. In other words, your behavior changes, which is a real plus! The change in behavior reduces the conflict in your life. It helps you have better relationships. The situational peace it brings can often facilitate a deeper spiritual walk. But it will not get you healed. And even though you have changed your pattern, this does not mean the feelings will not return. This is a benefit, but not a solution!

The solution is to affect yourself at the subconscious (heart/cellular) level. In counseling and personal use, I have seen incredible freedom come to people who have struggled with a particular issue their entire Christian life simply by learning how to deal with feelings and thoughts by following the proper biblical protocol. We sometimes call it "Releasing," but the biblical description is "Put off- Put on!" (For in-depth training in dealing with beliefs and cellular memories, go to www.HeartPhysics.com.) It was this personal and clinical application that gave birth to Heart Physics®.

Starting in the womb we develop cellular memories. They come from two sources: our parents and our genealogy. The strong emotions of the mother and father and environment have a dramatic effect on the unborn child. Because specific emotions affect specific organs, many of what we consider "genetic defects" are actually the result of cellular imprinting during the developmental phase of a particular organ. Additionally, many of our inherent emotional traits come from this same imprinting.

There is a popular doctrine among many Christian groups called "generational curses." This doctrine is a combination of misunderstanding the Scripture and thereby extrapolating an interpretation of empirical evidence. There is no doubt that we see moral, spiritual, and economic patterns pass from generation to generation. The Scripture does speak of iniquity being visited to the third and fourth generations. The problem with this doctrine is twofold. First, there is a wide possibility of what the word "visiting" means. Second, there is Scripture that states specifically that children cannot die for or be punished for the sins of their fathers.[3] Even when we do not understand the language issues, we cannot reach doctrinal interpretations that directly contradict other Scriptures. To do so always represents a need to satisfy the ego, to prove right that which we have already determined.

Science now tells us that children who are the third or fourth generation welfare family will probably never come out of poverty. Why? Science is finally coming to understand what the Bible told us, but we misinterpreted. Once a belief or lifestyle has been in a family for three or four generations, the children come into the world emotionally "hardwired," predisposed to that type of thinking. This phenomenon is seen in adopted children who are raised completely free from the environmental influence of their birth family, yet still take on so many of the emotional and behavioral similarities. God was not making a threat as to what He would do to the children of parents who lived in iniquity and idolatry; He was warning what the parents were, in fact, doing to their children.

Unless we know how to effectively free a person from cellular (subconscious) memories, they will stay a slave, or at least in a struggle their entire life. It's not like there is a secret formula. The New Testament tells us to cast down certain types of thoughts, put off the "old man" and put on the "new man," renew our mind, and many other such admonitions. But, since we really do not know what that looks like, we keep running to altar-calls, casting out demons, or expecting someone to lay hands on us and cause us to experience (know) the life of God, all of which is in direct contradiction to the New Covenant. Or we do the religious form of repentance. We do everything we can to feel bad about our thoughts and behaviors, yet we never change our mind. We totally ignore all the Scriptures that tell us to meditate, contemplate, and think of certain things, promising specific results. Our religious culture has no place for such activities and, while clearly directed to do so by the Bible, we relegate such activities to cultic or demonic activities. One way or another, we rationalize our resistance to the biblical prescriptions for transformation. We doggedly continue in our insanity... trying the same old religious junk that has never worked, expecting a different outcome and eventually, after enough disappointments, blaming, or at least questioning God!

> UNLESS WE KNOW HOW TO EFFECTIVELY FREE A PERSON FROM CELLULAR...MEMORIES, THEY WILL STAY A SLAVE

These cellular memories that evoke repeated feelings and thoughts eventually cause us to pass self-judgments or judgments about God. We assume the reason this is happening is because of something about me. Or, we come up with some works-oriented doctrine of God or, in the worst-case scenario, complete denial of God! After all, these feelings are real and they are powerful. If our religious formulas do not work, it is only a matter of time until our feelings win. These persistent feelings that start out as cellular memories become beliefs, which accomplish the ultimate death blow.

After enough continual, repeated experiences for which we find no explanation, we pass self-judgments that alter the way we see ourselves. The moment we reach any belief about our identity, it is now a heart belief. These heart beliefs alter our paradigm. They create a new "normal" within which we must live. They become the invisible boundaries which will define our life and our sense of self. So, cellular memories produce self-judgments that become heart beliefs. Remember, cellular memories deal with events, and heart beliefs pertain primarily to identity. Beliefs of the heart answer the question, "What does this mean about me?" Or even worse, "So what's wrong with me?" These destructive questions lead to destructive judgments about self, which forever alter our sense of identity and all the issues of our life!

None of these subconscious (heart beliefs/cellular memories) can be changed or removed at a conscious, intellectual level. In fact, as long as the intellectual mind is involved, one can be assured he will never gain victory over them! This is why it is crucial to learn to enter the HeartZone, that state of being where your intellectual mind loses its ability to control the process. Don't misunderstand! I am not talking about reaching a state of unconsciousness. I am not talking about losing conscious awareness. I am talking about reaching a state where the ego, the need to be right, the patterns of the brain, the self, or the "old man" cannot control the process. This only happens when we enter what I call the HeartZone!

In the HeartZone we can not only put off and send away these destructive beliefs and cellular memories, we can put on the "new man," and we can renew the mind. We can write the truth on our heart about who we are in Jesus. We can hear and recognize the voice of God! Entering the HeartZone is the end of behavioral modification. It is the place of rest where transformation is positive, painless, permanent, and effortless!

> # WE CAN WRITE THE TRUTH ON OUR HEART ABOUT WHO WE ARE IN JESUS.

Go to www.Heartphysics.com and download the free alpha-wave program. This program is designed to be used with headphones. It will slow your brain waves, making it much easier for you to enter into a meditative state. Sit in a quiet room listening to the waves through your headphones, and spend time worshipping, praying, or experiencing yourself enjoying a particular scriptural promise. Notice the difference it makes when your brain is not over-active. This is just a small indicator of what can happen when you develop a lifestyle of entering your HeartZone.

Endnotes

i. For extensive information about the power of judgments, see How To Stop The Pain by James B Richards.

ii. Prov. 18:20-21, A man's stomach shall be satisfied from the fruit of his mouth; *From* the produce of his lips he shall be filled. Death and life *are* in the power of the tongue, And those who love it will eat its fruit.
Prov. 12:6, The words of the wicked *are*, "Lie in wait for blood," But the mouth of the upright will deliver them.
Prov. 16:24, Pleasant words *are like* a honeycomb, Sweetness to the soul and health to the bones.

iii. Ex. 20:5, For I, the Lord your God, *am* a jealous God, visiting the iniquity of the fathers upon the children to the third and fourth *generations* of those who hate Me.
Jer. 31:29-30, In those days they shall say no more: 'The fathers have eaten sour grapes, And the children's teeth are set on edge.' But every one shall die for his own iniquity; every man who eats the sour grapes, his teeth shall be set on edge.

20

THE WAY OF PEACE

Zacharias, the father of John the Baptist, prophesied about John's ministry and the fact that God was doing a great work among His people: *Because of and through the heart of tender mercy and loving-kindness of our God, a Light from on high will dawn upon us and visit [us] To shine upon and give light to those who sit in darkness and in the shadow of death, to direct and guide our feet in a straight line into the way of peace* (Luke 1:78-79, AMP). From this verse we see that in order for people to come out of darkness, they need to be guided into the way of peace.

The New Covenant, which is established between God the Father and the Lord Jesus, is the Covenant of Peace. [1] He is referred to as the Prince of Peace. In Abraham's encounter with Melchizedek, who was a type of Jesus, he was called the King of Righteousness and the Prince of Peace (Salem).[2] One of God's covenant names, thereby revealing His nature, is Jehovah-Shalom: the God of Peace. And according to this prophecy based on Isaiah, Jesus will guide people into the way of peace.

> ## THE NEW COVENANT... IS... THE COVENANT OF PEACE.

Externalists have little regard for the way of peace. Attempting to establish the Kingdom by force has been the basis for worldwide contempt against the Church since soon after Jesus' resurrection. The externalist replaced the Gospel of peace with the message of condemnation, wrath, fear, and judgment. Instead of mercy and kindness being the tools that brought the fallen to repentance, they used exclusion, public humiliation, banishment, and excommunication. They fulfill Paul's repetition of Isaiah's prophecy: *And the way of peace they have not known* (Rom. 3:17).

The value for peace is lost on a generation that has replaced personal responsibility with external force. It seems that everything about being a "Christian" has become hard and strenuous. In fact, it has caused the believer to feel the need to strive to satisfy the false image of God projected onto the Church by those who know not the way of peace! The basic meaning of the word "temptation" is, "anything that causes one to strive." The difficult life legalists impose on us is a basis for temptation to follow another path.

In a total rejection of the New Covenant, the religious legalists have substituted repentance with penitence. They teach that God uses suffering and hardship as a way to test, try, and prove the believer. This "purging" directly renounces the substitutionary suffering of Jesus. In fact, James makes it clear for those who lack wisdom: *Let no one say when he is tempted, "I am tempted by God"; for God cannot be tempted by evil, nor does He Himself tempt anyone* (James 1:13). Based on the very best resources available, this verse could read as follows: Let no man say when he is tempted to do evil, tried, scrutinized, tested, inflicted with evils to prove your faith, or made to strive, [3] that it is from God!

The externalist creates doctrine in opposition to the cross that justifies his unbelief in the power of God's grace which works in the heart of the believer. They do not know the way of peace; they have not experienced the power of grace.

PEACE SHOULD BE THE HABITUAL STATE OF THE BELIEVER.

This form of doctrine makes it impossible for the believer to connect with his heart and know God for himself. His focus is completely turned outward; he is carnal minded. He cannot truly trust such a God as this. Fear overtakes any possibility of knowing and feeling the love of God. He is alienated from the life of God he so desperately seeks.

Peace should be the habitual state of the believer. It is rare when one leaves the place of peace that he or she is able to hear the voice of God in their heart. When we leave the place of peace, we block the messages that come from our heart and shift into thinking with a part of the brain that is used for survival. The nervous system goes into "fight or flight" and something happens that no one expects: we enter a hypnotic state.

I realize that if one simply mentions the word "hypnosis," most Christians rip off their clothes, start pulling out their hair, and run down the street shouting, "Unclean! Unclean! The devil is after me!" Nearly everything we have heard about hypnosis has come from ignorant Christians who didn't know what they were talking about. Or, you see a stage hypnotist that seems to get audience volunteers to do utterly foolish things against their will. Nothing could be further from the truth. I'm not here to defend hypnosis, but you must understand how it actually works in order to realize how you become hypnotized every time you enter the "fight or flight" state.

In hypnosis a person can never be made to do anything they do not want to do. You do not lose awareness, and you do not lose control. That's right! Those people on the stage know exactly what they are doing and they are in complete control. The stage hypnotist is a master at selecting people from the audience that are highly suggestible. They know and enjoy what they are doing! They accept a suggestion that is harmonious with their desires or intentions.

The hypnotic state is not a state whereby one becomes controlled by the hypnotist. The hypnotic state is when one becomes highly suggestible. In other words, we become more open to suggestions from external sources. But, even still, we must remember that we never become open to suggestions that we do not already desire or entertain. If hypnosis was control, we could cure every addiction and personality disorder in one hypnosis session. If only it was that easy!

> THE HYPNOTIC STATE IS WHEN ONE BECOMES HIGHLY SUGGESTIBLE.

Most people also wrongly think that hypnosis is induced through progressive relaxation, but that is not actually correct. Even if it were, we cannot reject relaxation, which is natural and healthy, because it is used in something we do not understand! Dr. George Kappas made astonishing breakthroughs in the field of hypnosis when he discovered that people enter a hypnotic (suggestible) state more quickly through "fight or flight," not progressive relaxation. When we are in a stressful state, we can enter into "fight or flight" physically and emotionally. When we retreat emotionally, we become open to suggestions (suggestible). For most of us this happens as a default mechanism and is only done to reinforce negative beliefs.

Let's say you are in a state of extreme stress. While in that state you will have strong emotions, i.e. fear, dread, feeling overwhelmed, or anxiety, just to name a few. While in the emotional state, which is inwardly trying to run from the threatening situation, you can be exposed to internal or external information. You now have the two components essential for influencing the subconscious: emotions plus information. In brainwashing the information is strategically planned to alter your perception of reality. In daily life external data can come from your parents, spouse, or anyone involved in the conflict.

The internal information comes from self-talk. Self-talk is such a powerful influence because it is your voice. You're saying things that may already be based on other things you believe; therefore, it is information the mind wants to believe, even if it is wrong or negative. Your voice is the most persuasive of all voices!

> SELF-TALK IS SUCH A POWERFUL INFLUENCE BECAUSE IT IS YOUR VOICE.

In this highly suggestible state, people say things about these circumstances, about themselves, or they make vows like, "I'll never trust anyone." In this hypnotic (suggestible) state, we can create subconscious beliefs (cellular memories) that could potentially stay with us for life. Or, even worse, we may pass judgments about ourselves which become heart beliefs. Remember, cellular memories only limit us in specific areas, but heart beliefs limit our life as a whole. Heart beliefs affect us at our most essential and basic functions as a human being: my ability to give and receive love; how I see God; my sense of worthiness, and so much more! Heart beliefs are the invisible boundaries of my life, the walls I cannot scale, the limitations I cannot exceed! Because heart beliefs affect our sense of identity, they always affect every area of our life!

Amazingly, in these times of "fight or flight," if we connected to God or our self-talk was personalizing the promises of God, we would see a reversal: that which was meant for evil would turn to our good! This is why some people emerge from a crisis stronger and more confident in God, while others emerge weaker, worn down, and with diminished faith! In "fight or flight" we become suggestible – we become suggestible to the things we say in our heart. By default, the things we say are usually fear-driven. Since every seed bears after its own kind, these words of fear produce a crop of fear. But when, by choice, we focus on the promises of God, these seeds sown in the heart produce life and faith.

It seems that chaos is the new normal for the world. In fact, it has been widely reported that governments of the world seek to create the feeling of impending doom as a way to manipulate the masses. Governments need the threat of war and bigger-than-life crises as a way to hypnotize and control the masses. We certainly know fear is the basis of most elections. Let me sell you the problem; then I'll be

> ## IT SEEMS THAT CHAOS IS THE NEW NORMAL FOR THE WORLD.

the cure. It's the same way at church. The pulpit is a place for attacking what people are doing wrong more than it is for telling people how to strengthen their heart in the faith!

Sadly, most of what we do to influence our heart is done by default. It is rare that we ever deliberately set ourselves apart to seek God in our heart. We seldom create a time and place of peace that facilitates our ability to hear the still, small voice of God. The externalist wants God to be in the fire and the earthquake, but like the Prophet Elijah discovered, they are listening for the wrong voice.

When Jesus prepared to leave Planet Earth, He began to teach the disciples about the ministry of the Holy Spirit. He began this process by warning, *do not let your heart be troubled*. A heart at peace can hear the still, small voice. A heart in chaos will often not even hear the earthquake. Chaos keeps us outward-focused. Peace hears both inwardly and outwardly. Chaos doesn't notice the warning until it is beyond our ability to resolve. Peace notices and makes corrections almost instantly.

Internal stress is usually based on external circumstances that demand our attention and trouble our heart. External noise demands an outward focus.

Even physical stress in the body takes our attention away from our heart. As we learned earlier, studies show that stress actually blocks the messages that are sent from our heart. Stress creates a physical energy that must be consumed. It can be spent by physical exercise, shaking our leg, tapping our fingers, or any number of annoying habits. Because it is a buildup of energy that must be released, it leads to insomnia and, eventually, a host of diseases. The key factor here is the demand to focus on the physical. Not only will twenty minutes of meditation give you a recovery that would take hours of sleep, it will also facilitate the releasing of stress. That's why all meditation exercises begin with physical relaxation.

The only way we will hear the voice of God in our heart is when we are in a state of inward peace. Fortunately, as we become more anchored in our faith and consistently inner-focused, it seems that outward influences distract us less and less. We become like the eye of the storm. The wind and waves may be crashing all around us, but in the eye of the storm we are in perfect calm. This is, no doubt, the basis for Scriptures that talk about standing on the rock, or abiding under the shadow, or God as our High Tower. These are all metaphoric of a person surrounded by turmoil and danger, yet abiding in safety and peace!

The Hebrew language gives us some great insight to how the prophets of old prepared themselves to hear from God. One word in particular, "Hitboden," means "to meditate." The root of this word means "to self-isolate." Based on how this word is used it can mean "physical isolation" as well as "internal isolation." When the prophets sanctified themselves, they were literally setting themselves apart. They set themselves apart physically, but they set their attention apart from the daily concerns to hear God! We naively think the prophets were simply going about their business and suddenly the Spirit would move in them and they would begin to prophesy. Or we think that sanctifying themselves was the process whereby they resolved all of their spiritual issues. More than anything, it was a time of preparation through internal and external isolation. . While spontaneous occurrences happened from time to time, that was the exception, not the rule. These men set themselves apart, they isolated themselves from daily activities, and they isolated their focus of attention from the external to their inner man, away from their physical body and the demands of life.

> THE SPIRIT OF GOD LIVES IN US. HE IS ALWAYS SEEKING TO SPEAK TO US.

The Spirit of God lives in us. He is always seeking to speak to us. But we are generally so outwardly focused that we cannot hear the still, small voice. Unlike the prophets of old, and in completely closing our eyes to the biblical directive to think, ponder, consider, imagine, and meditate, we keep waiting for the "big earthquake of God's voice." All the while, we are unable to hear the constant, still, small voice that is always offering wisdom, direction, and comfort.

There are many ways to create an inner focus. None are right or wrong within themselves, but different ones seem to be more effective for different people. All exercises that lead to a relaxed inner focus have at least one thing in common: they all slow the brain waves. "The normal state of mental awareness occurs when our brain waves are functioning at the beta state. Beta brainwaves are considered 'fast brain wave' activity. Beta brainwaves are brainwaves that cycle within the range of 12 – 38 Hz and are usually generated in the brain's left-hemisphere. Beta waves kick in when logically thinking, feeling stressed, and feeling tense. Beta is generally thought of as a 'normal' rhythm and is dominant in people who are alert, anxious, or have their eyes open. Beta brainwaves are considered to be the normal brainwave pattern in healthy adults."[4]

Beta is the optimal state for mental work; yet, in this state the brain is in control. To enter a worshipful or meditative state, the brain waves must be slowed. Any number of things can begin to slow the brain waves and, with each step down, we become less dominated by the mind and more open to the voice of our heart. It is at these states that we are able to overcome cellular memories, change heart beliefs, and develop our faith. Here the mind cannot hold us in the grip of our intellectual fixation.

It is interesting that so many of the physical forms of worship tend to slow down our brain waves. Music is very instrumental in affecting our brain waves. Chanting, which is done in many of the Psalms and is actually used in the Hebrew language to describe worship, slows the brain waves. Rolling our eyes up as if looking to Heaven, rocking, singing songs with repeated rhythmic patterns, bowing, dancing, and pretty much all of the physical expressions of praise and worship, slow the brain waves. When this happens, we think that God, who lives way off in Heaven, has suddenly been appeased to such a degree that He graces us with His presence. But the truth is just the opposite; God, who lives in us and is always expressing Himself to us, is finally realized by the shift in our awareness. We begin to experience what He has been expressing all along!

A good worship service provides so many of these actuators that are activated at one time, plus there is the intention to set this time aside to worship, i.e. focus on God, so we have the optimal environment and attitude for a meditative experience. The problem is it is rare after reaching this deep state that we use it to establish our heart in a truth that has eluded us or put off some aspect of the "old man" that seems to be dominating us. It has been my experience that altar calls given at this portion of a service facilitated some powerful transformations that were very different than what occurs at the end of a sermon! However, very few people ever develop the ability to enter into this quiet, reflective, peaceful, meditative state at home. If they did, and ever discussed it with the average Christian, they would be warned of the dangers of such activity.

Isaiah said, *They that wait upon the Lord shall renew their strength; they shall mount up with wings as the eagles. They shall run and not be weary, they shall walk and not faint* (Isaiah 40:31). This waiting on God is interpreted by some as passively waiting for God to decide to move. But this word for "wait" means, "to bind together, to entwine, to wrap around God."[5] This is a meditative process which results in an exchange. The word "renew" means "exchange." When we peacefully and prayerfully wrap ourselves around God, we exchange our weakness for His strength. But the resistance and outright refusal to set ourselves apart, both physically and emotionally, and entwine ourselves with God, ensures we will remain within the limits of our own strength. The intellectual, carnal-minded Church thinks God hears us because of our formulas, our vain repetitions, religious activity, or loud prayers. We have lost touch with, *be still and know that I am God* (Psalm 46:10). *In calmness and confidence you shall be made strong* (Isaiah 30:15, CJB). It is counter-intuitive to find strength in peace or to see strength in calmness. But *the way of peace we have not known!*

> THIS IS A MEDITATIVE PROCESS, WHICH RESULTS IN AN EXCHANGE.

Regardless of the method employed when one enters a state of physical and emotional peace, they are poised for an encounter with God. Some, because of what they believe about God, actually resist entering into relaxed peace. They are so afraid of what they will see or discover about themselves. Others expect to hear the voice of an angry God condemning them for their sins and failures, but actually the Holy Spirit will convince (convict) them of who they really are in Jesus, of His ability to empower their life, and of His abiding love. This mercy and kindness draws the struggling believer into repentance. They return to the light. In the face of mercy they have no need to hide with their sins in the darkness. By exposing themselves to the truth, they enter into fellowship with the resurrected Jesus. As they wrap themselves around God, they exchange their weakness for His strength (grace). They fellowship in His victories. That which was impossible by their own strength (dead works/flesh) now occurs effortlessly! They discover in peace what could not be known in striving!

The number one reason people do not set themselves apart is they do not have the time. Since there are only so many hours in a day, this will not begin because you get more time. This will begin because you make it a priority. It may be good to write a schedule of what you do with your time on a daily basis. Then make a list of what pleasure, benefit, or fulfillment each of those things brings you. Next write out the phrase: Spending time with God in prayer, meditation, and worship. Then beside it write: this is the key to living all my dreams, living in abundance, better health, and better relationships. Then decide, in light of the value each of these things bring to your life, which one you are ready to replace for time with God!

Endnotes

i. Isa. 54:10, For the mountains shall depart And the hills be removed, But My kindness shall not depart from you, Nor shall My covenant of peace be removed," Says the Lord, who has mercy on you.

ii. Heb. 7:1-2, For this Melchizedek, king of Salem, priest of the Most High God, who met Abraham returning from the slaughter of the kings and blessed him, to whom also Abraham gave a tenth part of all, first being translated "king of righteousness," and then also king of Salem, meaning "king of peace,"

iii. NT:3985

1. *to try whether a thing can be done; to attempt, endeavor:* with an infinitive, Acts 9:26

2. *to try, make trial of, test:*

    a.   in a good sense: Matt 22:35

    b.   in a bad sense: to test one maliciously, craftily to put to the proof his feelings or judgment, Matt 16:1

    c.   to try or test one's faith, virtue, character, by enticement to sin; James 1:13f

    d.   After the O.T. usage:

                a. of God; *to inflict evils upon one in order to prove his character and the steadfastness of his faith:* 1

(from Thayer's Greek Lexicon, Electronic Database. Copyright © 2000, 2003, 2006 by Biblesoft, Inc. All rights reserved.)

NT:3985

to try or strive," "to test,"

(from Theological Dictionary of the New Testament, abridged edition, Copyright © 1985 by William B. Eerdmans Publishing Company. All rights reserved.)

iv. http://4mind4life.com/blog/2008/02/09/beta-brain-waves/

v. OT:6960

1. to wait, to look for, to hope, to expect

    a.   (Qal) waiting (participle)

    b.   (Piel)

        1)   to wait or to look eagerly for

        2)   to lie in wait for

        3)   to wait for, to linger for

2. to collect, to bind together;

(from The Online Bible Thayer's Greek Lexicon and Brown Driver & Briggs Hebrew Lexicon, Copyright © 1993, Woodside Bible Fellowship, Ontario, Canada. Licensed from the Institute for Creation Research.)

21

BIBLICAL MEDITATION

The word "meditate" or "meditation" is only used twenty times in the King James Version of the Bible. However, certain Hebrew words that are thought to be linked to meditation are used numerous times. But even more important are all the words and instances where a meditative process is evident. Words like think, ponder, consider, wait on God, and imagine, or even the phrase "to know God" is referring to a meditative process. As we discussed, when the prophets set themselves apart, it was for a time of meditation while isolating themselves physically and emotionally to wait on God.

> YOU MUST LET GO OF ANY OF YOUR PRECONCEIVED IDEAS OR NARROW RELIGIOUS JUDGMENTS ABOUT MEDITATION...

At this point you must let go of any preconceived ideas or narrow religious judgments about meditation and allow yourself to consider biblical meditation as God's means of connecting with mankind in the heart. The word is in the Bible, the activities are in the Bible. It has been practiced by people who served God for thousands of years. For now, just think of meditation as a reflective process that a person could do at many different levels and brain states. When the brain waves begin to slow down through an action as simple as closing the eyes, we enter into a high alpha brainwave state which is a very shallow form of meditation. One can move through all the phases from high alpha to the lowest (slowest brain waves) delta state by employing different techniques or simply adding music.

These various states of brain wave activity are natural; God created them and, in fact, unless we process through them on a regular basis we cannot be physically or emotionally healthy. As we sleep, we pass through the alpha, theta, and delta states. In each of these states, the mind and body are nurtured and healed on different levels. Even our dreams are actually a meditative process whereby our mind rids itself of unwanted data. At different times of the night, our dreams are actually a representation of different mind-heart activities. According to Dr. George Kappas, in the first third of the night, our dreams are representative of useless information and emotional clutter that we are releasing. In the second third of the night, our dreams are symbolic representations of the things we desire like our goals, dreams, or decisions we have made. In the last third of the night, our dreams represent those things we are seeking to release. They are unwanted and, very probably, stand in the way of the things we do want that were represented in our earlier dreams.

Each of these phases of sleep and dreaming gives us insight into what we can accomplish through meditation. We can get rid of clutter that serves only to distract us from the more important life issues. We can see and believe our goals and dreams. We can even release and send away those things that inhibit us. Sleep and dreaming are the processes of our mind and body doing naturally what God designed them to do. By default, meditation is when we, by choice, use those same natural abilities, just as the prophets of old, the early New Testament believers, and very probably Jesus Himself.

When we read that Jesus went alone to a mountain and prayed, we interpret that in light of our twenty first century Western culture and externally-based concepts. We fail to realize this is precisely what the prophets did in the Old Testament. They isolated themselves both physically and emotionally to bond with, connect with, wrap around, and become one with God! It wasn't just talking; it was listening, it was reflection, and it was meditation. When Jesus was on the mountain at night praying,[1] the disciples set out across the sea. They were miles out on the water and it was dark. The Bible says Jesus saw them straining at rowing because of the wind and the waves. So my question is how could he see them? It was dark and they were miles away. This could not have been accomplished by the naked eye.

The word "see" could be translated as "to perceive with any of the senses or to know." Given all the factors it is probable that Jesus did not see them with His natural sight, but He saw them with the eyes of His heart. This would be similar to a vision. Some Hebrew scholars equate the word "prophecy" with "vision" and "meditate." The idea is that a prophecy, words of knowledge, or perceiving something inwardly emerges, or as the Hebrew says, "gushes forth" from a meditative state.

In 2 Cor. 4:18, Paul exposes his secret to facing and overcoming monumental obstacles like beatings, stoning, imprisonment, death threats, and all the hardship of ministry. He says, *we do not look at the things which are seen, but at the things which are not seen* (2 Cor. 4:18). The word "seen" refers to the ability to see with our eyes. So he sustained himself because he was seeing something that cannot be seen with the eyes. He followed the example of the patriarchs in Hebrews chapter 11, referred to as "the roll call of faith!" They endured every obstacle imaginable because they saw the promises, even though they were far off.[2] They heard the Word of God and then they perceived it with the eyes of their heart. Paul passed this same advice on to Timothy, the disciple he mentored. He wanted Timothy to know how to experience the Word in a life-producing way. So he told him, *Meditate on these things; give yourself entirely to them* (1 Tim. 4:15). Meditation was the way to give himself entirely to the things he had been taught. This would be the place he would incorporate them into his life beyond intellectualism.

Paul was following the example and teachings of King David, the prophets, Moses, and Jesus. They all knew and taught that our ability to give ourselves to God's Word was directly connected to the meditative process. Moses told Joshua that his ability to be strong and courageous, to prosper, and stay fully committed to God's Word was to *meditate on it day and night!*[3] They all knew what Jesus eventually taught His disciples and no doubt practiced: you

> OUR ABILITY TO GIVE OURSELVES TO GOD'S WORD WAS DIRECTLY CONNECTED TO THE MEDITATIVE PROCESS.

can only get life from God's Word to the degree that you bond with it through thought, study, prayer, reflection, contemplation… some form of meditation! In other words, *the measure you meet will be measured unto you!*

So, what is meditation? The word "meditate" or "meditation" in the Old Testament can mean "to murmur, to mutter, to ponder,[4] to be pensive (repeat a thought or word over and over), conceive, imagine, or utter out of the heart,"[5] Because of the use of the imagination which means "to form or shape," some translators also consider meditation to be framing or giving shape to something. This, of course, makes no provision for the Hebrew words that involve the process of bonding, cleaving, entwining, or other concepts of connecting to God. In the New Testament it is the same. There are so many words that have reflective or meditative connotation that it would be too time consuming to list and discuss them all.

There are many different types of meditation. The Psalmist would often look at things in nature and contemplate the wisdom, splendor, and greatness of God. I have spent hundreds of nights staring at the stars, contemplating these same things. Because the unseen things of God can be understood by His creation, biblical meditation has always included watching, observing, and reflecting on nature as a means of pondering the greatness of God. Just imagine; when men lived to be several hundred years old, they were able to see and grasp cycles and patterns in the earth that we will never live long enough to observe! As they pondered them, they came to understand aspects of God through His creation.

Praise, worship, and prayer are actually all meditative in nature. The idea of just repeating rote prayers or even singing Psalms straight from the Bible is of little value if we are not engaging every aspect of our being. The way the Church prays today did not come from the Bible; it emerged from Church leaders who brought their cultic, religious practices into the Church. Singing a song without envisioning its meaning or attempting to connect with God personally is of little value in general, and of no value to the heart. In fact, it could work against the heart. The Psalms often end a phrase with the word "Selah," which means "to pause and reflect." But that is completely ignored by most readers.

> **PRAISE AND WORSHIP SHOULD BE AN INTIMATE EXPERIENCE.**

Studies show that when a Christian prays he or she activates a part of the brain that does not become activated when other religions pray or with general non-personal meditations. When I sing any song, I change all the pronouns so they will be personal. If the song says, "praise Him," I change it to "I praise You!" I never want to be singing *about* God, I want to be singing *to* Him. And by all means, make sure the words do not deny the finished work of Jesus. The last thing you want in a meditative state is to repeat words that work against your faith! I also make all the words about God's promises or His deliverance present tense, positive, and personal. I change all the instances of "we" to "I." I make all the promises now! I really don't care what everyone else is doing, I am connecting to my God on the basis of the finished work of Jesus, fellowshipping and sharing in His resurrected life that is mine now! I want this to be personal and intimate.

Praise and worship should be an intimate experience. The Psalmist, because of the Hebrew words used, equated prayer, praise, and worship with meditation. They had no concept of singing songs with your mouth when your mind is elsewhere. They sang, prayed, and worshipped to bind themselves to God. To sing songs, even scriptural songs, without connecting personally to God is nothing more than an exercise in personal motivation. Just as true as intimate, heartfelt, love making is when a man and woman "know" one another and build a stronger connection and oneness, meditative prayer and worship causes us to "know" God and bind ourselves to Him more deeply!

Everyone knows that music has great emotional power. King David appointed musicians to prophecy on their harps, providing worship continually before God. David saw the power of music on the soul when he would play for King Saul and the evil spirit would depart from him. This is the effect music has on the soul, producing a meditative state that gives it power. The more simple and repetitive the music, the more meditative in nature it becomes. This was the unrealized power behind the choruses of the early charismatic movement. They were usually very short. You could memorize the songs after singing them just a few times, and they were very repetitious. But the most wonderful part was... they were scriptural. Most of the songs in the early days were exact quotes from the Bible.

As the second generation of "spirit-filled" believers arose, they didn't really have the same heart for worship as their predecessors. The songs became more "wordy," harder to remember, and the melody lines became more complicated. Thus, all of the other factors that induce a meditative state of worship were abandoned. People couldn't close their eyes because they couldn't easily memorize the words. The melody lines became too complicated. The intellectual mind had to stay engaged. The focus was no longer on God; the focus was on the words on the screen and the difficult melody line.

Praise and worship that is simple, scriptural, and directed toward God allows the worshipper to engage himself or herself in a personal exchange with God. As they sing of the greatness and splendor of God, they magnify Him (make Him larger) in their life experience. This not only does something in that very moment, it also makes them see life differently. God starts looking bigger in their circumstance. Because we are created in the likeness and image of God, anything that magnifies God in our heart and binds us to Him changes our sense of self. As He gets larger in us, we get larger in life. We experience that exchange spoken of by Isaiah, the prophet!

Then there is the meditation in God's Word. Meditation in the Word has incredible potential to change our life. The Western approach to this is to recite a verse over and over and contemplate its meaning. This is meditating *about* the Word, not me *in* the Word and the Word *in* me. While that no doubt has value, it could easily become an exercise in intellectualism. We are disciples, not just students. We want to live the Word more than interpret the Word. We are not looking for the "perfect" scriptural interpretation as much as we are looking for how the Scripture would be translated into life application.

> MEDITATION IN THE WORD HAS INCREDIBLE POTENTIAL TO CHANGE OUR LIFE.

If I engage my heart and this is in direct communication with God (not about God), then I have to see me in this equation. I don't want to meditate *on* the Word as much as I want to meditate *in* the Word! What does that look like in me? What do I look like in that verse? I want to fellowship (participate in the life of God I have) in Jesus. Since all the promises of God are "yes" for us in Christ (2 Cor. 1:20), I can't separate my meditation of the Word from my life in Him! I want to see and experience my life living in the promises. The Word is true for me because I am in Him. He obtained it; He is my Source; He is my qualification; outside of Him, pondering the promises is just positive thinking!

So, when I consider a verse that says *I have everything that pertains to life and godliness...* I always add "because I am in You!" I never claim a promise apart from him. I recreate an awareness of the fact that it is all because of Him! Faith in Jesus is not faith in Him as He walked Planet Earth, even though that has great merit. Faith in Jesus is faith in what was accomplished through His death, burial, resurrection, and subsequent inheritance that I now share with Him! I want to see, perceive, experience, and grasp what I would look like, how my life would be, and what I would be feeling if I were experiencing that promise in my life at this moment. When I acknowledge my righteousness in Jesus, I want to experience what it is to be righteous. In other words, I don't want to say anything that I do not in some way allow myself to experience!

To get biblical meditation down to a simple functional concept, I would describe it as follows: biblical meditation is when you think about, ponder, imagine, or consider any biblical promise until you have all the emotions of it being true at this moment. After spending years meditating in my personal life and developing many of these concepts, I heard the late Kenneth Hagin, Sr. describe faith using this same concept. He said something to this effect: Faith experiences the Word as if it is true right now. I don't know what all he knew about it because I am certain, like all men of God, he knew more than he said. But I am certain that coming to the place of faith (immovable trust) is a meditative process. He could not have been more correct!

Some people say they can't experience things when they meditate. But that is never true. I always ask, "Do you ever think of negative things from your past and start to feel depressed?" The answer is always "yes." This means that you do meditate, and you meditate until you change your emotional state. The problem is you have trained your mind to meditate on negative, painful things but not positive, pleasant things.

A good way to learn to connect to the positives in life is to think of any positive experience. Try to recall every detail possible. Then notice and acknowledge even the slightest positive emotions that emerge. In time you will be able to use the Word of God to create positive emotions about the fulfillment of the promises in your life. Besides learning to meditate on the Word, this will also help you learn to stop negative default meditation and turn your emotions around any time or any place. This is a great life management tool!

Endnotes

i.   Mark 6:45-52
ii. Heb. 11:13, These all died in faith, not having received the promises, but having seen them afar off were assured of them,* embraced *them* and confessed that they were strangers and pilgrims on the earth.
iii. Josh. 1:7-8, Only be strong and very courageous, that you may observe to do according to all the law which Moses My servant commanded you; do not turn from it to the right hand or to the left, that you may prosper wherever you go. This Book of the Law shall not depart from your mouth, but you shall meditate in it day and night, that you may observe to do according to all that is written in it. For then you will make your way prosperous, and then you will have good success.
iv. (Biblesoft's New Exhaustive Strong's Numbers and Concordance with Expanded Greek-Hebrew Dictionary. Copyright © 1994, 2003, 2006 Biblesoft, Inc. and International Bible Translators, Inc.)
v.   (from Brown-Driver-Briggs Hebrew and English Lexicon, Unabridged, Electronic Database. Copyright © 2002, 2003, 2006 by Biblesoft, Inc. All rights reserved.)

22

GATHERING EVIDENCE

Faith or belief, which is the same word in the Greek, is a matter of the heart. It is faith in the heart that moves mountains, experiences rest, does the impossible, and connects to the finished work of Jesus. In our external religious paradigm, intellectual acknowledgment has been substituted for faith. But intellectual acknowledgment is the mere giving of consent or approval to the information. This intellectual consent is a form of judging God. When God's Word makes sense to us, we give it our intellectual approval. In doing so we set ourselves above God! It is a form of determining good and evil.

Intellectual consent has nothing to do with trusting God, it is about trusting self. Through intellectual acknowledgment we don't give ourselves to the Word because we trust God or His wisdom; we give ourselves to the Word because it seems to be in agreement with our opinion, i.e. it feeds our ego! It fits into our

> INTELLECTUAL CONSENT HAS NOTHING TO DO WITH TRUSTING GOD...

"known," so we feel safe with it. After all… we trust our opinion. Because this is a mere intellectual pursuit; we could easily be swayed by a more reasonable argument. It is not immovable trust for God! This has been the demise of many Christians who thought God had failed them when, in fact, they never really trusted Him in their heart.

Faith is not just about the information; it is about the character and dependability of the One who provides the information. Faith grows as we walk with God. The more we put His Word to the test of faith, the more we see how utterly dependable are His promises! It is an immovable trust for the facts which is so certain that one commits to it. In fact, it is a conviction that is so absolute there is no separating ourselves from the Word. Therefore, obedience to the Word grows out of the fact that this Word is my character, my shared opinion, my point of view... my identity! But more than anything, faith is trusting the One who spoke the Word!

Sadly, most people have their first challenge to operate faith when they are facing some type of crisis! So they find a promise and attempt to "believe" it. It's usually a "hit and miss" proposition. When it works, they don't know why; and when it fails, they don't know why! They do know that when they look at Jesus as their model, faith should always work.[1]

Mark 11:22-23[2] gives us some interesting insight into the working of faith from the heart. Many scholars agree that verse 22 should read "have the faith of God," not *in* God. So this passage is telling us to operate faith the same way God does. It then lays out a brief overview of the process whereby God Himself operates faith. Faith speaks something; it has no doubt, and is immovable... And at this point we insert something the Bible does not say. We insert that we must believe God will do it. While that may be implied, that is not what it says. It says we must *believe that those things we say will be done!*

This begins to overlap with concepts of the heart. *Of the abundance of the heart the mouth speaks.* We know that physiologically the heart reflects its health in the tongue. The words of Jesus make a direct connection between the heart and the tongue, i.e. speech! Therefore, confidence in our words is directly affected by the heart.

We all know God's Word is absolute. We all know what God says will come to pass. Our problem is not usually what we believe about God, but what we believe about us. Do I have enough confidence in the words I speak to believe they will come to pass? The Apostle John warned of the negative effects of our heart condemning us.[3] It makes it impossible for us to receive from God. But it also makes it impossible for us to believe that what we say will come to pass. Do I believe what I say will come to pass? This touches on the core of the heart that answers the question: who am I? My identity, my sense of self, has to be one with my confidence in God. This is only found when there is an abiding "in Him" awareness!"

Our heart becomes immovable in the promises of God not because we have "mega-versed" our brain with Scriptures about faith but becomes immovable about the promises of God because we are immovable about who we are in Him, immovable because He is our qualification for the promises, immovable because every aspect of our hope and trust is in Him. He is the reason all the promises are "yes" for us! This is the fellowship (joint participation) we have in Him!

> OUR HEART BECOMES IMMOVABLE ABOUT THE PROMISES OF GOD BECAUSE WE ARE IMMOVABLE ABOUT WHO WE ARE IN HIM...

The book of 1 John was written to believers who, among other things, believed sin had no consequences in their life. From his pointing out that their hearts condemned them based on the way they lived, we can discover many helpful insights. If my heart is about my identity, and I profess righteousness, my behavior should not deny my profession of faith! This creates disharmony between my heart, my spirit, my mind, and my confession (profession of righteousness). My heart needs evidence that I am righteous. This disharmony robs me of evidence, and my heart condemns me, destroying faith and confidence!

The writer of Hebrews recognized this interesting but overlooked reality. *Now faith is the substance of things hoped for, the evidence of things not seen* (Heb. 11:1-2). The heart is not blind-- quite the opposite! It is the seat of perception. We have spiritual sight! The heart needs evidence to believe! This evidence comes to us in everything from the way we live our life to the things we imagine. Faith, unwavering trust, is the title deed, the proof of ownership, the substructure for things that have been accomplished and are confidently expected. Unwavering trust that permeates every aspect of our being is the evidence our heart needs to be immovable. The problem is the evidence which comes to us from our five senses is relentless. It never stops! Our heart will believe that for which we have the most evidence and the strongest, most consistent emotions!

When our heart is overwhelmed by the constant barrage of physical evidence, we have to see the unseen with the eyes of our heart. If we cannot gather more evidence to support God's promises than we have evidence to the contrary, we will either waver or doubt. Meditating on the Word of God, specifically fellowshipping with Jesus (participating in our joint inheritance), is the place we must go to gather evidence.

In addressing the issue of faith, there are four things we must define from a biblical perspective. There is doubt. Doubt is when we believe something more than we believe the Word of God. The word "doubt" literally means "to choose between two." Doubt chooses the physical world over the unseen world. Then there is unbelief; that is, no belief (the absence of immovable trust in anything.) Then there is wavering. Wavering is when we shift from one position to another. And finally there is belief, which is being sure or unwavering in our trust in God's promise through the Lord Jesus.

> ## MOST SERIOUS BELIEVERS HAVE THEIR GREATEST STRUGGLE WITH WAVERING.

Most serious believers have their greatest struggle with wavering. They know intellectually that God's Word is true, but their heart beliefs cause them to have feelings to the contrary. Those feelings direct their thoughts, and eventually those thoughts cause them to move their attention from God's Word to their circumstances. Since intellectualism produces very little emotion, it can never maintain a fixed focus, particularly when faced with strong opposing feelings or emotions.

Wavering is the product of shifting your focus of attention. When we look at the promise, we have one emotion. When we look at the problem, we have another emotion. If we were in faith, we would not waver. So, what is the solution? I want to be in faith! How can I get there when I am wavering? Simple! You gather evidence. Evidence persuades your heart. At the end of the day, you will focus your attention on the place that provides the most consistent, compelling evidence.

Not only does the physical world provide a constant stream of thoughts leading to emotions, but we have also trained our senses to feel these emotions, especially the negative emotions associated with fear, worry, and pessimism. There is no way a casual glance at the promise of God can compete with such a thoroughly developed process… unless we can create emotions that are equally compelling! Remember, emotions are created by where we place our focus. If the promise was written on our heart we would have deep feelings of confidence, hope, and peace emerging to move us toward a godly faith-focus. But if a truth is not believed in the heart, negative, conflicting feelings will emerge to move us toward wavering and doubt.

Walking through this process from despair to delight is not as mystical as it seems. Jesus gave us the way in Mark 11:22: *Have the faith of God.*[4] In other words, operate faith just like God! God is a faith God. Everything that exists was brought into being by the same process that we must use when seeking to manifest what has been given to us. It is important to realize before God created the physical or seen worlds, He first had to create what I call "the field." The field was the subatomic world and all the laws that governed them. Then He spoke into that field of limitless potential from a heart that had already seen or given shape to what He was prepared to speak. Then He spoke words filled with faith. These words gave rise to and organized the invisible subatomic energies into matter. Hebrews 11:6 confirms this: *things which are seen were not made of things which are visible.* That which is seen was not made from *nothing;* it was made from something unseen! The potential for everything we need already exists in the field. We are not using our faith to make something from nothing, which I find encouraging. Our faith becomes the substructure, the organizing factor for the unseen realities to manifest in this physical realm.

> THESE WORDS GAVE RISE TO AND ORGANIZED THE INVISIBLE SUBATOMIC ENERGIES INTO MATTER.

It seems God employed four phases of operating faith, all of which coincide with Mark 11:23. First, God had to choose the outcome He wanted. This concept is seen in the fact that spoken words emerge from thought. This is implied in the fact that the person speaking to the mountain had to first decide he wanted the mountain to move. To operate the God-like faith, we must first choose the desired outcome within the scope of God's promises. The Bible says, God *declares the end from the beginning (Isaiah 46:10.)* The word "declares" has a causative effect. He doesn't declare it just because He knows it. His declaration causes it to come to pass.

Next, we must believe in our heart that what we say will be done. These words must be spoken from the place of immovable faith. Before faith speaks it "frames up" the outcome in its heart. The heart must be persuaded of the desired outcome in opposition to the evidence and emotions that declare otherwise. This happens as we meditate on the Word. When we see and experience ourselves living in the end result promised in His Word, it becomes real in our experience!

Faith in the heart ventures into the realm of the eternal where there is no time. Therefore, for something to be real in the heart it must be real now, i.e. experienced as a present tense reality. We cannot project it into the future as something we will experience one day. We live it in our heart today! When I close my eyes and ponder myself living in the promise, I want to experience every possibility of what it would be like to be living in that promise at this moment. I only become immovable to the degree that I experience it as being real now.

This is not a mind game. This is the way the heart works. This is not a denial of the reality of the circumstance. I am simply experiencing another reality more powerfully than the circumstance. When God made Abraham and Sarah the promise of their heirs, the KJV gives us a faulty rendering of what he had to face. Romans 4:19 says Abraham didn't consider his own body or the deadness of Sarah's womb, which seems like denial. But that is not what the original says, which is revealed in almost every other translation. *Without weakening in his faith, he faced the fact that his body was as good as dead — since he was about a hundred years old — and that Sarah's womb was also dead* (NIV, emphasis mine). He did not deny reality. He was not afraid to look at reality. Faith and denial are not compatible. He faced the facts, but the facts did not move him.

FAITH AND DENIAL ARE NOT COMPATIBLE.

Verse 21 explains why he did not waver when he faced those negative facts; he was fully persuaded. We have to face the realities of our circumstances, and then we have to gather evidence in our heart that outweighs what the physical world presents. God gave Abraham meditative exercises to help him overcome the limitations. He had him look at the stars and even try to count them. He then connected that visual representation with the promise of the greatness of his offspring. He did the same thing with sand. This is what we do in our heart. We see the end from the beginning. We involve all of our God-given senses to experience the reality and base our experience of reality on what has been accomplished by the Lord Jesus.

Next, we have to not doubt. Doubt is when we choose between two options. In this case we choose the promise of God or the circumstance. We will usually shift over to doubt through the process of wavering. This occurs because we are not single-minded. We shift from one focus to another, and each time we do our emotions change. Therefore, the moment we feel our emotions change, we need to go back and observe the evidence of God's Word by getting into our HeartZone and experiencing (knowing) the in-Him truth! This is why the truth only sets you free when it is known (experienced).

When I waver, I will experience a negative emotion. The moment I realize this, I should go back to my HeartZone and observe myself living and experiencing the promise... without hesitation. The longer I wait, the stronger the emotions or feelings grow that oppose my faith. The more I waver, the harder it is to go back and even consider the promise. I must abide in that place of having what is promised until my emotions change. When the promise is established in your heart, your deep feelings continually move you toward the truth. In time you will find the methodology that works most effectively for you. Depending on the greatness of the problem, this can be done in minutes or it could take hours.

We are not earning the blessings of God by these efforts. The effort we put into this is not because of what it takes to move God; it is because of what it takes to move our heart from doubt to faith. Hebrews give us insight into this paradox: *Let us labour therefore to enter into that rest, lest any man fall after the same example of unbelief* (Heb. 4:12, KJV). The rest occurs when we enter into belief, i.e. faith. The labor is what it takes for us to reach that place. The laboring is what I call persuading my heart, but once I am fully persuaded all laboring ends.

God gave us our left brain, our right brain, and our capacity to think and imagine as tools to use for godliness. Our left brain has the facts. This is true because it has been accomplished by Jesus. Taking all the promises back to the finished work of Jesus satisfies the needs of the left brain. Then our right brain gives us the power of emotion and imagination. As we ponder and imagine ourselves living in the promise, we are combining the logic of truth and our imagination. The word "imagine" means "to form, fashion, or to squeeze into a shape." Imagination is a powerful, godly tool essential for effective heart work. It is key to shaping the outcome we desire!

Isaiah 26:3 shows us the incredible value of a godly imagination: *You will keep him in perfect peace, Whose mind (imagination) is stayed on You, Because he trusts in You.* The word "mind" would be better translated as "imagination." It is the same root word.[5] But we also see that in addition to "squeezing something into," it is also the conception. God is able to keep him in peace because of where he keeps his trust, which is the fruit of his imagination. Paul echoed these same words when he told the Philippian believers to think on, meditate, or imagine specific things and the God of peace would be with them. Obviously he is speaking metaphorically. God was with them. He was speaking of God being with them in a way they could experience as He manifests His peace.[6]

It is from this place of being fully persuaded that we speak or confess the Word as a reality that we have already experienced in our heart. We know what it feels like to be real. In our experience it is, in fact, more real than anything in the physical world! We do not waver or become impatient, regardless of how long it takes to manifest. In our experience it is already ours! We have gathered and considered all the evidence. We are immovable in our trust for God! This is the way of the God-like faith!

> IT IS FROM THIS PLACE OF BEING FULLY PERSUADED THAT WE SPEAK OR CONFESS THE WORD AS A REALITY THAT WE HAVE ALREADY EXPERIENCED IN OUR HEART.

In the areas of your struggle, are you gathering as much evidence that promises a good outcome as you are the evidence of a bad outcome? People often come to me and tell me they have prayed about something and are still struggling. I ask them what they did to assess and attempt to resolve the problem. I try to determine the time they invested in the problem. Then I ask, "How did you pray about this? Show me what you prayed." If they ever actually show me what they prayed it usually stacks up something like, "You spent four hours focusing on the problem and you spent 30 seconds focusing on God's answer, and never actually experienced it as being real. So which one do you have the most evidence to believe?"

Be realistic about where you place your attention and for how long. Where you place your attention is the source of evidence. If the majority of your evidence is about the problem, the problem is growing in your life, and possibly in your heart! Take steps to become more deliberate and more honest about the evidence you are gathering.

Endnotes

i. John 14:12-14 "Most assuredly, I say to you, he who believes in Me, the *works* that I do he will do also; and greater works than these he will do, because I go to My Father.[13] And whatever you ask in My name, that I will do, that the Father may be glorified in the Son. If you ask* anything in My name, I will do *it.*

ii. Mark 11:22-24, "Have faith in God. For assuredly, I say to you, whoever says to this mountain, 'Be removed and be cast into the sea,' and does not doubt in his heart, but believes that those things he says will be done, he will have whatever he says.

iii. 1 John 3:21-23, Beloved, if our heart does not condemn us, we have confidence toward God. And whatever we ask we receive from Him, because we keep His commandments and do those things that are pleasing in His sight.

iv. Young's Literal Translation

v. OT:3336 rx#y@ yetser (yay'-tser); from OT:3335; a form; figuratively, conception (i.e. purpose): (Biblesoft's New Exhaustive Strong's Numbers and Concordance with Expanded Greek-Hebrew Dictionary. Copyright © 1994, 2003, 2006 Biblesoft, Inc. and International Bible Translators, Inc.)

vi. Phil. 4:8-9, Finally, brethren, whatever things are true, whatever things are noble, whatever things are just, whatever things are pure, whatever things are lovely, whatever things are of good report, if there is any virtue and if there is anything praiseworthy — meditate on these things. The things which you learned and received and heard and saw in me, these do, and the God of peace will be with you.

23

CONTROLLING THE PROCESS

"Resistance" is a term that describes what happens when the mind "resists" following the heart. There are many forms of resistance. They range from incredibly subtle to outright defiant. Resistance can present itself in very reasonable ways or extremely illogical ways. For example, at least a hundred times I have been seeking to develop myself in a particular area. Then, before I actually initiated any heart work, I would get the idea, "I should buy a book about this." That not only sounds logical, but it seems supportive of my original idea. Very often when I would get quiet and peaceful I would hear that still, small voice say, "You don't need to read a book about it. You need to put into practice the things you already know." I always knew that

> MOST OF US ALREADY KNOW EVERYTHING WE NEED TO KNOW TO LIVE A GREAT LIFE.

was a call to get into my heart and experience myself living the things I sought before I started taking in more information. Most of us already know everything we need to know to live a great life. We simply resist actuating what we know in our heart because to do so would actually require change!

Reading a book about anything is not a problem unless you think your answers lie in the pages of the book. That causes you to begin with information. If, on the other hand, you first went to your HeartZone and created a vision for what you wanted to do, then your heart would lead your mind instead of your mind leading your heart. Proverbs 29:18 says, *Where there is no vision, the people perish.* The word "vision" can mean a spiritual vision, it can mean vision with the eyes, or it can mean a mental vision. The most common usage is, "a divine revelation."[1]

When we launch out on any endeavor, we need a revelation. Remember, a revelation is not when God decides to show me something He has been withholding. A revelation is what I see when I surrender my opinion. A revelation emerges in a heart that doesn't have a predetermined, strongly held opinion. A revelation provides me with a clear mental picture of the end goal. When I begin any endeavor with the outcome in mind, I am able to recognize the signposts along the journey. But more importantly, when I get a revelation in my heart, it will always support my sense of identity.

It is important to always begin any new endeavor from your heart. When an idea or inspiration comes, spend time previewing your life in that situation. So many times by seeing what it would really be like to follow through on a certain decision, I have discovered that I didn't really want what I thought I wanted. Remember, before man fell he was a living soul. In other words, his soul was led by the life of his spiritual walk with God. But after he fell he became flesh. His soul was dominated by the five senses. Always allow God to lead you from your heart, otherwise your emotions (soul) will take a direction that does not support who you really are and where you really want to go.

We need what can be discovered by our intellect, but we should never be led by our intellect. The mind was created to provide us with the capacity of observation. But what we observe must be evaluated in our heart as we commune with God! The intellect tries to keep you within the bounds of your current sense of self as a means to protect your ego. Because the unknown presents the possibility of pain, the ego seeks to avoid the unknown. With your intellect you have created some definitions of pain and pleasure that are not at all congruent with God's definitions. These twisted concepts keep us from what will help us and lead us into what will hurt us. But all the while our intellect and our emotions are driving us and we think it's God!

The intellect will keep us within the bounds of where we have been and what we know. The heart will keep you within the bounds of who you are. Hence, the more you develop your sense of identity in Christ, the more you move the boundaries of your life. Limitless living can only be found by an identity capable of supporting it. My sharing in Jesus' inheritance is the only true source of limitless living! All that God has is ours in Him! This is why

> LIMITLESS LIVING CAN ONLY BE FOUND BY AN IDENTITY CAPABLE OF SUPPORTING IT.

fellowship, entwining ourselves around our shared experience of the cross and the resurrection, is the power of the Gospel; it is the place where we experience the exchanged life!

Another subtle way the mind resists is when we think we should fix ourselves. We are not capable of fixing ourselves. In fact, any attempt to fix myself is usually an effort to clean up the "old man." There is only one cure for the "old man:" death. Any other approach is a vain, unscriptural imagination. Paul's prescription is three basic steps: Put off the "old man;" renew the mind; and put on the "new man!" But it sounds reasonable to want to fix your problems before you pursue some new aspect of your life's dream. We do not need to understand our problems or where they came from to make the choice to send them away (put off).

In the parable of the wheat and the tares (Matt. 13:24-30), the master would not allow the servants to pull up the tares that had been planted in his field because they might unintentionally pull up the wheat. That is what happens to the person who self-prescribes and then attempts to fix themselves. They do more damage than good. Those who listened to this parable realized that tares and wheat look alike until they bear fruit. They understood Jesus was telling them they could not dig all their problems out of their own life, lest they damage themselves more.

Most attempts at fixing ourselves are based on self-judgment. Judgment is when we assume to know why someone is doing what they are doing. We have the right and obligation to know what people (we) do and to observe the fruit of their (our) actions, but we are never allowed to judge others or ourselves. But the intellectual mind (which got us into our problem) seeks to control the process by causing the problem, diagnosing the symptoms, and offering a cure. It's like allowing the same politician who stole from us to write laws to protect us against corruption. It never works out like we think.

When we walk with God through any healing process in our heart, we will always be led to deal with issues in the order that brings the most amount of healing and the least amount of pain in the quickest possible time. As a medical practitioner, I realized that people who came to my clinic with serious illnesses had often received treatment that should have helped them. The problem was, however, the treatment was provided in the wrong sequence. What should have been effective was not. Sometimes it even made the problem worse. Just as the body seeks to heal itself in an intelligent sequence that most effectively supports life and health, so does the heart.

The intellectual mind is always jumping on some fad or bouncing back to some religious practice we tried in the past. In other words, the mind ignores the heart as God attempts to lead us through the healing process and comes up with some intellectual reasoning for why we should follow a process we consider logical! At the end of all intellectual pursuits to fix ourselves are limited and temporary results, all of which are soon lost and bring more discouragement and disappointment!

> THE INTELLECTUAL MIND IS ALWAYS JUMPING ON SOME FAD, OR BOUNCING BACK TO SOME RELIGIOUS PRACTICE.

In my clinic most people who had been experimenting with alternative medicine tended toward a logic that said "no pain, no gain." Personally, I have seen this to rarely be accurate. A seasoned physician always sticks to the motto, "above all else, do no harm." So many times I would be making great progress with someone, and they would sabotage the process by jumping into some extreme "cleanse" recommended by an unqualified practitioner. Why? Their intellect told them if they were not feeling pain, they were not making gains. Then, when they would lose the progress they had made with more sensible treatments, they would become discouraged and give up on their health. This is exactly what happens to the carnally minded believer who does not listen to the voice of God in their heart! We sabotage what would work by following our own plan. Proverbs calls this leaning to our own understanding!

In "put off, put on" exercises, we discover the beliefs we incorporated in the past, but we do not try to fix ourselves. The problem is simple: we have held onto beliefs and offenses that affect us today. Once we identify the unwanted belief, feeling, emotion, or behavior, we send it away. Then we renew our mind (enter into fellowship) around the shared victories we have in Jesus. Then we put on that "new man" by connecting with Jesus in our heart. It's not rocket science, but it works. Ironically, it is too simple for the person who needs their problem to be complex. After all, if my problem is not complex and difficult to resolve, how can I justify doing nothing about it for all these years (ego)?

All of these forms of resistance point to one major fear: I don't want to die! You have to put off the "old man" before you put on the "new man." However, putting off the old is never an attempt to fix the "old man." Likewise, putting on the "new man" is never about mere behavior modification; it is about fellowshipping in His suffering and sharing in His death on the cross. Then it is about knowing Him and the power of His resurrection. It is about acknowledging every good thing in us because we are in Christ.[2] When it becomes a real experience in our heart that we share in all those good things which are in Him, transformation becomes effortless (grace). We enter into the rest that only comes from believing the truth in our heart!

Then there are forms of resistance where a person goes to sleep while doing heart exercises. A person can even become physically ill every time they attempt to venture beyond their current limitations. Resistance can come in many forms. No matter how it takes shape, there is always a common denominator. It is the thing that keeps you from venturing into the person you truly want to be, experiencing what you have never experienced before. Besides the dread of dying to self, one of the top reasons we are drawn into all

> NO ONE CAN TEACH ANYONE TO HEAR AND KNOW THE VOICE OF GOD.

forms of resistance is we do not quickly and easily recognize the difference between the voice of our mind and the voice of God in our heart!

When I first began this journey of the heart over 40 years ago, I had no one to teach me. It was all trial and error. What I have since learned is that no one can teach anyone to hear and know the voice of God. That is one of the unique factors of God speaking in your heart. No one can do this for you and no one can bring this to you! Therefore, everyone who chooses to make this journey will do so by trial and error. After you hear His voice enough times, it will become unmistakable to you!

Every time I made a decision that did not go well, I would get into as reflective of a state as I knew how. I would then attempt to recall the moment that I made the decision. I tried to notice the feelings or emotions that were compelling me. I viewed the entire event as an outsider, with absolutely no self-judgment. The more I did this exercise, the more I came to realize the types of feelings, attitudes, emotions, and desires that would tend to take me off track. During this time of development, I determined that I would not make any life decisions without thought and contemplation. Taking that extra time to listen to my heart gave me a chance to recognize what was really driving me. Eventually I came to notice in the moment what was really driving my choices, and I was able to make much better decisions that supported my true identity in Christ!

So many times serious, dedicated believers start out on a life-journey because they know they have heard the voice of God in their heart, or they have experienced a strong inspiration. They launch with the pure intention to follow God, but it's not long until self-intellect and ego lead them off course and leave them utterly confused. They know they heard God in the beginning and have no clue how things could have gone wrong. At that point they pass judgments on themselves, others, and even God to create an understanding of "why" their pursuits did not end well. Whatever their conclusion, it usually takes them even further off course.

The mind resists the unknown. Therefore, anytime we seek to improve our life, we are venturing into an unknown. After all, if we knew how to have a better life we would already be putting it into practice. So, God inspires us; we know it is His leading. But what usually happens is we immediately take the inspiration and decide how we want to pursue it. In other words, we want to follow a path that we understand. We may even use some Scriptures or lessons God has taught us in the past. But both of those scenarios depend on either your intellect or your memory and neither of them is actually allowing God to lead you today.

The Psalms tell us, "The Lord is my Shepherd." The first thing we must realize is following Him as Shepherd means we have surrendered to Him as Lord. We intend to follow, not lead! Our Savior is not necessarily our Shepherd.

When we surrender to Him as Lord, we will follow Him as our Shepherd. The very first thing that happens when we follow Him as our Shepherd is He leads us away from lack and into righteousness (that which is equitable, moral, legal, and prosperous, i.e. how it should be). He never leads us into lack. That would be a denial of His Covenant as well as a denial of the finished work of Jesus. The feeling of lack is the beginning of every temptation. The feeling of lack gives rise to desire (lust) and we know *every man is tempted when he is drawn away of his own lust* (desire).

Psalm 23 walks through incredible benefits from following Him as our Shepherd. For this discussion one of the most interesting is found in verse four: *though I walk through the valley of the shadow of death, I will fear no evil; For You are with me; Your rod and Your staff, they comfort me.* "The valley of the shadow of death" can be what we pass through as we surrender and die to self, venture into the unknown, or face the possibility of actual death. At this point the believer who started out in faith is tempted to devise his own plan, lean on his own understanding,[3] and rely on his own wisdom. What we realize is that we do not actually trust Him, we trust ourselves.

To venture into the unknown, one must know and trust the process or know and trust the one who leads them through the process. It's like getting a serious surgery. You rarely understand all the complexities of your surgery; instead you rely on your doctor's wisdom. You don't know the process, but you know your doctor. He becomes your source of peace through a dangerous process. Our need to find a way we understand, according to Proverbs 3:5, points to our lack of trust for Him. This is not willful or defiant; it is the natural result of spending our life using our natural instincts for survival. We have trained ourselves in life patterns that the "old man" employed to stay alive. They were at one time essential for survival, but now become the thing that keeps us from following Jesus as Lord into life as it should be (righteousness).

> SEND AWAY CONTROL EVERY TIME IT EMERGES IN ANY AREA OF YOUR LIFE, WHETHER IT IS IN YOUR MARRIAGE, BUSINESS, OR FRIENDSHIPS.

The only way out of this quagmire is to make a renewed, informed, full commitment to Jesus as Lord! Send away control every time it emerges in any area of your life, whether it is in your marriage, business, or friendships. A little leaven leavens the whole lump. You will never free yourself from trying to control your walk with God if you allow control in other areas of your life. Spend time in your HeartZone communing with Him, coming to know and recognize His voice. Utilize Heart Physics® exercises that get you in touch with Christ in you. Reflect on your decisions to determine what was driving them. Own the selfishness or personal agendas that were cloaked beneath a seemingly benign choice. Spend time worshipping and acknowledging who God is and your decision to trust Him. Come to know Him so deeply that you trust His Word, His Spirit, and His voice more than you trust your own logic. Every time you find yourself taking control repent, let go, and commune with God until you know how to recover your path.

Get quiet and relaxed. Close your eyes and go back in your mind to the last decision you made that did not come out as you thought it would. Imagine a movie screen where you see yourself just at the time you were making the decision. Tell yourself you are able to hear the thoughts you had at that moment. Allow yourself to feel the feelings you felt. As you watch from a distance, you will recognize subtle feelings or emotions that you didn't recognize at the time. Or you may realize that when you recognized them, you pushed them down because your mind argued why you would benefit from the decision. Doing this exercise will help you realize which emotions tend to lead you into bad decisions. When you feel them emerge in the future, interrupt the thought and remind yourself of your original goals. Soon it will become a natural process that keeps you on track.

Endnotes

i.   The literal sense, perception with physical organs of sight (from Theological Wordbook of the Old Testament. Copyright © 1980 by The Moody Bible Institute of Chicago. All rights reserved. Used by permission.)
from OT:2372; a sight (mentally), i.e. a dream, revelation, or oracle: (Biblesoft's New Exhaustive Strong's Numbers and Concordance with Expanded Greek-Hebrew Dictionary. Copyright © 1994, 2003, 2006 Biblesoft, Inc. and International Bible Translators, Inc.)

ii. Philemon 6, That the communication of thy faith may become effectual by the acknowledging of every good thing which is in you in Christ Jesus (KJV).

iii. Prov. 3:4-8.

24

CHRIST IN YOU:
THE STARTING PLACE

Before any believer can participate in the finished work of Jesus, he or she must come to terms with what is probably the most disbelieved, underappreciated Scripture in the New Testament: *you are complete in Him* (Col. 2:10). The word "complete" has an obvious meaning: to fill up, to be replete, to finish, to cause to abound, and to render perfect. Our response to this verse determines our entire journey as a believer. If we do not believe this, we deny the finished work of Jesus in our heart and live the rest of our Christian life in the flesh trying to become what we believe God would have us be. If we believe it to be true, we spend the rest of our life making this heart journey, metamorphous transformation of putting off the "old man," renewing our mind, and putting on the "new man"!

When we look a little deeper at this word "complete," it becomes even more interesting. One source says this is an idiom which means "to fill the heart; or literally, to throw into the heart; to cause someone to think in a particular manner, often as a means of inducing some behavior -- to make think, to fill the heart, to cause to decide."[1] In the Greek this verse reads: *And you are in Him complete* (emphasis mine). This completeness is "thrown into the heart" on the basis of our faith in Him as the resurrected Lord and our faith that we are in Him and share in His resurrection life.

Before making this pivotal New Covenant statement, Paul warns of philosophies based on the world's logic and tradition which would deceive and rob the believer of what he has in Jesus. That deception would be ANY doctrine, teaching, or theology that makes us believe there is something else we must do to become complete. Then he presents the key element in his logic: *For in Him dwells all the fullness of the Godhead bodily* (Col. 2:9). If all that God is dwells in Jesus, and if we dwell in Jesus, we obviously already have (share in) all we need. In other words, if Jesus is not enough, there isn't enough!

None of this means anything, however, if it is not "thrown into the heart." We know that God writes His laws on the part of our heart that pertains to the spirit, but we have to write on that part of our heart that pertains to the soul by the renewing of our mind and fellowship with Jesus!

> WE HAVE TO WRITE ON THAT PART OF OUR HEART THAT PERTAINS TO THE SOUL BY THE RENEWING OF OUR MIND AND FELLOWSHIP WITH JESUS!

Paul's next verse shines another light onto this puzzle; *In Him you were also circumcised with the circumcision made without hands, by putting off the body of the sins of the flesh, by the circumcision of Christ* (Col. 2:11). We know, based on both Old and New Testament Scriptures, he is referring to the circumcision of the heart![2]

Too often we forget that everything in the Old Testament found its ultimate expression in the inner realities of the New Covenant. Circumcision is the most graphic and accurate concept of what needs to happen to our heart. It needs to be as sensitive to God as a freshly circumcised penis. In Genesis 34:13-29 we have a story about some of the inhabitants of the land raping and then wanting to marry one of the daughters of Jacob. Two of Jacob's sons convinced them they would comply with their request if all the men in the city would agree to be circumcised. Blinded by their greed to get the wealth of Jacob's family, the inhabitants yielded to the request. The third day after their circumcision, two of the sons of Jacob slaughtered **all** of the inhabitants of the city. The reason two men could kill an entire city is because the sensitivity of circumcision rendered them totally incapable of relying on their natural strength.

A true circumcision of the heart renders us completely incapable of trusting in our own strength. It makes us hypersensitive to the Spirit of God. As we connect with Jesus in our heart, we will not only be freed from confidence in our flesh, the very thought of it will be crippling! Our completeness is in Him, not in us, not in our strength. In the Old Covenant a stranger could not partake of the Passover unless he was first circumcised.[3] So it is

> OUR COMPLETENESS IS IN HIM, NOT IN US, NOT IN OUR STRENGTH.

with Christ, our true Passover; we can only partake of Him when our heart has been circumcised. It is in this level of sensitivity that we experience the meaning and value of our Passover Lamb!

Circumcision was received by Abraham as...*a seal of the righteousness of the faith* (Rom. 4:11). And this righteousness, which is by faith, is all about the finished work of Jesus experienced in the heart! Interestingly, Abraham is hailed by many as the father of the faith. But the truth is, he is the father of faith righteousness,[4] and his circumcision was a "type" of a heart that could benefit from it!

Paul goes on in Colossians to explain: *Christ in you is the hope of glory!* This Scripture is the core of Heart Physics®. In fact, it's the very core of Christianity. It is the reality around which the entire Gospel works. It is the truth upon which we should build our entire life. Without this truth as our reality nothing in the Gospel ever really works as it should: *Christ in you is the hope of glory.* This is one of the simplest, yet most overlooked nuggets in the New Testament, especially when coupled with, *you are complete in Him!*

The word "glory" is an incredible word that would take pages to explain. In fact, my attempts to explain the glory of God would never exhaust all there is about the subject. The truth is, we will spend eternity exploring and experiencing the never-ending depths of His glory. There is no end to it. But one aspect of the word "glory" has to do with reality. As we have already discovered, there are many versions of reality available for us to experience. There is the reality observed by the five senses, and there is the reality of God. We don't deny physical reality, but we do choose to place our attention on a higher reality!

243

God's glory is a reality that is created by His will. In fact, the words "view," "opinion," and "reality" are among the vast explanations of the glory of God. This is His truth, His reality which exists in a realm called the Kingdom of God, which can only be accessed in the heart. The glory of God cannot be separated from the person of God. It is completely consistent with His character. It is, in fact, a perfect expression of who He is. It is the essence of His divine nature. In addition to the concepts of greatness, splendor, and majesty, here are just a few interesting things Thayer's Lexicon expresses to explain the glory of God:

> ... the absolutely perfect inward or personal excellence of; a most glorious condition, most exalted state; the glorious condition of blessedness into which it is appointed and promised that true Christians shall enter after their Saviour's return from heaven, which condition begins to be enjoyed even now through the devout contemplation of the divine majesty of Christ, and its influence upon those who contemplate it.[5]

The glory of God is a reality that expresses all God is. It is His glory that manifests in us as eternal life. His reality is embodied in the thousands of promises He made to mankind. It is revealed in the many names given to the Father, Son, and Holy Spirit. It is seen in His vast creation! It was made flesh in the person and life of Jesus! We don't experience these promises because we beg God who reluctantly gives them after enough prayer and sacrifice. No! We experience His promises when they become a part of our reality. As Thayer's says, this condition is enjoyed by those who contemplate (meditate on) it. Pondering the glory of God in you creates a fusion of two becoming one. It erases the boundaries of where you stop and He starts. It is the place where you lose yourself in Him!

THE GLORY OF GOD IS A REALITY THAT EXPRESSES ALL GOD IS.

You see, when we accept His view and opinion as our own, and it becomes our primary awareness, we become immersed in His reality. In other words, His reality becomes our own. In Heart Physics® you will learn that different realities can exist simultaneously on several levels. Just as in the case of the natural laws of physics, the reality one experiences is determined by perception, a fact well known by those who attempt to experiment or take measurements at the subatomic level. Where you are determines your view, and your view determines the reality you perceive and experience.

For example, a person standing in the middle of the street watching his car roll down the hill sees his car rolling away from him. That is real. A man standing in the middle of the street farther down the hill sees the car rolling toward him. Both of those perceptions are real. One man stands to lose his car because of his reality. The other stands to lose his life because of his reality. In Christ we can experience an exchange; when we exchange our life for His, we also change our reality for His. We now have the opportunity to see every promise from a new perspective...in Him. Or we can cling to the reality that we have learned to embrace through the course of our entire life. They are both real, and they both have the power to influence the quality of our life. But you have to choose which one you will embrace, and you have to make that your heart belief.

This is the greatest challenge of the Gospel: will I surrender my view and opinion and accept God's view and opinion? Remember, this is death to self. We have lived from our view and opinion all the years of our life; it's the way we have survived. That which has made us safe in the past is not easy to surrender. God does not desire surrender as a way to humiliate us. He desires that we humble ourselves, surrender our

> WILL I SURRENDER MY VIEW AND OPINION AND ACCEPT GOD'S VIEW AND OPINION?

view and opinion, so we can be lifted up to our rightful place as joint heirs with Jesus;[6] so we can see life from His perspective, thereby experiencing all the benefits of His reality.

Having a relationship with God is all about empowerment. Surrendering ourselves is not designed to bring us to the point of helplessness. It is to bring us to the place of complete access to God's unlimited power, completeness as a child of God! And that is exactly what will happen as you make this journey into your heart to discover Christ in you. This is the starting place of experiencing God's reality as your own.

When there is an abiding sense of Christ in you, you will never spend another minute trying to get the power to live the life of your dreams. You will be empowered by the supernatural revelation of Christ in you. Empowerment comes by acknowledging the truth, not by trying to get more power. The Bible says, *you are complete in Him, you can do all things through Christ, you have all things that pertain to life and godliness, by His stripes you were healed, you have the power to get wealth, you are blessed, prospered and protected, and made whole.* If this is true, why am I trying to get God to give me these things? Simple! It may be true, but it is not the reality I am experiencing. Because I am not experiencing it, my belief is: It is not true; it is not real! Remember, I can only experience the realities of my own heart!

We start every person seeking to make this journey of the heart with a program we call Essential Heart Physics®. This is essential because this is where we take the believer through thirty days of biblical meditation with daily cognitive support to connect them to Christ in their own heart. It is a combination of renewing the mind and putting truth into practice. As the intimate connection with "Christ in me" comes alive, my focus changes from outward to inward, from "me-centered" to "Christ-centered," from relying on my strength to relying on His strength. Unlike most programs, the root of this is the personal experience with Christ. Until we have an interactive experience with Christ in our heart, we are not ready to move into the deeper aspects of Kingdom Living. Christ in you is the hope of glory, or as I translate it from the original: "Christ in you is the basis of your confident expectation of God's view and opinion of you becoming your reality!" because in Him you are complete. That is God's reality and it can become yours!

> ## I CAN ONLY EXPERIENCE THE REALITIES OF MY OWN HEART!

Please don't think you must purchase Heart Physics® to develop this in your own heart. You can do as I did. I took hundreds of identity Scriptures, coupled them with the names of God, and spent time every day acknowledging the truth of these Scriptures in me, because I was in Him. I did this at a time when I was desperately ill with an incurable, genetic disorder, and had more debt than I thought I would ever pay. I experienced Christ in me. I experienced the reality of His promises. When His view and opinion became more real to me than what my five senses were telling me, my five senses lost control of my life. After helping hundreds of people walk through this process one-on-one, I finally realized I could better serve the masses if I put this in a program that was readily available. Since then thousands of people have experienced life transformation using Essential Heart Physics®.

Endnotes

i. (from Greek-English Lexicon Based on Semantic Domain. Copyright © 1988 United Bible Societies, New York. Used by permission.)

ii. Jer. 4:4, Circumcise yourselves to the LORD, And take away the foreskins of your hearts,

Rom. 2:28-29, For he is not a Jew who *is one* outwardly, nor is circumcision that which *is* outward in the flesh; but *he is* a Jew who *is one* inwardly; and circumcision *is that* of the heart, in the Spirit, not in the letter; whose praise *is* not from men but from God.

Phil. 3:3, For we are the circumcision, who worship God in the Spirit, rejoice in Christ Jesus, and have no confidence in the flesh,

iii. Ex. 12:48-49, And when a stranger dwells with you *and wants* to keep the Passover to the LORD, let all his males be circumcised, and then let him come near and keep it; and he shall be as a native of the land. For no uncircumcised person shall eat it.

iv. Rom. 4:1-3, What then shall we say that Abraham our father has found according to the flesh?*For if Abraham was justified by works, he has *something* to boast about, but not before God. For what does the Scripture say? *"Abraham believed God, and it was accounted to him for righteousness."*

v. (from Thayer's Greek Lexicon, PC Study Bible formatted Electronic Database. Copyright © 2006 by Biblesoft, Inc. All rights reserved.)

vi. James 4:10, Humble yourselves in the sight of the Lord, and He will lift you up.

25

Participating
in the Exchange

After creating a dynamic awareness of Christ in you, the next step is to become intimately and actively involved in the death, burial, and resurrection of Jesus! This is where we move past mere information to an active *fellowship* experience. This is the place where the message of the cross ceases to be information and becomes a divine influence on the heart … on every aspect of our being. As simple as this sounds, fellowshipping with Jesus around the death, burial, and resurrection will bring more of a personal, life-altering paradigm shift than you can imagine. This is where you lose "you" completely!

Sadly, very little accurate information is taught about the three days Jesus spent from the cross to the throne. We have become so steeped in religion we don't even believe He was in the grave for three days. No matter how you count it, from Friday afternoon until Sunday morning, which is the religious spin, is not three days and three nights! Every aspect of our faith related to salvation is based on what happened in those three days, and was consummated at the resurrection and receiving of the inheritance. Amazingly, this is the only basis for faith; the place of fellowship is seldom, if ever, preached.

The life of Christ was a model. He emptied Himself of His divine power and depended on the Holy Spirit, thereby showing us what we could be if we fully yielded to the Holy Spirit. Additionally, He showed us the character and nature of God. As a man without sin, He was the perfect sacrifice, without which there would be no salvation. None of that should be minimized! But it is all meaningless apart from the resurrection. Our faith is not based on the historical life of Jesus. No! Our faith is based on the resurrected life of Jesus!

OUR FAITH IS BASED ON THE RESURRECTED LIFE OF JESUS!

Christ's experience from the cross to the throne is the basis of our fellowship. It is what we share in common with Him! Prayer is not fellowship. Worship is not necessarily fellowship. All that we do with Him that does not involve His finished work is activity that is aimed at Him. Fellowship is a shared experience *with* Him! It is not a shared interest; it is a shared life! Until we experience the cross, the grave, and the resurrected life, our faith has no basis to take hold of (receive) the inheritance!

I spent years imagining what it would be like to be in Him when He died, in Him in the grave, in Him at the resurrection, and in Him with His inheritance. Like every journey, it started as an intellectual pursuit. Then, through prayer and meditation, it has progressively become my life experience. I don't say that as a basis of pride; as Paul said, not that I have arrived on the goal of my journey. But I can assure you I am traveling the right road!

Like every other area that I share with believers, I developed this into a program. Until it was put in a program, I could only help one person at a time. I want to help one billion people at one time. New Beginnings is the Heart Physics® module that follows Essential Heart Physics®. Only after we have created the awareness of Christ in us and developed our capacity to connect with Him in our heart at will do we have the ability to deliberately experience the cross! We all have moments of experiencing Christ in our hearts. We all have insights and inspirations that are connected to His death, burial, and resurrection, but we usually have no idea how or why they come or go. But we are not called to visit Jesus occasionally; we are called to abide in Him![1] This is more than a casual visit or an accidental glimpse in glory. This means, "I know where you live and I'm moving in with you!"

In the Book of Colossians, Paul points out that when we are baptized we participate in His death and resurrection by faith in the working or operation of God.[2] Water baptism should be one of the most dynamic and transformative events in the life of new believer; instead, it has become a near-meaningless ceremony whose power has been exchanged for religious activity. There is more debate about the proper means of baptism (sprinkling or immersion) or the formula one should invoke than what is supposed to happen in our heart.

Water baptism, like any "ceremony," only has value when it is a heart-engaged, interactive experience! This is the time a pastor should explain what happened from the cross to the throne.[3] The believer should be made aware that his faith is based solely on what Jesus accomplished through this event which we refer to as 'the cross of Christ.' He should understand that he is now dead, and his new life is hidden with Christ, in God![4] Therefore, as the New International Version translates it, the new believer should *set your heart on these things.*

When he is immersed[5] he should focus all of his capacity to believe on this: "I died with Christ and just as He was buried, I am burying my "old man" and all that pertains to him." As he is raised up out of the water, he should focus all of his capacity to believe on this fact: "Just as Jesus was raised from the dead and seated at the right hand of God, I am raised up with Him; I am seated with Him in heavenly places,[6] and all His victories are my victories."[7]

Just as there is no overall word for repentance, it is the same for faith. We believe on Jesus to be saved. But we believe on the finished work of Jesus, one situation at a time, to experience salvation in each area of our life. We must use our faith to enter into the exchange. I have been exchanged; my life for His, my sin for His righteousness, He took my punishment, and I take His inheritance.[8] But I experience the exchange (reconciliation) as I wrap myself around Him moment by moment, choice by choice,[9] and exchange my weakness for His strength!

I HAVE BEEN EXCHANGED...MY LIFE FOR HIS...

The fact that this legal reality is not an actuated experience until we use our faith is recognized when Paul appealed to believers in Corinth: *we implore you on Christ's behalf, be reconciled to God* (2 Cor. 5:20). Legally and positionally they were reconciled. None of that is of any value unless it is experienced! The heart is the variable between Jesus' finished work and our finished experience. Until we believe a truth, it is of little benefit in this life.

Through fellowshipping with Jesus utilizing the truths of the New Beginnings Heart Physics® module, you experience the exchange (reconciliation). You see yourself die with Him. You experience His death. But you also experience the resurrection, conquering all the opposing power and inheriting all the promises! I have laid on my pillow and imagined being raised from the dead with Him hundreds of times. I want to know this resurrection power!

Heart Physics® modules are not designed to become a substitute for your individual experience. They are tools designed to lead you down a path, but at the end of that path you have to step into your own experience with God. In time you find yourself communing with your own heart at night, seeing and experiencing yourself in Him raised up. You find yourself dealing with problems in a completely different way.

A believer who has fellowship with Jesus around the resurrection finds problem-solving quite easy. When any situation arises, simply ask yourself, "Did Jesus pay the price to free me from this?" Look to the cross for your answer. If your answer is yes, follow with this, "When Jesus rose from the dead did He conquer this?" Look to what He accomplished through the resurrection! Then ask, "Did Jesus receive an inheritance that ensures I do not have to settle for this?" Your answer is found in the promises of God. Then the final qualifying question is, "Am I in Jesus and do I share in the benefits of His death, burial, resurrection, and inheritance?" Every victory is won based on these questions, and these alone. Based on your answers you make a final decision and use your own authority. "I don't want you; I don't need you; you are not from God, I send you away." I like to do this in a meditative state so I can imagine the problem leaving me. I want to see it go. I want evidence. Then while in my HeartZone, I want to experience personal victory! I sometimes imagine myself putting on a suit of clothes that looks like the robe of righteousness. Or sometimes I imagine my entire being filled with the life of God and driving all darkness from me. Every battle ends with a new beginning based on the inheritance you share <u>with</u> Him, <u>in</u> Him, and <u>through</u> Him!

> "DID JESUS PAY THE PRICE TO FREE ME FROM THIS?"

Endnotes

i. John 15:5-8, "I am the vine, you *are* the branches. He who abides in Me, and I in him, bears much fruit; for without Me you can do nothing. If anyone does not abide in Me, he is cast out as a branch and is withered; and they gather them and throw *them* into the fire, and they are burned. If you abide in Me, and My words abide in you, you will ask what you desire, and it shall be done for you. By this My Father is glorified, that you bear much fruit; so you will be My disciples.

ii.   Col 2:11-13, In Him you were also circumcised with the circumcision made without hands, by putting off the body of the sins of the flesh, by the circumcision of Christ, buried with Him in baptism, in which you also were raised with *Him* through faith in the working of God, who raised Him from the dead.

iii.   For detailed information about what happened from the cross to the throne go to: http://impactministries.com/Store/tabid/1092/List/1/ProductID/809/

iv.   Col. 3:1-4, Since, then, you have been raised with Christ, set your hearts on things above, where Christ is seated at the right hand of God. Set your minds on things above, not on earthly things. For you died, and your life is now hidden with Christ in God. When Christ, who is your life, appears, then you also will appear with him in glory (NIV).

v.   Church history indicates that immersion was the only acceptable means of baptism by the early church. But the dogmatic arguments about it are meaningless compared to the need for the new believer to grasp the concept of death, burial, and resurrection in Jesus.

vi.   Eph. 2:4-6, But God, who is rich in mercy, because of His great love with which He loved us, even when we were dead in trespasses, made us alive together with Christ (by grace you have been saved), and raised *us* up together, and made *us* sit together in the heavenly *places* in Christ Jesus,

vii.   Eph. 1:18-23, that you may know what is the hope of His calling, what are the riches of the glory of His inheritance in the saints, and what *is* the exceeding greatness of His power toward us who believe, according to the working of His mighty power which He worked in Christ when He raised Him from the dead and seated *Him* at His right hand in the heavenly *places*, far above all principality and power and might and dominion, and every name that is named, not only in this age but also in that which is to come. And He put all *things* under His feet, and gave Him *to be* head over all *things* to the church, which is His body, the fullness of Him who fills all in all.

viii.   2 Cor. 5:21, He made Him who knew no sin *to be* sin for us, that we might become the righteousness of God in Him.

ix.   Rom. 5:11, …we also rejoice in God through our Lord Jesus Christ, through whom we have now received the reconciliation.

26

PUT OFF - PUT ON

Put off – Put on is the biblical solution to all problems facing the believer. I have developed many different ways to do this. They range from simple to extreme for difficult cases. The many different ways of doing this are because of the barriers we have created in our own beliefs. Too many times we subconsciously establish the prerequisite conditions for our healings, both physical and emotional. For example, some people determine they can only get free from a past offense if the offender apologizes. While biblically this is not true, if it is a determination made in your own heart, it is true for you.

> PUT OFF – PUT ON IS THE BIBLICAL SOLUTION TO ALL PROBLEMS FACING THE BELIEVER.

The clearest example of this in the Gospels is the woman with the issue of blood. There was no reason for her to touch the hem of Jesus' garment. Despite all the religious teaching about this woman, there was no special healing in His garment. The truth is it was a religious superstition found nowhere in Scripture nor seen in Jesus' ministry. Jesus healed people by laying on hands, rubbing them with mud, telling them to go dip in water, or simply speaking the Word.

Like this woman, we often set a condition for our healing in our own heart. That condition becomes the barrier we must cross to experience our freedom. Many times we want to know where the problem came from. Some of the more advanced forms of put off – put on make that information possible.

The Ultimate Put Off – Put On Experience is the third Heart Physics® module we recommend before becoming a coach, presenter, or receiving any of the other Heart Physics® training or certifications. "Put off – put on" is the ultimate ministry goal. By establishing ourselves in who we really are in Jesus, we eliminate obstacles to believing the truth about ourselves and God! We facilitate Jesus' stated goal of knowing the Father and experiencing His life! Everything else in ministry is a waste of time if it does not bring the believer to the "put off – put on" process!

When it gets down to the bottom line, all ministry aimed at solving problems, helping believers overcome sin, or developing what we call "spiritual growth" is either going to be the "put off – put on" process, or it will be some form of dead works! Many ministers do a great job of getting people to repent or change their mind about a particular sin, but it is rare they have any process for putting on a new belief or new identity once the old one has been rejected.

"Put off – put on" starts with the assumption that we have been *made* righteous. It is never aimed at *becoming* or *getting* righteous. It never attributes destructive works of the flesh to the devil, thereby implying that any entity has power over us. "Put off – put on" asserts that we all have liberty in Jesus, and we have a choice as to how we will use that liberty. Paul, Peter, and other New Testament writers warned against the misuse of liberty (freedom). They make it very clear that we have the freedom to choose. But they point out the unwise and destructive ways we tend to abuse our freedom (liberty). The first is to get back in bondage to religious legalism.[1] The second is to use our freedom to justify yielding to the flesh.[2] Both make us slaves to sin!

> WE ALL HAVE LIBERTY IN JESUS, AND WE HAVE A CHOICE AS TO HOW WE WILL USE THAT LIBERTY.

The idea of liberty is completely foreign to the Church. It is a place where we have deliberately blinded ourselves. It is so far beyond our natural/religious/carnal/worldly logic we cannot process how it can possibly be part of the Gospel. We forget that loving relationships are based on total freedom of choice. There are foundational, doctrinal[3] truths missing from our belief system that would make it impossible for us to embrace some of the deeper issues of the heart. Some of the most essential of these truths are: the overriding foundation of love as the primary character of God and the true essence of spirituality, knowing and experiencing God as the reason Jesus came, repentance from dead works as the doctrinal starting place, belief as a heart issue, the covenant of peace as our covenant with God, faith righteousness as our standing before God, the fellowship of the resurrected life as the absolute and total basis for our life of faith, and grace as God's power, ability, and capacity that works in our heart. Without these foundational truths to build on, little of the biblical truth we know can be actuated, which leaves us with mysticism, superstition, and outright opposition to the finished work of Jesus.

One word used for "liberty" refers to a slave who has been set free to make his own choices. He may make bad choices or he may make good choices, but they must be his own choices. It should never be our goal as ministers to control the choices of another. He or she must *work out his own salvation… with fear and trembling (Phil. 2:12)*. The point is not that we should be afraid of God; the point is we should realize we are dealing with eternity. In this Kingdom we are sons, not slaves. As sons we make our own choices for good or bad. We should, however, make our choices wisely! Can you be a son and make destructive choices that will have negative consequences for you and your offspring for generations to come? Yes! Theologians have debated the eternal consequences of those decisions for two thousand years; there is no reason to address that here. But we must always count the cost of all of our behavior, beliefs, and choices, and recognize the gravity of destructive choices!

> UNFORTUNATELY, RELATIVELY FEW BELIEVERS KNOW THEY HAVE BEEN MADE RIGHTEOUS.

Unfortunately, relatively few believers know they have been made righteous. Therefore, they have no concept of "put off – put on!" Their every effort to solve problems tends to make their problems more difficult to manage and more deeply rooted in their heart. Remember, we have two choices in solving problems: "put off – put on," or dead works. We can choose between the finished work of Jesus or works of the flesh; faith righteousness or works righteousness; faith in Jesus or faith in self! There is no in-between and there is no third option!

Paul said the process for dealing with ungodly behavior is to put off the "old man," renew the mind, and put on the "new man" (Eph. 4:17-24)! The words "put off" are related to these words: send away, forgive, remit, lay aside, deliverance, and liberty. When Jesus said He came to bring deliverance to the captives and liberty to the bruised, the fact that "liberty" and "deliverance" are the same Greek word, "send away," we realize the thing that had them captive was not a demon in the traditional sense; it was the bruising, i.e. brokenness of the heart, the footprints on the heart, and the pain of life that crushes the heart. That is what takes us captive. We are enslaved as our sense of self and of God is so distorted, making it impossible for us to embrace the truth.

While I believe deliverance is a legitimate New Testament ministry, I do not believe the way it is done toward believers necessarily represents the finished work of Jesus. Jesus' ministry of deliverance and healing was delivered to those who had not been born again. They did not have the resources we have today. You do not see the emphasis on the same type of healing and deliverance ministry for the body of Christ after the resurrection. So I must assume there is something we are missing when we attempt to apply Jesus' ministry to the lost as the model for ministry to believers! The same terminology for having a demon is also used in regard to having Christ. Therefore, we know this word cannot imply something that occurs by force or against our will. Even in the issue of demon possession, the language makes it questionable: who is doing the possessing, the demon or the person? When people reach unscriptural beliefs, they become captive to a lie. They enter darkness, and they become slaves to sin. When people believe the truth, they are captivated by it, and they become slaves of righteousness. People take hold of truth or lies and when they give their heart to them, those beliefs then have a hold on them.

All lies are of the devil; therefore, by their choice or beliefs, believers become what the Greek more appropriately calls "demonized!" But the demonic doctrine did not take them; they took the doctrine, thought, or belief. Paul attributes most of what we call "demonic activity" to the works of the flesh, even witchcraft and idolatry![4] His solution to these types of problems is to walk in the Spirit —

or as John said, *walk in the light* — but to reach this place, we must put off the "old man," renew the mind, put on the "new man," and fellowship with Jesus! Remember, the words "put off" are from the same Greek word as "deliverance" or "send away."[5]

In Scriptures cited in the previous reference, we are told to put off specific behaviors. We know these behaviors to be based on beliefs connected to the old identity. So I must be specific about what types of behavior I am sending away. Then, these same Scriptures tell me the type of behavior to put on in place of that behavior. For instance, if I tend to lie, I need to put off lying and put on speaking the truth in love.

> # I MUST BE SPECIFIC ABOUT WHAT TYPES OF BEHAVIOR I AM SENDING AWAY.

In The Ultimate Put Off – Put On Experience, we teach believers how to identify the specific emotion, feeling, or belief driving the destructive behavior. We know that all behavior is the result of emotions, feelings, or beliefs! Until we deal with the underlying cause, we could have a constant drawing back into the behavior. For example, let's say when I lie, I do it for fear of rejection. Like most behavioral issues, lying is not the root; it is the fruit. I could have a cellular memory of being rejected by my father when I was truthful. Therefore, when I am put in a situation that seems similar to the earlier event, cellular memories are triggered, causing a flood of negative feelings. I feel and anticipate rejection. Then, in an instant I yield to the lust (desire) to lie. Why? I want to avoid the pain of the anticipated rejection.

When Paul talked about something that warred in his members, I believe this could be a reference to cellular memories. *But I see another law in my members, warring against the law of my mind* (Rom. 7:23). As previously discussed, experiences in the form of memories can be imprinted into the very cells of our body. Not only do they cause sickness in those cells, they host feelings that emerge when triggered, but we have the ability to send these away.

Likewise, past offenses that are not resolved can be embedded in my cells and *lie in wait for my blood!* When we suffer an offense or trespass as a result of someone's actions the typical process is to wait for that person to apologize and then "forgive" them. By forgive, we mean, "I will no longer hold this against you!" While that may be an aspect of forgiveness, it is not the key factor. Regardless of whether or not the other person comes and asks forgiveness, the real question is, "What will I do with this offense, this emotion that compels me to act in an ungodly manner?" It is more important that I focus on forgiving the offense than forgiving the person.

Jesus said, *If you forgive the sins of any, they are forgiven them; if you retain the sins of any, they are retained* (John 20:23). So when someone sins against me I have two options: forgive, i.e. send away, or retain (hold on to). There is not a third option. Furthermore, if I do not send it away by choice, I have chosen to hold it. If I hold it, it becomes an offense, an occasion for stumbling, and has the potential to become a cellular memory.

All things exist in the form of energy. Healthy cells and organs must vibrate at specific frequencies to be healthy. When the negative, hurtful memories are stored in my cells, it is like playing a piano with a string out of tune. It will sound great except for when you play anything that involves that note. The same thing happens in our life. Every time we do anything that involves certain issues, that frequency is triggered and produces discord in that situation. Even more deadly is the fact that the discord I produced in that cell is giving rise to inflammation, pain, and disease!

This is why people often experience physical healing after extending forgiveness. God is not giving healing in response to their act of kindness; they are simply releasing that which brought disharmony to their physical body!

Anytime I recognize in my life or the life of someone I am seeking to help a repetitive pattern of behavior, emotions, or even sickness, I want to determine if there is an emotion, feeling, or belief contributing to this pattern. Then I will put off the emotion, feeling, or belief, and I will put on the specific feeling, emotion, belief, or behavior that I choose as a new creation in Christ! It's really that simple!

The Book of James offers a solution for the misuse of our liberty.[6] He warns of the self- deception involved in the life of the person who only hears the Word. He says it is like looking into a mirror, walking away, and forgetting what you look like. He reminds us that the goal is to look into the perfect law of liberty, and then continue in it! He says the way to make this happen is to be *a doer of the Word.*

A doer of the Word is obviously one who puts it into practice, but like many Greek words, there is a much deeper connotation than is revealed through a casual glance. A doer of the Word is a "poetic performer" of the Word![7] A performer doesn't just read the Word, they perform it poetically. When one performs the Word poetically, it is read with all the voice inflection and emotions that bring the Word to life!

> A PERFORMER DOESN'T JUST READ THE WORD, THEY PERFORM IT POETICALLY.

It could be that a poetic performer of God's Word is someone who does their confession of Scripture or meditation and contemplation of Scripture in a way that brings all of the emotional feeling to life, just as a poetic performer or entertainer would do. When this Word comes alive in us, we experience it as real. We then walk away with an experience, not just some more information that will soon be forgotten!

We must put on Christ in our experience. We must see all that we are, all that we have, and all that we can do because we share this life with Him. We must use our imagination, our every capacity to make that as real to us as any life experience. It must become our identity. When it becomes real in our heart, we cannot separate that sense of reality from any other life experience. When we put on Christ, we cannot separate ourselves from Him. We become lost in Him, one with Him. We abide in Him and He in us! We experience the same access to God that He has at His right hand! This is the heart of the New Covenant: knowing God! AND this is where we experience His life!

One of the simplest starting places for put off – put on is to pray The Prayer of Transformation. Any time you see a repetitive thought, feeling, behavior, or sickness, pray the Prayer of Transformation:
(http://impactministries.com/Resources/PrayerofTransformation.aspx).
Any time you see a repetitive thought, feeling, behavior, or sickness, pray the Prayer of Transformation. This is a great first step in initiating Put off – Put on!

Endnotes

i. Gal. 5:1, Stand fast therefore in the liberty wherewith Christ hath made us free, and be not entangled again with the yoke of bondage.

ii. Gal. 5:13-15, For you, brethren, have been called to liberty; only do not *use* liberty as an opportunity for the flesh, but through love serve one another. For all the law is fulfilled in one word, *even* in this: *"You shall love your neighbor as yourself."* But if you bite and devour one another, beware lest you be consumed by one another!

iii. Foundations of Faith is a free online audio course provided at http://impactministries.com/Resources/FoundationsofFaith.aspx

iv. Gal. 5:19-21, Now the works of the flesh are evident, which are: adultery,*fornication, uncleanness, lewdness, idolatry, sorcery, hatred, contentions, jealousies, outbursts of wrath, selfish ambitions, dissensions, heresies, envy, murders,*drunkenness, revelries, and the like

v. Send away scriptures. Highlighted words are the same in the Greek.
Luke 4:18-19, to preach deliverance to the captives, and recovering of sight to the blind, to set at liberty them that are bruised, To preach the acceptable year of the Lord.
Rom. 13:12, The night is far spent, the day is at hand: let us therefore cast off the works of darkness, and let us put on the armour of light.
Eph. 4:25-5:8, Wherefore putting away lying, speak every man truth with his neighbour: for we are members one of another. Be ye angry, and sin not: let not the sun go down upon your wrath: Neither give place to the devil. Let him that stole steal no more: but rather let him labour, working with his hands the thing which is good, that he may have to give to him that needeth. Let no corrupt communication proceed out of your mouth, but that which is good to the use of edifying, that it may minister grace unto the hearers. And grieve not the holy Spirit of God, whereby ye are sealed unto the day of redemption. Let all bitterness, and wrath, and anger, and clamour, and evil speaking, be put away from you, with all malice: And be ye kind one to another, tenderhearted, forgiving one another, even as God for Christ's sake hath forgiven you.5:1 Be ye therefore followers

of God, as dear children; And walk in love, as Christ also hath loved us, and hath given himself for us an offering and a sacrifice to God for a sweet smelling savour. But fornication, and all uncleanness, or covetousness, let it not be once named among you, as becometh saints; Neither filthiness, nor foolish talking, nor jesting, which are not convenient: but rather giving of thanks. For this ye know, that no whoremonger, nor unclean person, nor covetous man, who is an idolater, hath any inheritance in the kingdom of Christ and of God. Let no man deceive you with vain words: for because of these things cometh the wrath of God upon the children of disobedience. Be not ye therefore partakers with them. For ye were sometimes darkness, but now are ye light in the Lord: walk as children of light.

Col. 3:8-10, But now ye also put off all these; anger, wrath, malice, blasphemy, filthy communication out of your mouth. Lie not one to another, seeing that ye have put off the old man with his deeds; And have put on the new man, which is renewed in knowledge after the image of him that created him.

Heb. 12:1, Wherefore seeing we also are compassed about with so great a cloud of witnesses, let us lay aside every weight, and the sin which doth so easily beset us, and let us run with patience the race that is set before us.

James 1:21-25, Therefore lay apart all filthiness and superfluity of naughtiness, and receive with meekness the engrafted word, which is able to save your souls. But be ye doers of the word, and not hearers only, deceiving your own selves. For if any be a hearer of the word, and not a doer, he is like unto a man beholding his natural face in a glass: For he beholdeth himself, and goeth his way, and straightway forgetteth what manner of man he was. But whoso looketh into the perfect law of liberty, and continueth therein, he being not a forgetful hearer, but a doer of the work, this man shall be blessed in his deed.

1 Peter 2:1, Therefore laying aside all malice, and all guile, and hypocrisies, and envies, and all evil speakings...

vi. James 1:22-25, But be doers of the word, and not hearers only, deceiving yourselves. For if anyone is a hearer of the word and not a doer, he is like a man observing his natural face in a mirror; for he observes himself, goes away, and immediately forgets what kind of man he was. But he who looks into the perfect law of liberty and continues *in it*, and is not a forgetful hearer but a doer of the work, this one will be blessed in what he does.

vii. NT:4163, fromNT:4160; a performer; specifically, a "poet"; (Biblesoft's New Exhaustive Strong's Numbers and Concordance with Expanded Greek-Hebrew Dictionary. Copyright © 1994, 2003, 2006 Biblesoft, Inc. and International Bible Translators, Inc.)

27

LIFE WITHOUT LIMITS

Most of us came to Jesus in pursuit of a better quality of life often known through a feeling of inner peace, freedom from a destructive lifestyle or the need to experience forgiveness for wrongs against others. Whatever the reason, we reached an end to the life we had and wanted better. Even though we may not have known the scripture to back it up, the Spirit of God was drawing us with the promise of a better life. Jesus called it the *abundant life* (Jn 10:10): better in quality and quantity, exceptional, being more than expected, superior, remarkable, more than is needed, extraordinary, unusual, uncommon, giving an advantage... and more![1] This is what is promised so this and nothing less should be the goal of our faith. After all, we only experience grace to fulfill the goal of our own faith. [2] Just because it has been freely given does not mean we have received it (taken hold of it and brought it to ourselves). This biblical type of receiving only happens when we believe it in our heart.

Although many of us enjoyed a flood of new life in the beginning, most of us lost that initial experience because of the failure to renew our mind or the acceptance of religious externalism! When we didn't understand why all of these promises did not instantaneously happen, instead of connecting with God in our heart the way we did in the beginning, we turned to religion, tradition, and in some cases outright superstition. We accepted man's vain philosophies and ignored the Holy Spirit as our Teacher. We yielded to carnal logic over the Word of God and although we were sincere, our sincerity did not deliver us from the choices we made.

Paul encouraged believers to continue in their journey with Jesus in the same manner they began it,[3] in faith! Then he gave us a serious warning: *Beware lest anyone cheat you through philosophy and empty deceit, according to the tradition of men!* But we didn't know the difference between truth and that which deceives. Most of us did not trust the truth in our hearts. We relied on the peer pressure of man and for most of our lives have been cheated out of what could have been. But the great thing is no matter when you choose to begin this journey God is always ready. He doesn't penalize you. In fact, He will take everything that worked against you and find a way to use it for your good.

> HE WILL TAKE EVERYTHING THAT WORKED AGAINST YOU AND FIND A WAY TO USE IT FOR YOUR GOOD.

Now we realize what God wants to do in our lives is not magic, it is miraculous. It is a process that is based on the finished work of Jesus and comes into our experience *by grace through faith.* In the beginning we wanted it all immediately. The realization that it was a journey wearied us. Today we rejoice in the fact that this is a never-ending experience of the heart. It is an eternal journey of knowing and experiencing God, thereby becoming one with Him through the knowledge of the Lord Jesus and our life in Him.

We are not trying to fix ourselves; instead we are yielding to a metamorphosis that defies the world's and religion's logic. It is such an alien concept that it can only be grasped by the heart and never fully explained by the intellect. It is dying to self and entering into the Kingdom of Heaven now through the door of our heart! It is leaving the death we thought was life and discovering a life we thought was death!

In the beginning of this journey death-to-self was all about trying to overcome and break free from the past. We anticipated pain and hardship, but we now realize that anticipation of pain and hardship was simply a form of resistance created in our mind because we still trusted self. The self-life we struggled to justify and keep, we now despise and reject. We once thought that walking with Jesus would narrow our life choices. We thought we were losing our freedom. Now we see walking with God as entering into true freedom. The life we once loved we no longer want or need. As we realize and trust that which is available to us through Kingdom living our concept of death-to-self changes. We shift our focus from the illusion of what we imagined to be giving up to the hope (confident expectation) of what we gain. We discover that death-to-self is of little concern; it is merely letting go of our limitations.

These revelations are the natural fruit of abiding with Him in your heart! The days of trying are over, *being* is your new norm. When your life is ruled by Christ in you and not ruled by your own mind, you CANNOT think the same. Those who utilize the Heart Physics® exercises share some common experiences and the first is the abiding awareness of "Christ in me." What this does in each person's life will be different. For those who are lonely, it may mean never feeling alone again. For those struggling with a particular sin, it may manifest as a grace to overcome that sin. I have known people with poor financial habits break free and establish new, successful careers. There is no way to predict what will change in your life when you have a living awareness of Christ in you! Regardless of the initial experience, Christ in you is the starting place for living in Christ from your heart!

One of the most interesting ironies we have seen in this area is that those who try to control the outcomes seldom experience the outcome they had hoped. We cannot dictate how Jesus will express Himself in us. The very idea defies the concept of Lordship and following Him as our Shepherd. What it really says is, "I will lead; you will follow. I am lord, you work for me as I choose!" When we allow Christ to work in our heart we cannot control the process or the priority of events. A financial miracle may be the most pressing emotional relief you desire but other far more important life priorities may exist.

> WHEN WE ALLOW CHRIST TO WORK IN OUR HEART WE CANNOT CONTROL THE PROCESS OR THE PRIORITY OF EVENTS.

In fact, there may be issues in your life that need to be resolved first in order to prevent self-destruction after your goal is reached. Be assured God is not playing games or testing you. He is leading you into abundant life through the best means possible.

Another experience shared with those who practice Heart Physics® is a sense of limitlessness! Because all things are His and we are in Him, all things are ours. There is no way to express in words the boundless possibilities available to us as we participate in the "in Him" life. This reality can be experienced but not explained. The uninitiated might interpret this sense of limitlessness as greed or ego, but nothing could be further from the truth. In reality, this sense of limitlessness is the result of the peace we can only experience in Jesus. This peace is more than a feeling; it is a tranquil state of mind that comes from knowing all our needs are met in Him, knowing the abundant life is ours, knowing we are safe in Him, knowing we will live and never taste death, even if our physical body is slain!

We have *tried* to find a state of faith where all things are possible to him who believes. Bu tit has been done in a selfish, convoluted way for the primary purpose of fulfilling our lusts. We have worked every imaginable formula attempting to "get enough faith" - in itself a contradiction of terms. Faith is not an *amount* of trust; it is a *quality* of trust! James' description of those who sought to use faith to satisfy their greed aptly applies to many who seek a magic formula to fix their problems apart from actually transforming their lives…*you do not have because you do not ask. You ask and do not receive, because you ask amiss, that you may spend it on your pleasures* (James 4:2-3).

Righteousness is when things are as they should be. We want things to be as they should be in our finances, but not in our spending; in our health, but not in our eating; in our marriage, but not in our loving. We want our circumstances to change while we're allowed to stay the same. We waste our faith on useless things that perish and have little value in the larger scope of our lives. We attempt to use the same corrupt priorities and logic that got us into trouble to tell God how He should get us out of trouble. But God's righteousness works in our lives from the inside out. It expresses itself in every aspect of our being as it should.

> RIGHTEOUSNESS IS WHEN THINGS ARE AS THEY SHOULD BE.

Vines Expository Dictionary points out that this life we have in Him is not a mere principle or power; it has moral associations which are inseparable from it. Outwardly focused people would twist this to mean that we *earn* righteousness by the life we live - our behavior. This reversal of cause and effect is actually part of the religious thinking that The New Testament labels as being of this world's system, thereby opposed to God and His Kingdom. This life of God doesn't allow for a distinction between *who* God is in character and *what* He experiences in quality. Likewise, our capacity to yield to (not earn) the quality of life that exists in the Kingdom is inseparable from yielding to its character. This speaks to the mystery of righteousness. Jesus is the light and the life. It is, therefore, impossible to embrace Him as one and not the other. Life, health, circumstances, emotions, etc. are a continuum of the life of God. We must allow God to work in us as He wills and trust His ways above our ways!

Because what we believe in our heart determines all the boundaries of our life, trying to correct or move the external boundaries without resolving the beliefs of our heart will result in self-destruction! Since the Word of God is written on our heart when we are born again, it may be that all of our heart work after that comes down to seeing ourselves as being one with this truth. What I see, experience, and believe in my heart (to the point that it is immovable) about myself as a success brings about an inner transformation that moves my external boundaries.

> TRYING TO CORRECT OR MOVE THE EXTERNAL BOUNDARIES WITHOUT RESOLVING THE BELIEFS OF OUR HEART WILL RESULT IN SELF-DESTRUCTION!

Seeing myself, in my heart as whole, well, energetic, and healthy moves my outward physical boundaries. As boundaries are moved in my heart (how I see myself inwardly) in any area I am able to live a better outward quality of life. However, expanding my outward life without expanding the boundaries of my heart (my inner sense of self) will cause stress, resistance, self-destruction, and fear. This is why some people experience an improvement in a particular area of life and then grow anxious, expecting something to wrong. This is a form of condemnation - the expectation of punishment! It would be injurious for the Holy Spirit to fix an external problem that is not yet supported by heart beliefs. His work in our lives is individualized and personal. If we simply trust and follow, God will lead us away from lack and into abundant life.

The common denominator of those who make this journey is that they walk in love. God is love. If we abide in Him we abide in love.[4] The one and only way to determine if we are abiding in Him is to examine ourselves in light of love. 1 John 4:8 explains that if we are not walking in love we are not experiencing God![5] So I must always ask, "Am I doing this because I value God and the person with whom I am dealing?" My intention should always be to convey value to every human, even if I despise his or her behavior. If I am still unsure I must ask, "Are my actions aligned with the expressions of love laid out in 1 Corinthians 13?" No matter what the Spirit is leading me to do, it must be done in love or I have missed the goal. I may have heard God's voice, but it's me who determines if I will apply what I have heard in a way that conveys love!

Jesus said all the law and all the prophets were fulfilled in two commandments: *Love God with all your heart, soul and mind, and love others as yourself.*[6] Paul told Timothy there were three goals in everything he taught: *love from a pure heart, a good conscience and faith unfeigned.*[7] Then Paul told the Galatian believers: *For all the law is fulfilled in one word, even in this: "You shall love your neighbor as yourself* (Gal 5:14). If righteousness is fulfilled in those of us who walk after the Spirit and if all the law is summed up in walking in love, it is safe to say that our ultimate transformation goal should be to walk in love. Knowing His love should be our ultimate relationship goal. We only know Him if we know His love. Walking in love will make us more like God than any other attribute. Any godly expression or characteristic can be perverted if it is not qualified by love.

> LOVE IS THE LANGUAGE OF GOD AND IT IS THE LANGUAGE OF THE HEART.

Love is the language of God and it is the language of the heart. The only healing for our wounded hearts is found in God's love. Love is the beginning and end of all that is God. It is both our experience from and our expression of knowing God. It is the cause *and* the effect! Knowing, believing, and experiencing this love becomes the launching pad into a life without limits.

In this prayer Paul wanted us to comprehend this continuum of inner and outer power that's source is this continuous flow of God's limitless love.

> *For this reason I bow my knees to the Father of our Lord Jesus Christ, from whom the whole family in heaven and earth is named, that He would grant you, according to the riches of His glory, to be strengthened with might through His Spirit in the inner man, that Christ may dwell in your hearts through faith; that you, being rooted and grounded in love, may be able to comprehend with all the saints what is the width and length and depth and height — to know the love of Christ which passes knowledge; that you may be filled with all the fullness of God. Now to Him who is able to do exceedingly abundantly above all that we ask or think, according to the power that works in us, to Him be glory in the church by Christ Jesus to all generations, forever and ever. Amen.* (Eph 3:14-21).

Many have sought a life of limitless power apart from limitless love, not realizing how totally destructive such a life would be. God is seeking to move us into a life of limitless love, limitless power, and limitless promises. All of this is restored though a limitless, never-ending journey of the heart wherein we experience "Christ in me!"

Endnotes

i. (from Greek-English Lexicon Based on Semantic Domain. Copyright © 1988 United Bible Societies, New York. Used by permission.) NT:4053, *exceeding some number or measure or rank or need*
(from Thayer's Greek Lexicon, Electronic Database. Copyright © 2000, 2003, 2006 by Biblesoft, Inc. All rights reserved.)
(from Theological Dictionary of the New Testament, abridged edition, Copyright © 1985 by William B. Eerdmans Publishing Company. All rights reserved.)

ii. 1 Peter 1:9, receiving the end of your faith — the salvation of *your* souls.

iii. Col 2:6-10, As you therefore have received Christ Jesus the Lord, so walk in Him,[7] rooted and built up in Him and established in the faith, as you have been taught, abounding in it* with thanksgiving.[8] Beware lest anyone cheat you through philosophy and empty deceit, according to the tradition of men, according to the basic principles of the world, and not according to Christ.[9] For in Him dwells all the fullness of the Godhead bodily;[10] and you are complete in Him, who is the head of all principality and power.

iv. 1 John 4:16, God is love, and he who abides in love abides in God, and God in him.

v. 1 John 4:8, He who does not love does not know God, for God is love.

vi. Matt 22:37

vii. 1 Tim 1:5-6

28

Making
Your Own Journey

You are now armed with an incredibly powerful resource. You now know how to make all biblically-based knowledge come to life. You never have to wonder how to get any truth to work. You never have to try to *find* God; He is with you and in you! There will be no more need for formulas or fads. You know how to make the truth work: believe it in your heart! This is the most phenomenal mystery ever revealed to mankind! This is something prophets, priests, and kings didn't see in advance. It has been hidden from generations but is revealed to us, the Church. You know what few people in the world know, but what all men have longed to know! You have the key to knowing and experiencing God intimately. You can now conquer any personal problem. There is no need for you to ever be limited by any boundary! You can change all the issues of your life! You know the mystery!

> ## YOU CAN NOW CONQUER ANY PERSONAL PROBLEM.

Old Covenant believers knew a Savior was coming. The mystery, however, was not just the fact that a Savior and Deliverer would come, but that He would come and live in our hearts. This was beyond the comprehension of the externally focused, legalistic world into which Jesus was born. Even though it was clearly written in the Scriptures and modeled by Old Testament saints, they were not willing to accept that God was a heart God.

They, like us, wanted a Savior who would come and change their external world. They imagined Israel ruling the Earth. With deep hatred, they imagined their natural enemies conquered. It was their hope that a Savior would come and break the power of Rome in a humiliating supernatural victory! They wanted an external Savior and an external salvation! They didn't want to change ... they wanted everyone else to change. Therefore, according to Jesus' teaching, they closed their eyes so they would not see the obvious truth that challenged their fear of dying to self!

This truth about the heart, like all truth, presents an interesting paradox. This gives you incredible freedom hand-in-hand with incredible responsibility. You have immediate access to God and all His resources, yet if you choose to be irresponsible you will attempt to justify your unbelief just as those who hoped and prayed for a Savior were the same who crucified Him because He was not what they wanted. You may create excuses like, "I don't understand! I just don't see how that will work!" Or, "That's just not what I believe!" Although your excuses will never actually give you peace, they may seduce and sedate your conscience enough to ignore the continual still, small voice of God speaking in your heart, calling you to fellowship with your Father and Creator.

> YOU HAVE IMMEDIATE ACCESS TO GOD AND ALL HIS RESOURCES...

It really doesn't matter if you agree with all of my concepts. What matters is that you see the need to relate to God from your heart. Jesus revealed our capacity to recognize truth by our intention to put it into practice. If any part of this is true, how will you put it into practice? Do you have any intention to act on what is going on inside you? If so, you can start just as I did over forty years ago by asking yourself questions. Seek the answers in the Bible, not in the pulpit, not in philosophy, and not in subjective interpretation of your experiences. But more than anything else, determine that you will know and follow God from the deepest part of your being. You will bring all of your motives and intentions in line with His truth.

Most people who twist truth have one guiding factor that is used to interpret Scripture. Because the mind wants to be right they can't consider possibilities that may present a different answer. But those who learn to live from their heart are capable of seeing the paradoxes of truth. They are able to allow guiding factors to interpret the application of truth, independent of their need to be right. They are secure in their relationship with God, independent of the need to be right!

In ancient times fires were lit in the harbors to guide the ships safely into port at night. If sailors only had one fire to follow, they would easily see the light and head in the approximate direction, but still be in danger of sailing in from a wrong angle and crash on the rocks. To remedy the problem those on shore would light more than one fire. When looking at the fires from sea, if the ship was aligned properly, the multiple fires would appear as one and sailors would know they were navigating safely into the harbor. But if they saw more than one fire, they knew they were heading for disaster. When we relate to God from our heart, we are able to light more than one guiding light! When determining our relationship to a potential truth we must align three fires: Is this based on the inheritance Jesus received through His resurrection? Is this consistent with Jesus' teaching and lifestyle? Am I applying this from the motive of God's love for me and His love for the world? There are, no doubt, other guiding lights, but I assure you, if these three are aligned as one you will find yourself "safe in the harbor."[1]

The following will provide a brief summary of essential truth and Crucial Points for Transformation. This list is designed to serve as a quick reference tool so you can begin applying what you have learned right away. The sooner you begin, the sooner you will experience your invisible boundaries expanding.

Endnotes

[i.] Safe in the Harbor, Cindy Richardson Walker, Crusader CD, Florence, AL

Summary

1. God is a heart God.
   a. God meets with us, speaks with us leads and empowers us in our heart.
   b. God looks on the heart, therefore, regardless of our words or deeds, they are false if they are not from our heart.
2. My heart is the real me.
   a. The heart is some combination of spirit and soul; this combination is what gives me my unique identity.
   b. The beliefs of the heart are primarily about my identity.
   c. All that is genuine emerges from my heart.
3. According the parable of the sower:
   a. Truth not sown in the soil of my heart cannot take root and bear fruit, therefore it is of no value, nor influence in our life.
   b. Truth is sown in the heart by thoughts, study, consideration, pondering and meditation.
   c. We take ownership by seeking to understand how it would work, and what it would look like if it were true in our own life.
   d. If we do not change the beliefs of our heart, whether good or bad, we will keep getting more of what we've got.
4. All the boundaries of life are projected onto the world through my heart.
   a. If I focus my attention outward to expand my life boundaries, without first dealing with the beliefs of my heart I will fail.
   b. Self-sabotage, and even many health issues occur when I push past my boundaries without resolving my heart beliefs.
   c. Expanding my sense of identity in Christ is the primary manner.
5. All transformation occurs in the heart by the grace of God, change occurs in the mind by will power.
   a. All transformation occurs through some type of meditative reflective process.
   b. I am not attempting to become what I am not, I am transforming into who I really am!

6. I have the ability to write God's truth on my heart.
    a. When I believe the truth in my heart it alters my sense of self, my identity!
    b. When I believe the truth in my heart, its application is effortless.
    c. There is no promise of transformation apart from some type of meditative process.
    d. When I believe the truth in my heart I am free from internal conflict, my conscience is harmonious.
    e. Information plus emotion write information on my heart.
7. All the promises of God belong to Jesus because I am in Him I share in those promises.
    a. I am a new creation in Christ, the righteous me!
    b. In Christ I am qualified for all the inheritance of the Kingdom.
    c. Because Jesus suffered all the curses of the law, I am free from those curses
    d. Because I am one with Him, I cannot accept as lawful in my life any curse of the law.
    e. Because I am one with Christ, I am as He is before God.
8. Love must be the motivating factor of all my actions.
    a. Without love I have nothing, am nothing and profit nothing.
    b. Love is expressed primarily through our value for others.
    c. In the absence of love truth always gets corrupted.
9. Meditation, contemplation and reflection is crucial to every aspect of interacting with God.
    a. Prayer, worship and praise should all be a meditative process wherein I experience God in my heart.
    b. God keeps me in perfect peace when I keep Him in my imagination.
    c. My imagination shaped and forms my life.
    d. Meditation is where I think and imagine something until I experience it as real.
10. All the issues of the heart are resolved by believing on the resurrection in my heart and confessing Jesus as Lord.
    a. Unless I my commitment to Jesus as Lord, is based on trust in the death, burial and resurrection, my faith is in vain.
    b. The heart journey only works for those who are fully committed to following Jesus as Lord.
    c. If he is my Lord, I will always surrender my view, opinion and will to His.

Crucial Points for Transformation
Review Put Off – Put On

1. Identity any negative repetitive thought, feeling, emotion or behavior. Any behavior thought feeling or behavior that would be unacceptable by Jesus at the right hand of God has no right in your life. You do not have to tolerate or accept it!
2. Send it away. Identify it and use your authority as a believer to send it away from you.
3. Renew your mind. Gather the biblical information about what you have in Christ as a result of His death (setting you free from the curse of the law & the punishment you deserve), His burial (and the burial of all you are outside of Christ), and His resurrection (all that is yours because you are in Christ and share in His inheritance).
4. Put in the new man. Begin to acknowledge to God that you accept the terms of His Covenant, Jesus as your Lord and the fact that you are in Him. Acknowledge and meditate on all you are, all you have, and all you can do as a result of being in Jesus.

If you desire to accelerate your journey and want access to the tools and resources that will help you along your way go to www.heartphysics.com. But remember, you now possess all you need to make this journey. The same Holy Spirit that taught me will teach you. Heart Physics® tools and resources are not a substitute for the Holy Spirit; they are only tools designed to help you avoid the mistakes that I made, while accelerating you progress.

Free Online Support!

Want to put what you're reading into practice right now? Please visit this link (http://www.heartphysics.com/MYIBsupport/) for free online cognitive support, exercises and chapter questions.

About the Author

James Richards is a pioneer in the field of faith-based human development. He has combined spirituality, energy medicine, scientific concepts, and human intuition into a philosophical approach that brings about congruence in spirit, soul, and body, resulting in incredible breakthroughs in health, emotional management, financial abundance, and intimate connection with God. He is a life coach, consultant, teacher, and motivational trainer. He holds doctorates in Theology, Alternative Medicine, and Human Behavior. He was awarded an honorary doctorate in World Evangelism for years of service in the Philippines. His many certifications include: substance abuse counselor, detox specialist, herbalist, handwriting analysis, EFT, energy medicine, and an impressive number of additional certifications and training certificates.

Dr. Richards has been successful as an entrepreneur who has built several profitable businesses ranging from contracting to real estate to marketing. As a national best-selling author, Dr. Richards has written several books that have sold million of copies around the world. His most noted work is Heart Physics®, a life-renewal program designed to equip people to transform any aspect of their life through changing the beliefs of their heart.

When asked why he has studied such a broad field his answer is simple: "If it helps people, I want to understand it!" The goal of all his work is to "help people experience wholeness in spirit, soul, and body!"

To contact Dr. Richards call or write:

Impact Ministries
3516 S. Broad Place
Huntsville, AL 35805

256-536-9402
www.impactministries.com

Other Publications by Dr. James B. Richards

Taking the Limits Off God

Grace: The Power to Change

Supernatural Ministry

The Gospel of Peace

The Prayer Organizer

Leadership That Builds People, Volumes 1 and 2

The Lost Art of Leadership

My Church, My Family: How to Have a
Healthy Relationship with the Church

Becoming the Person You Want to Be:
Discovering Your Dignity and Worth

Breaking the Cycle

How to Stop the Pain

We Still Kiss

Effective Small Group Ministry

Satan Unmasked: The Truth Behind the Lie

The Anatomy of a Miracle

Wired for Success, Programmed for Failure

Heart Physics®

How to Write, Publish, and Market Your Own Bestseller eBook

Take Control of Your Life

The Greatest Threat to American Freedom eBook

**For more information on these and
Dr. Richards' other materials please visit:**

www.impactministries.com